D0789999

Ira...

A Beginner's Guide

"Homa Katouzian's book offers a comprehensive overview of Iran's history. He sheds light on the most complex aspects of Iran's social, political, and cultural history and yet does so in a concise and accessible way."

> **Nasrin Rahimieh** - Maseeh Chair and Director of the
> Samuel Jordan Center for Persian Studies and Culture
> at the University of California, Irvine

"Drawing on the author's encyclopedic knowledge of Iran's history, politics, economy, and culture, Homa Katouzian's *Iran: A Beginner's Guide* is the most lucid, engaging, and authoritative introduction to the study of Iran available in any language today."

> **Ali Banuazizi** - Professor of Political Science and Director,
> Program in Islamic Civilization & Societies, Boston College

"An excellent historical introduction to Iranian politics and political culture from ancient Persia to the contemporary Islamic Republic. It is a must-read book for beginners and an exemplary textbook for undergraduate courses."

> **Mohamad Tavakoli-Targhi** - Professor of History
> and Near and Middle Eastern Civilizations
> at the University of Toronto

"A must read for those who want to know Iran really well. Short, lucid, and highly informative, it could only have been written by a doyen of Iranian Studies."

> **Fariba Adelkhah** - author of *Being Modern in Iran* and
> Director of Research at SciencesPo/CERI

ONEWORLD BEGINNER'S GUIDES combine an original, inventive, and engaging approach with expert analysis on subjects ranging from art and history to religion and politics, and everything in-between. Innovative and affordable, books in the series are perfect for anyone curious about the way the world works and the big ideas of our time.

aesthetics
africa
American Politics
anarchism
Animal Behaviour
Anthropology
Anti-capitalism
aquinas
art
artificial intelligence
biodiversity
bioterror & biowarfare
british politics
cancer
censorship
christianity
civil liberties
classical music
climate change
cloning
cold war
conservation
crimes against humanity
criminal psychology
critical thinking
daoism
democracy
descartes
Dewey
dyslexia
energy
engineering
epistemology
European Union
evolution
evolutionary psychology
existentialism
fair trade
feminism
forensic science
French Literature
french revolution
genetics

global terrorism
hinduism
history of science
Homer
humanism
Huxley
Iran
islamic philosophy
Islamic Veil
journalism
judaism
lacan
life in the universe
literary theory
machiavelli
mafia & organized
crime
magic
marx
medieval philosophy
middle east
Modern Slavery
NATO
nietzsche
Nutrition
oil
opera
Particle Physics
paul
Philosophy
philosophy of mind
philosophy of religion
philosophy of science

planet earth
postmodernism
psychology
quantum physics
racism
Reductionism
Religion
renaissance art
shakespeare
sufism
the bahai faith
the beat generation
The Bible
the brain
the Buddha
the enlightenment
the northern ireland
conflict
the palestine–israeli
conflict
the qur'an
the small arms trade
the torah
United Nations
volcanoes

Iran
A Beginner's Guide

Homa Katouzian

ONEWORLD

A Oneworld Book

Published by Oneworld Publications 2013

Copyright © Homa Katouzian 2013

The moral right of Homa Katouzian to be identified as the Author
of this work has been asserted by him in accordance with
the Copyright, Designs and Patents Act 1988

ISBN 978–1–78074–272–4
ISBN (ebook) 978–1–78074–273–1

Typeset by Cenveo, India
Printed and bound in Great Britain by
TJ International Ltd, Cornwall.

Oneworld Publications
10 Bloomsbury Street
London WC1B 3SR
UK

To Peter and Marianne Reed
for a debt of honour

Contents

Introduction
Iran: The land and the people

In the last few decades Iran has been at the centre stage of world affairs, more in the international news perhaps than some other major countries. The revolution of February 1979, the establishment of the Islamic Republic, the hostage-taking of American diplomats in November 1979 and subsequent stand-off with the United States, the 1980–8 war with Iraq, the international conflict over Iran's nuclear policy and the resulting sanctions against it – these are but some of the key events that explain Iran's present situation and the negative attitude of Western powers towards it.

But interest in this fascinating nation is not just a modern phenomenon. Iran boasts thousands of years of history. It is an ancient land of the utmost variety in nature, history, art and architecture, languages, literature and culture. Until the early twentieth century, Iran was known in the West as Persia. When the Greeks first came across the Iranians, Persian Iranians were ruling the country as the Persian empire, and they called it 'Persis'. Just as when the Persians first came into contact with Ionian Greeks, they called the entire Greek lands 'Ionia'.

In parts of Iran, civilization goes back several millennia, and includes that of the ancient, pre-Persian Elamites. Aryan tribes arrived in the land in the third and second millennium BCE in more than one wave of immigration. Nomadic Iranian tribes settled across the Iranian plateau, and by the first millennium BCE,

Medes, Persians, Bactrians and Parthians populated the western and central part, while the Iranian Pashtuns and Baluch settled in the eastern parts of the plateau. There were still other Iranian peoples, such as the Scythian and Alan tribes, the former of which later harassed various Persian empires with their border raids.

Originally, Iranians were more of a race than a nation, the Persians being only one people among many. Afghanistan and Tajikistan also belong to the wider Iranian entity in historical as well as cultural terms, and the Iranian cultural region – sometimes described as Persianate societies – is even wider than the sum of these three countries, extending to parts of northern India, Central Asia, the Caucasus and Anatolia. Persian is just one of the Iranian languages: there have been many others, of which Kurdish, Baluchi and a few other languages, as well as Pashto, Ossetic, and so on still survive as living tongues, while other languages are also spoken in Iran, notably Turkish and Arabic. On the other hand, other varieties of Persian are spoken both in Afghanistan and Tajikistan, such that the people of the three countries can understand each other in conversation as well as literary communication. Many more Persian dialects are spoken in Iran. 'Farsi' is the *Persian* word for the Persian language; the correct English word is 'Persian'.

As mentioned above, Persia was only part of Iran, in that the Persians made up one of the Iranian peoples. Yet at times it had an even wider meaning than Iran because what was historically known as Persia or the Persian empire not only included a much wider territory than present-day Iran, but also encompassed non-Iranian countries and peoples such as Egypt.

The country and its peoples

Today's Iran is part of the much larger Iranian plateau, the whole of which was at times included in the Persian empire.

The country is vast, bigger than Britain, France, Spain and Germany combined. It is rugged and arid, and except for two lowland regions is made up of mountains and deserts. There are two great mountain ranges, the Alborz (Elburz) in the north, stretching from the Caucasus in the north-west to Khorasan in the east, and the Zagros, which extends from the west to the south-east. The two great deserts, Dasht-e Kavir and Dasht-e Lut, both in the east, are virtually uninhabitable. The two lowland areas are the Caspian littoral, which is below sea level and has a subtropical climate, and the plain of Khuzistan in the south-west, which is a continuation of the fertile lands of Mesopotamia and is watered by Iran's only great river, the Karun.

Thus land is plentiful but water is scarce, an issue that has played a major role not just in influencing the character and system of Iranian agriculture but a number of key sociological factors, including the causes and nature of Iranian states and the relationship between state and society. The spread of mountains and deserts naturally divided the Iranian population into relatively isolated groups. But aridity played an even greater role in this, and at the level of the smallest social units. In most of the country, cultivation and flock-keeping was possible only where natural rainwater, a little stream, a subterranean water channel known as *qanat*, or a combination of these, provided the minimum necessary water supply.

The typical Iranian village – small, isolated and almost self-sufficient – was a product of the dryness of the land, the general lack of water typically putting a long distance between a village and its nearest neighbour. The village thus became an independent social and productive unit, too small to provide a feudal base, since that would require a surplus of production much above the sustenance of the peasantry to provide for a feudal lord, his court and his retinue. The villages were far too distant from each other to provide such a base taken together. The aridity of the land and the remoteness of the social units to which it was related thus combined to prevent the rise of a feudal society and state the like of which prevailed throughout a long stretch of European history.

Feudalism describes a system which, with a good deal of variation through time and place, stretched for a thousand years from the fall of the Western Roman empire to the rise of the Renaissance and absolutist states of Europe, although some of its features survived beyond that, and in the case of Russia it both came late and was abolished too late.

Some people may still be surprised to learn that Iran was never a feudal society. The reason for this is that feudalism is often thought of simply as a traditional system in which there are landlords and peasants. These are certainly some of the basic features of the feudal society, but not all. If feudalism were to be described by these features alone, it could be claimed that virtually every society from the dawn of civilization until recent times has been feudal. This was not true even of Europe, where the feudal system flourished for ten centuries, being preceded by the classical Graeco-Roman system and followed by the Renaissance and absolutist states and other systems following them.

In a feudal society, landlords formed the ruling classes, which were first and foremost represented by the state. The state was thus dependent on and representative of the ruling classes. In Iran, it was the landlords and other social classes who depended on the state because the state nominally owned the whole of the land, actually owned parts of it and assigned the rest to various landlords and tax farmers, from whom it could take land away whenever it wished. Thus, in Iran, the state stood over and above the social pyramid and looked upon the whole of society, both high and low, as its servants or 'flocks'. In general, Iranian states had the power of life and property over their subjects regardless of their social class, a power that not even the absolutist states of Europe – which flourished only for four centuries for the continent taken as a whole – ever possessed.

State and society

Feudal landownership in Europe was free and independent of the state. Land was owned by a long-term and continuous aristocratic class even beyond the feudal period. That was not the case in Iran precisely because landlords were basically creations of the state and did not have any *independent rights* of ownership, only the more or less temporary *privilege* of enjoying its benefits. This privilege could be withdrawn if and when the state so wished, as long as it had the physical power to enforce it. Landlords could not automatically pass their estates on to their descendants. They did not form a continuous class because their possession normally lasted for a relatively short period, passing to others at the will of the state and its officials. This does not exclude the long-term existence of autonomous nomadic tribes and principalities, which the state was not able to subdue. The point is that within the confines of the power of the state *long-term and continuous* peers and aristocratic classes did not and could not exist.

In every type of European society, even in the absolutist or despotic states of Europe between 1500 and 1900, the power of the state was to a greater or lesser extent constrained by laws or deeply entrenched traditions. For example, it was not normally possible even under the absolutist rule of the English Tudors, the French Bourbons, the Austrian Hapsburgs, and so on for a prince, a member of the aristocracy, a leader of the church or a member of the bourgeoisie to be killed at the whim of the king without charge, hearing and trial. In Iran, on the other hand, all power was concentrated in the hands of the state, and more specifically the shah.

In principle, the shah had the power of life and death over every member of society, from princes of the blood and the chief minister downwards. He could expropriate any prince, vizier, landlord or merchant so long as he had the physical power to do so at the time: no independent law or custom existed that could stop him. Thus, the most central characteristic of government – and of all social power – was that it was arbitrary, unimpeded by any established written or unwritten laws outside itself.

This does not mean that government was necessarily centralized, or that there was extensive intervention by the state in everyday living, which is characteristic of modern states everywhere. It simply means that, in all the areas in which the state had the will as well as the physical means to act, it could do so without restraint from any external body of laws or entrenched traditions. It was a system the like of which never existed anywhere in Europe, except for very short periods, although similar systems may have prevailed in some other Asian societies.

All power and fortune emanated from the shah, and all life and possession was at his will. He was God's vicegerent on earth and several cuts above all other human beings, including his sons and other princes. Even if he was the first son of the previous shah, which often he was not, his fundamental legitimacy was not due to that or even to his belonging to the ruling dynasty. It came directly from Divine Grace, called *farr*. Thus, Persian shahs did not draw their legitimacy from an aristocratic and/or priestly class, but directly from God by possessing the *farr* or Divine Grace. This concept of kingship survived into Islamic times, when both the term *farr* and such titles as Shadow of the Almighty, and Pivot of the Universe, were used to describe the shah's glory.

State–society conflict

The Iranians were typically opposed to their rulers, precisely because their life and property was in the ruler's power. But they nearly always welcomed a ruler who emerged in the midst of chaos and stamped it out, although shortly afterwards the society went back to its habit of adopting a negative attitude towards the state. And they became increasingly rebellious whenever the state was in trouble. There was a fundamental antagonism between state and society throughout Iranian history, putting aside a few short-term exceptions: the state tended towards absolute and arbitrary rule (*estebdad*); the society tended towards rebellion and chaos. One of four situations normally prevailed in Iranian history: absolute and arbitrary rule; weak arbitrary rule; revolution; and chaos – which was usually followed by absolute and arbitrary rule.

It was never clear who would succeed a ruler because it was Divine Grace, not primogeniture that was the basis of legitimacy, and in practice this could be claimed by anyone who managed, often by force, to succeed. That was why almost invariably there was conflict over succession, sometimes resulting in civil war among different claimants. He who won had the Divine Grace by virtue of his victory.

Absence of law of the kind that existed throughout the history of Europe did not mean that there did not exist rules and regulations at any point in time. It meant that there were no enduring laws or unshakable traditions by which the state was bound. Regarding judicial laws, for example, the *shari'a* supplied an extensive and elaborate civil and criminal code in Islamic times. The restrictive factor, however, was that they could be applied only so far as they did not conflict with the wishes of the state. That is why the state could deal out such punishments against persons, families or whole towns which had no sanction in *shari'a* law; and how the condemned could sometimes escape punishment if they could make the shah or the local ruler laugh at the right time.

Society, on the other hand, tended to be rebellious precisely because of its endemic rejection of the state, even though in every short term there existed methods of legitimation and bargaining between state and society. It was not perpetually engaged in rebellion, which was not possible except on the occasions when the state was considerably weakened by domestic or foreign factors or a combination of both. But society did not regard the state's rule as legitimate, and therefore often viewed it as an alien force. Voluntary cooperation of society with state – as opposed to enforced submission – was a rare occurrence in Iranian history.

Traditional Iranian revolutions were intended to remove an 'unjust' ruler and replace him with a 'just' one. Thus in practice they were focused on removing the existing ruler rather than the overturning of the system of arbitrary rule, which, until the nineteenth century, was believed to be natural and therefore unavoidable. This became the central objective only at the turn of the twentieth century in the Constitutional Revolution, and it had been inspired by the realization in the nineteenth century that European governments were based in law.

However, it must be stated that none of the above arguments is 'ahistorical', implying that Iranian society remained stagnant throughout history. On the contrary, because of the short-term nature of the society, change was more frequent than in European history. What persisted as the norm in Iranian history was the arbitrary nature of power, exactly as law had always existed in Europe as the basis of state power.

The short-term society

All this gave rise to the 'short-term society'. A shah was not sure that his favourite son would succeed him after his death. A minister, governor or other official knew that at any moment he might lose his post, together with his property and frequently his life as well. A rich man was not sure if he could hold on to some or all of his wealth vis-à-vis the ruler, governor or other powerful persons. Hardly anyone could be sure that his position or possessions or both would be passed on to his descendants, for example, a minister's grandson becoming an important person and a merchant's a well-to-do man. Hence, seldom if ever were decisions made according to long-term considerations. The Persian expression 'Six months from now, who is dead, who is alive?' summed up the general attitude towards time, prediction and planning.

Nomads and ethnicity

No discussion of Iran's history, economy, society, polity or culture may be complete without taking full account of its nomadic peoples, beginning with the Persians who built its first empire to the Qajars who ruled until the twentieth century. Looking for greener pastures, a variety of Iranian as well as Turkic peoples of different origins were attracted to the region from the north, north-east and east, and once they were established they had to face the menace of other incoming or native hordes. Both aridity and the pressure of population in their own lands were causes of nomadic migration to Persia, and water scarcity within Iran was the cause of the internal movements of nomads from their winter to their summer quarters and back again every year. It was these nomads who from the beginning created the Iranian states, since they were both martial and mobile and could gather the surplus product of a vast territory to establish powerful central states.

Historically, Iran has been the crossroads between Asia and Europe, East and West. People and goods as well as beliefs and cultural norms have passed through the country, usually but not always from the East to the West. Its peculiar geographical location gave rise to what may be termed 'the crossroads effect', both destabilizing and enriching the country; at once making its people hospitable and friendly towards individual foreign persons and highly self-conscious vis-à-vis foreigners in general; both making the acquisition of foreign ways, habits, techniques and fashions desirable, and yet making the fear of the foreigners' designs normal, although the tendency towards xenophobia and suspicion of foreign conspiracies has been at least in part a product of arbitrary rule and the habitual alienation of the society from the state.

One product of the crossroads effect is the fact that Iran now inhabits a variety of ethnic and linguistic communities. No reliable statistics are available, but it is likely that a century ago the native Turkic speakers outnumbered the native Persian speakers, though that is no longer so if only because of the high growth of bilingualism, such that most native Turkic or Arabic speakers also use Persian like a native language. The Turkic speakers are mainly concentrated in the north-western region of Azerbaijan – bordering Turkey and the Caucasus – as well as the north-east.

The Kurds are an Iranian people and their language is an Iranian language. Today, about five million Iranian Kurds form a minority of other Kurdish people who live in Turkey, Iraq and Syria. They live mainly in the Kurdistan region in the highlands of the Zagros in western Iran. The Kurds are largely settled, but the tribal structures still survive among many Kurdish communities. The majority of Kurds are Sunni Muslims.

Iranian Arabs are almost entirely located in Khuzistan, next to the Iraqi border. Arab tribes settled in other provinces in the early days of Islam, having lost their identity through the passage of time. Iranian Arabs are Shi'a. The Baluchis, on the other hand, are Sunni and live in the south-east on the Pakistani border. Their language is Iranian and their region is one of the least developed parts of the country. Parts of greater Baluchistan are in Pakistan and Afghanistan.

This does not exhaust the list of ethnic and linguistic Iranians, which includes small numbers of Armenian, Assyrian and Jewish peoples. Lors and Bakhtiari, for example, are still partly tribal. There are still others, such as the people of Laristan on the Persian Gulf, who speak an entirely independent Iranian language.

Iranianism

Yet although ancient and medieval Iranian empires sometimes included even more diverse peoples than at the present time, a quality and characteristic of Iranianism (Iranian-ness or *Iraniyat*) always distinguished the country from its neighbouring lands and peoples. It was not nationalism in any modern sense of the term, but consciousness of a social and cultural collectivity which made the country and its peoples different and distinct from their historical neighbours: Greeks, Romans, Arabs, Turks, Chinese and Indians.

The factors which bound them together and determined the shared identity of Iranian-ness have not been the same throughout the ages, although some of them have always played an important role in it. Three factors have been most important in this since medieval times. One is the Persian language as the lingua franca and the medium of high literature and culture, which often went beyond Iranian borders and even became the official and cultural language in other countries such as Mogul India. Another factor is Shi'a Islam which is unique to Iran as a state, is followed by the great majority of Iranians and has aspects and implications that are deeply ingrained in Iranian culture since ancient pre-Islamic times. The third factor is territoriality, the fact that, despite national expansion and contraction through the ages, which for many centuries led to the formation of several states in Iranian lands, there was a fairly distinct Iranian territory, at least as a cultural region.

Conspiracy theories

Iranians seldom take things – events, phenomena, opinions, suggestions – at face value. On the contrary, they are more inclined to believe that appearances are deceptive and that the truth is hidden beneath them. This trait is best known and most conspicuous in the conspiracy theories concerning politics, and is by no means exclusive to Iran and, in recent times, has even spread to some Western societies, although in Iran and a few other Eastern countries it tends to be deep-rooted, strong and widespread.

The constant interference of Imperial Russia and Britain in Iranian politics over a large part of the last two centuries, followed by the influence between 1953 and 1979 of the United States, played an important role in intensifying such theories. In the twentieth century, in particular, the belief that the slightest event in the life of the country was caused and manipulated by the hidden hand of the British became so widespread that almost everyone, from shah and minister to teacher and taxi driver, tended to believe that their country was little more than a pawn in the hands of the British or *Ingilis-ha*, who masterfully – indeed magically – plotted and executed some of the minutest happenings regarding the least important issues in Iranian society. *My Uncle Napoleon (Da'i jan Napoleon)* is a famous Persian satirical novel which has brilliantly portrayed this problem.

Personalism

Few foreign observers have failed to comment on what they describe as 'Iranian individualism'. They certainly refer to something special in Iranian attitude and behaviour, but it has never quite been defined clearly, and the term itself is misleading in that it may be confused with the liberal individualist movement of Europe. Let us for the sake of convenience call this Iranian 'personalism', rather than 'individualism'. There are two sides to this phenomenon. On the one hand, Iranians unusually tend to be detached from one another if they are not related by family bond or friendship. That is, the sense of social cohesion and regard for *unknown individuals* among Iranians at large is not very strong. Exceptions to this rule occur in rare circumstances such as a revolution, in which Iranians become passionately attached to each other even if they are perfect strangers, for the sake of the common objective of bringing down the state. In such circumstances they behave and act as one big family.

The other side of personalism runs in the opposite direction and results in unusual care for, and attachment to others. Iranians are uncommonly close to members of their own family, extended family, clan and close friends, and would help, defend and even make sacrifices for them when they are in greater or lesser need.

In any realistic analysis of Iranian society, it is vital to take into account this deep-seated personalism in all its manifestations. For it both results and is reflected in an extraordinarily strong sense of security and degree of protection within the clan and familiar community, and a markedly strong sense of insecurity and vulnerability outside it, among strangers in society at large.

Iranians, as a people, are intelligent, inventive and artistic. They are versatile and adaptable to different situations. They love fun, gaiety and outdoor activity. They almost make an art of eating, and Persian cuisine is one of the best in the world. They enjoy fiction, tales, jokes and rumours. They tend to accept rumours and anecdotes spread against the state without question, and are experts at making the funniest jokes at the expense of those who wield power and authority, especially the government.

A leading modern poet once wrote in a verse: 'Our life is poetry, legend and myth'. And – although there is much more to Iranian life – poetry, myth, legend, mysticism and religion form a substantial part of everyday living. Emotion has the upper hand among Iranians and reason takes a lower seat in forming opinions. An average Iranian is more likely to be convinced of the truth of a statement if it is justified by an anecdote, an appropriate verse or an extraordinary and extra-rational explanation than by mere logical argument or empirical evidence.

These fundamental aspects of Iranian culture and society, both ancient and modern, will be explored in the following chapters, as they need to be borne firmly in mind for a realistic understanding of this ancient and complex country.

1

Ancient Persia

Iran is a very old country. Dozens of prehistoric sites across the Iranian plateau point to the existence of ancient cultures and urban settlements in the fourth millennium BCE, and there are records of numerous ancient civilizations living on the plateau before the arrival of the Aryan tribes. One of the main civilizations was Elam, to the east of Iraq, which started from around 3000 BCE. Later the Elamites were absorbed into the Persian empire.

The Persian empire was the very first world empire. Founded more than two and a half thousand years ago in 550 BCE by Cyrus the Great, it covered vast swathes of what are today the Middle East, Central Asia and the eastern Mediterranean. Until Alexander the Great brought about their downfall in 330 BCE, the Achaemenid dynasty ruled myriad peoples subsumed under the mighty Persian banner. Great cities rose from the rocks, while opulent palaces and audacious monuments ensured that their legacy remained in the memory even after the empire had crumbled. Following Alexander's death, successive dynasties would rebuild the empire but none would achieve the same magnificence.

Achaemenid Persia (550–330 BCE)

Of the various Aryan nomads who, looking for new pastures, began to move into the Iranian lands from the north-east and north-west sometime in the second millennium BCE, the Medes and the Persians were destined to form, respectively, a local and a world empire. At the beginnings of the eighth century BCE the

Iranian Median tribes managed to unite under the leadership of one of their chiefs, Dayukku (Greek, Deioces). He thus became the founder of the nascent Median state, which, from its inception, had to struggle for survival against powerful neighbours such as Assyria, Armenia and the Scythian nomads, who were also Iranian by race. The Median capital city was Ecbatana, built on the site of the modern Hamadan. In time, the small city would expand into an empire.

The Medes spoke a north-western Iranian language simply referred to as the Median language. They had an ancient Iranian religion (a cult of the god Mithra, which later became a major Roman deity) with a priesthood known as magi (which we know of from the three kings in the Christmas tradition); although during the reigns of the last Median kings, Zoroastrianism was becoming increasingly popular in the west. Evidence of the history and culture of the Median state is scant, but the few archaeological sites and textual sources that have been discovered demonstrate the lasting impact that the Medians had on Iranian culture.

Meanwhile, sometime in the eighth century the Iranian Persian tribes moved down from the north-west and, by the late sixth century BCE, had already established, through the dynastic line of Achaemenid (a legendary Persian chief), a Persian kingdom in the south and south-western parts of modern Iran. Born around 600 BCE, in 550 BCE Cyrus the Great (600–530 BCE) captured Media, defeating his own maternal grandfather in the process and uniting the Medes and the Persians.

Herodotus tells the story that after the birth of Cyrus, Azhdahag (Greek, Astyages) the last Median emperor had a dream that his magi interpreted to mean that his grandson would eventually overthrow him. Immediately upon hearing the prophecy he ordered his steward to kill the infant boy. The steward, however, couldn't bring himself to murder. Instead he asked a herdsman to do it for him, but the herdsman disobeyed and kept the

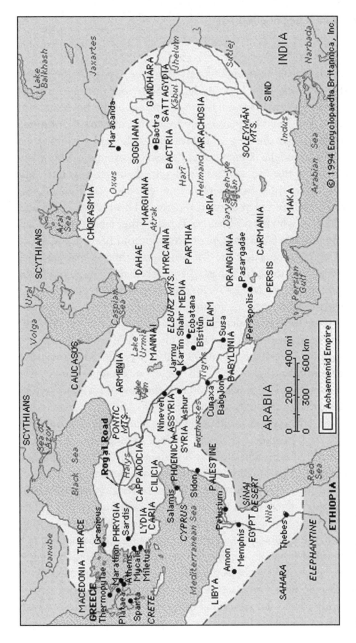

The Achaemenid empire

child, raising him as his own. By the time Cyrus was ten years old, it was clear from his attitude and behaviour that he could not be a common man's son. Hearing rumours of the boy's superior character, the old emperor summoned his steward. Confronted with the truth, the steward confessed that he had not killed the boy. Angered, the king wrought terrible revenge, seeking out and killing the old steward's real son, then tricking him into eating the corpse's flesh. Yet in a strange twist of fortune, Cyrus was allowed to return to his real parents. This is clearly a legend, the likes of which have been told about other fabled and historical figures, but it may not be entirely without historical interest.

Having subjugated the Medes, Cyrus then embarked on a career of conquest. In 547 BCE he attacked and conquered Lydia and much of Asia Minor, including some of its Greek cities. Two years later he turned his attention to the east to secure his frontiers there from nomadic violations, and conquered vast territories in the process. But the jewel in his imperial crown came with the conquest of Babylon in 539 BCE. It was the oldest surviving civilization in the region and included Mesopotamia, Syria, Phoenicia and Palestine. By 530 BCE, the year of his death, Cyrus had created the first global empire.

The fairness and moderation with which Cyrus treated the conquered people is the stuff of legend, and has been fairly extensively covered in the Old Testament. The Cyrus Cylinder – now in the British Museum – on which is proclaimed the freedom of the subject peoples in matters of religion and culture is sometimes described as the first charter of human rights. While 'human rights' is a modern concept no more than a few centuries old, the Cylinder does reflect moderation and toleration by a supreme overlord in a generally immoderate and intolerant age. Cyrus even went as far as worshipping the great god Marduk of the Babylonians. He also famously released the Jews from captivity and ordered the rebuilding of the temple at Jerusalem, which had been destroyed by previous conquerors. A letter from Cyrus to the Jews, quoted by Josephus, the first-century Romano-Jewish historian, demonstrates this tolerant attitude perfectly:

> I have given leave to as many of the Jews that dwell in my country as please to return to their own country, and to rebuild their city, and to build the temple of God at Jerusalem on the same place where it was before. I have also sent my treasurer . . . and . . . the governor of the Jews, that they may lay the foundations of the temple. I require also that the expenses for these things may be given out of my revenues. Moreover, I have also sent the vessels which [the Babylonian] king Nebuchadnezzar pillaged out of the temple, and have given them to . . . the treasurer, and to . . . the governor of the Jews, that they may have them carried to Jerusalem, and may restore them to the temple of God . . . I permit them to have the same honour which they were used to have from their forefathers, as also for their small cattle, and for wine and oil . . . The priests shall also offer these sacrifices according to the laws of Moses in Jerusalem; and when they offer them, they shall pray to God for the preservation of the king and of his family, that the kingdom of Persia may continue. But my will is, that those who disobey these injunctions, and make them void, shall be hung upon a cross, and their substance brought into the king's treasury.

Cyrus also made his mark on the landscape. Apart from the original Achaemenid capital, Anshan, and those of the conquered empires, Cyrus built his own capital, Pasargadae, some 120 kilometres from the modern city of Shiraz. The archaeological site covers 1.6 square kilometres and includes the tomb of Cyrus, the fortress of Tall-e Takht, sitting on top of a nearby hill, and the remains of two royal palaces and gardens. To stress Cyrus' lordship, carved above the gate was a message in Old Persian – Elamite – and Babylonian: *I, Cyrus, the king, an Achaemenian*. The gardens are the earliest known example of the Persian *chahar bagh*, or four-fold garden design, looking somewhat like modern tree-lined boulevards. Now in ruins, Pasargadae represented Persian art at its best during the period. Architectural and decorative borrowings from Babylonia, Egypt and other foreign lands were infused with the original Iranian arts to produce a unique composite effect, an artistic wonder that some scholars have even put above the much more majestic and less ruined complex at Persepolis.

According to Xenophon, Cyrus created the first postal system in the world, and this must have helped with intra-empire communications: he was not only a conqueror but also an empire-builder. Almost nothing is known about Cyrus' personal beliefs, but Xenophon reports that in religious matters he followed the guidance of the magians at his court.

Around 530 BCE, Cyrus the Great died. He had rushed to the east to face intruding nomads of Iranian origin when he was struck down in battle. He was succeeded by his first son, Cambyses. According to legend, before setting out to conquer Egypt in 525 BCE, Cambyses had his brother Bardiya secretly murdered for fear that he might revolt in his absence. Having conquered Egypt, and heard that in Persia an impostor named Gaumata had claimed to be Bardiya and usurped the throne, he was charging back when he died of a dagger wound on the way. The usurper ruled for some three years until, in 522, Darius (Persian, Dariyush), a high-born Achaemenid, and his fellow plotters succeeded in overthrowing him. It is worth noting that this account follows Darius' version of events. There is however some doubt as to whether or not the 'usurper' himself had not been the real Bardiya.

Thus began Darius' strong rule (522–486). A very able administrator, he divided his vast empire into twenty satrapies or governorates, each with a governor or satrap and a military commander whose activities were checked by a secret intelligence service, overseen by Darius.

The king's power was absolute and arbitrary, and the satraps enjoyed the same kind of power in their satrapies. The empire, as shaped by Cyrus, was truly vast and made up of numerous peoples who spoke many languages and worshipped according to various cults and religions. Thus it is not surprising that the social organization was not centralized, and that the people lived within their own local customs and culture. Persian definitions of justice meant that the satraps and other state officials were not to exercise their powers beyond what the king regarded as legitimate. And, as explained in the Introduction, the king's power was limited by no law or custom, only by the physical limits to his power.

One of Darius' most significant achievements was to fix the coinage and introduce the Darik or Zarik gold coins. The tax rate was standardized, though it varied from the richer to poorer satrapies. Each satrapy was assigned a gold and silver quota, which in some cases, such as Babylonia, was too heavy and led to economic decline. Tax farming was introduced, a policy which persisted in various forms down to the nineteenth century, whereby the province's revenues would be contracted to a rich and powerful tax farmer against a fixed annual payment by him to the state. Then an efficient method of filling the state treasury, in effect it delivered the people to the mercy of the tax farmer.

Not only was Darius a very able civil and military ruler, but he was also a man of vision and grandeur, conscious of building monuments to his name and leaving his version of events to posterity. Around 518 BCE he began building the complex of palaces known as Persepolis, some 70 kilometres north-east of Shiraz. It was a structure dedicated to power, to glory and to art. Persepolis was the newest and most important capital of the empire, the others being at Babylon, Ecbatana and Susa. At Susa Darius also built a monumental palace, of which, unfortunately, no part still stands. Usually on the move, the king and his retinue could then winter in Susa, spend the spring in Persepolis and go to the cool elevations of Ecbatana during the summer.

Archaeological evidence suggests that the earliest remains of Persepolis date from just four years after the accession of Darius. Consequently, some scholars have suggested that it was Cyrus who chose the site of Persepolis, with Darius continuing the plan and Xerxes (Darius' son) bringing it to completion. However, it was certainly Darius who ordered the construction of Apadana Palace, the Debating Hall and the main imperial Treasury and its surroundings. Further construction of the buildings on the Terrace at Persepolis continued until the downfall of the Achaemenid dynasty.

Apadana was the greatest and most glorious palace at Persepolis, and was used for the King of Kings' official audiences. It was a marvel of architecture, ornately decorated and lavishly adorned. The work began in 515 BCE and was completed thirty years later. The palace had a grand hall in the shape of a square with seventy-two columns, thirteen of which still stand on the enormous platform in the surviving ruins of the city. The columns carried the weight of the vast and heavy ceiling. Their capitals were made from animal sculptures such as two-headed bulls, lions and eagles. The columns were joined to each other with the help of oak and cedar beams. The walls were tiled and decorated with pictures of lions, bulls and flowers. Darius' name and the details of his empire were written in gold and silver on plates which were placed in covered stone boxes in the foundations under the four corners of the palace. The external front views of the palace were covered with pictures of the Immortals, the king's elite guards.

But perhaps no less spectacular as a feat of civil engineering was the construction of the royal road from Susa to Lydia, the capital of Sardis. It had 111 stations (where the royal party could break their journey), was patrolled by army units, could be travelled between its two ends in three months, which was very fast for the time, and was used by the king's couriers to receive information and convey commands. Almost equally impressive was the construction of a canal in Egypt (already begun before the

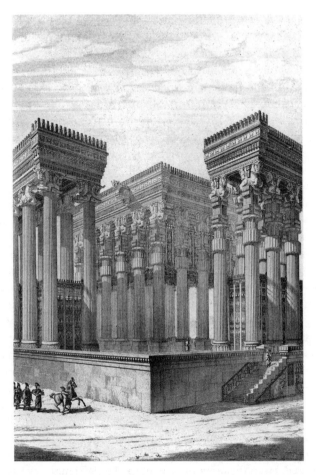

Nineteenth-century drawing of the Apadana, Persepolis by Charles Chipiez. (Source: Charles Chipiez, via Wikimedia Commons)

Persian conquest) from the Nile to the Red sea, thus connecting the Mediterranean to the Indian Ocean and anticipating the Suez Canal.

Regarding religion, in his expansive inscriptions on Mount Bisotun in the modern province of Kermanshah, Darius proclaimed himself victorious in all battles during the period of upheaval, attributing his success to the 'grace of Ahura Mazda'. Some historians take this as evidence that he was a Zoroastrian, since Ahura Mazda is the supreme deity in the Zoroastrian faith. But other evidence makes this unlikely. First, Zoroastrianism could not have been the state religion or else Darius, like Cyrus, would not have tolerated and sometimes even paid tribute to other people's cults and gods. Second, Zoroaster's name is not mentioned in any of the inscriptions. Third, the Achaemenid kings, including Darius, were buried in tombs contrary to the strict Zoroastrian rule that the dead be exposed to the elements. Fourth, Ahura Mazda was also one of the pre-Zoroastrian Iranian triad, Ahura Mazda-Mithra-Anahita. The interest in whether or not the Achaemenids and the Parthians after them were Zoroastrians arises from the fact that the prophet Zoroaster or Zarathustra predates them, and that, as mentioned below, it became the state religion under the Sasanians, the last dynasty to rule Persia before the advent of Islam.

Like Cyrus, Darius too was a conqueror though not of the same scale. Darius' war with Athens followed his subjugation of the Ionians and the conquest of some Aegean islands. The decisive battle was fought at Marathon in 490 in which the Persians were defeated. From the point of view of the Persian empire this was a relatively minor setback, but from the vantage point of Europe as the inheritor of the Greek civilization, it was a historic event.

Xerxes (486–465 BCE) had been viceroy of Babylon when his father died and he succeeded to the imperial throne. He possessed nothing of the genius of his father or of Cyrus the Great (his maternal grandfather). The victory of Athens had led to a series of revolts in Asia Minor as well as Egypt, which, typically of Iranian history, had been worsened merely because of the death of the great shah.

In 480 BCE Xerxes the Shahanshah (King of Kings) gathered the greatest army the world had yet seen and crossed the Hellespont, broke the heroic resistance of the Spartans at Thermopylae, captured Athens and set fire to the Acropolis. Despite this crushing defeat, the Greeks refused to give up. Instead they concentrated their fleet on Salamis and defeated the King of Kings' forces at sea before his own eyes, watching as he was from his throne placed on the shore. This critical victory ended Persian ambitions for further advances in Europe.

Xerxes was an ill-tempered ruler with proclivities to impulsive and cruel behaviour. He was assassinated in a palace coup, and, unsurprisingly, the assassin was his own son.

The Achaemenid empire was to survive for more than 130 years after the death of Xerxes before Alexander the Great conquered it. But although the empire remained unrivalled in its vastness and power, it had already passed its peak and was never to attain the glory that its founders had brought to it. The rest of the Achaemenid rule was generally distinguished by two series of events: court intrigues, assassinations and struggles for succession; and frequent rebellions, often in more than one province at a time. Bloodletting became virtually a regular feature of the court and the royal family. Some of the satrapies in effect passed out of the Great King's rule.

During this period, several king-emperors ruled the empire. They were often incompetent and their rules were seldom of long duration. The beginning of the end came when Philip, ruler of Macedon, who had annexed some Greek territories, began to be recognized as the leader capable of standing up to the Persians. At first Philip moved cautiously and concluded a peace treaty with Artaxerxes III (359–338 BCE). The Greeks were not so fortunate, and not long afterwards, in 338 BCE, Philip attacked and put an end to Greek independence. In the same year the strong Persian king was poisoned to death by his general, Bagoas.

Bagoas went on to poison Artaxerxes' son as well, leaving the succession to the ill-fated Darius III (335–330 BCE), a relative. Darius III would have been poisoned by Bagoas too, had he not moved swiftly and poisoned Bagoas first.

Philip of Macedon had gathered a strong army for the invasion of Persia when he fell victim to assassination and was succeeded by his young son Alexander. Leading an army of 40,000 men, Alexander went on to conquer Persia's Greek colonies. Having been defeated twice in the battles of Granicus and Issus, Darius' peace offerings were rejected by Alexander. He lost the final battle in 331 and fled to Ecbatana, where he was killed by two of his satraps. The gateway to Susa and Persepolis was then open to Alexander's forces, but, due to conflicting historical accounts, it is not clear whether Persepolis was burned intentionally or by accident. Thus the mighty Persian empire crumbled even more swiftly than it had been built.

The Achaemenids built an empire and created a world civilization. Never before had such diverse and distant peoples and lands been brought under one rule. The achievement is made even more impressive when we consider the sheer diversity of ethnicities, religions, languages and cultures that thrived as part of the empire. This diversity, combined with massive expenditure by the central government on buildings, in addition to the luxury consumption of the upper classes, led to the emergence of a distinct Persian style of art in architecture, sculpture, decoration and craft, which even spread to foreign lands such as India.

The Hellenistic interlude (306–c. 150 BCE)

Alexander died in 323 BCE, and within twenty years his vast empire had been divided up between Macedonia (including Greece) led by Zeos the Great, the Ptolemys of Egypt and the Seleucids of Iran. This is the beginning of Greek cultural influence in Iran: although not ruling Greece, the Seleucid culture was largely Hellenistic. The Seleucids basically adopted the Achaemenid system of administration and, as before, the state owned all the land. Where they diverged from the Achaemenids was in building Greek-style cities. The Seleucids founded many new cities and also rebuilt some old cities under new names. These were run along the lines of the Greek *polis*, with its assembly of peoples, its council and its officials appointed annually.

At first, the Seleucids adopted Darius' principle of a centralized state, but later necessity compelled them to loosen their grip in the style of Cyrus the Great. Various Greek colonies had already been founded as far east as Bactria (Afghanistan). Greek as the official language as well as the language of the upper classes replaced Aramaic, the official language under the Achaemenids. Many Greeks and Macedonians married Persian women and settled in Persia. Thus Hellenization took place without compulsion or a special official policy for its promotion. Indeed, it was a two-way process since the intermingling and intermarriage of the two peoples also led to the Persianization of some Greeks, even in matters of religion. The place least affected was Persis or Persia proper, which, being the heartland of the old civilization and not on the major trade routes, maintained its linguistic, cultural and religious character better than most other Iranian provinces.

Achaemenid art was inevitably interrupted because the patronage of art passed on to the Seleucid court, the Greek settlers and colonies in Persia, and the Hellenized Persian upper classes. The resultant style was neither Greek nor Persian art but hybrid forms of both, which reflected a conscious or unconscious artistic compromise.

The vast Seleucid empire, stretching from the Mediterranean to Jaxartes (Persian, Syr Darya) and Indus (Sind), made up of various Iranian and non-Iranian peoples proved more difficult to unite as one political body than the Achaemenid empire. After all, the Seleucids were outsiders in Iran. By the middle of the third century BCE they had effectively lost control over Bactria and Parthia in the east, while the Romans were gradually advancing from the west. After losing Mesopotamia to the Parthians about a century later, they were reduced to little more than a monarchy made up of a couple of provinces which were in effect mostly independent. Shortly thereafter, and without much of a fight, they were absorbed into the Roman empire like the rest of the Greek monarchies, and the Seleucid empire was over.

Arsacid Parthians (247 BCE–CE 224)

Long before the fall of the Seleucids, however, two brothers of Iranian Scythian origins managed to dislodge them in the north-east of their empire in 247 BCE, shortly after the Bactrian Greeks had declared independence from them. Arsaces (Persian, Arshak or Ashk) was a chief of the Scythian Parni tribe whose rebellion led to the defeat of the local Seleucid forces and the conquest of Parthia. The Parthians themselves had originally been a nomadic Iranian people who raided the eastern marches of Achaemenid Persia until they settled in Parthia and became subjects of that empire. At about the same time, Arsaces' brother Tiridates (Persian, Tirdad) managed to wrest Hyrcania (Gorgan) out of Seleucid hands and went on to build a new capital named after his brother Ashk (cf. Ashgabat or Ashkabad, the capital of modern Turkmenistan).

However, the true founder of the Parthian empire was Mithridates (Persian, Mehrdad) I, who, between 160 and 140 BCE succeeded in conquering most of the already crumbling posses-sions of the Seleucids, including Media and Babylon, and reviv-ing the Achaemenid title of King of Kings.

The Parthians were semi-nomadic, north-eastern strangers to the central and western Iranian lands that they conquered.

They were therefore greeted with a good deal of hostility by their newly won Greek as well as Persian subjects. The Greek Seleucids made one final attempt under Phraates (Persian, Farhad) II to hold on to their lands, and for a time it looked as if the Parthians would have to concede defeat. But in 129 BCE Mithridates I struck a decisive blow and managed to drive the Seleucids all the way back to Syria.

It was while Mithridates ruled that Rome reached the Euphrates and for the first time became a neighbour to the Parthians. He tried to woo the Romans into an alliance against the kingdoms of Armenia and Asia Minor, which had successfully resisted Roman advances. But the famous Roman leader Sulla, who knew little about the Parthians, responded with virtual contempt. Slighted, Mithridates entered an alliance with those two kingdoms instead. Typically, however, for Iran, fortunes were changing from one short term to the next. It was after a few years of weakness and chaos that the able and powerful Mithridates II became emperor in 123 BCE, and managed to restore order and power, though predictably, his death in 88 BCE was followed by almost three decades of decadence and decline. At the time it looked as if the sun had completely set on the Arsacid empire, reducing them almost to the level of a vassal state of the Armenians. The turning point came when the Romans, alarmed by the expansion of Armenia and Asia Minor, offered a treaty to Phraates III.

The peace, however, was short-lived and a few years later, in 53 BCE, Crassus the famous Roman triumvir and consul of Syria decided to score a great victory over his fellow triumvirs in Rome by attacking in the hope of inflicting a heavy defeat on the Parthians. But all did not go to plan when his army was met by the able Iranian general, Sorena. Crassus' army was routed and Crassus lost his life in the process. Once again there was a meteoric rise in the star of the Iranians. Some of this fortune quickly turned however when Orodes, who having killed his father Phraates III was now ruler, decided to take advantage of

Crassus' defeat and march through Syria to the Mediterranean. Some of the failure of this campaign was because Orodes had killed the great general Sorena in a fit of jealousy. In true Iranian style, Orodes was in turn killed by his son around 29 BCE, despite the fact that he had nominated him as his successor. The new king then had all his brothers killed for good measure. It was a killing party, the likes of which have not been rare in Iranian history.

From then on, the Parthians had to face the Romans in the west as well as the recurring invasion of nomads of Iranian race from Outer Iran in the east. The first major Roman invasion in CE 115 resulted in the fall of Ctesiphon, the Parthian capital near modern Baghdad. For a while it looked as if Parthia was lost for ever, but for a while pressure from forces in the north-east pushed the Romans back.

Under Vologases (Persian, Balash) III the Parthians renewed their offensive and made some advances but the Romans turned the tide against them, and in 165 BCE once again entered Ctesiphon. This did not last, but still some of the western Iranian provinces had to be ceded to Rome, especially as the Parthians' continual struggle for succession to the throne resulted in feeble and divided leadership.

This indeed was what enabled Rome to attack and capture Ctesiphon again in CE 197. On the other hand, in CE 217 Artabanus (Persian, Ardavan) V defeated the Romans heavily and exacted a high price from them. But luck had now permanently turned against the Parthians, for while Artabanus and his brother were busy fighting for the throne, the rebellion in Persis eventually led to the downfall of the Parthians in CE 224.

The Parthian system of administration was loose and decentralized relative to the Achaemenid system. In fact, it did not change much from the late Seleucid system, when the vassal states had become stronger and largely autonomous. The Arsacids did not and perhaps could not change that system, partly because their own origin was nomadic and partly also because the old western provinces did not view them as culturally equal. Indeed, when there was a clash with the Seleucids and later the Romans the old countries of the empire often welcomed the invaders. That is why whenever the Arsacids were in dire trouble they tried to organize support from the people of their own origin in the north-east, east of the Caspian Sea.

Nevertheless, they were in charge of the empire as a whole and the vassal states had to pay tributes and taxes and contribute to the military forces whenever there was an external war. That is why the early Islamic historians described the Arsacids as *Muluk al-Tawa'if*, literally meaning Kings of Tribes. There were some differences with the Achaemenid system even at the centre, especially with the existence of two councils – one, of the great nobles, and another of the elders and magi, who advised the king.

While there were always men under arms both at the centre and in the vassal states, there was no organized central army and, as noted, levies would be called in from all regions at times of war. The cream of the Parthian army was made up of heavy cavalry and light cavalry, the latter consisting of mounted archers who were especially noted for their mobility and ease of manoeuvring.

For a long time the inscription Philhellene (Greece-friendly) appeared on the Arsacid coinage, indicating their amenity towards Greek culture, or, in truth, Hellenistic Iran. Twentieth-century Iranian historians tended to interpret this as lack of nationalism. In fact, it is likely that the Parthians, being simple and undeveloped nomads were influenced by Hellenized Persians of the Iranian hinterland. However, the first signs of a neo-Iranian cultural revival appeared under Vologases I in the first century CE. On the reverse side of his coinage an indigenous fire altar was depicted together with a sacrificing priest, and the money bore letters of the Arsacid Pahlavi (Parthavi or Parti) alphabet, Parti evolving under the Parthians from Old Persian and later developing into the Sasanian Middle Persian or Pahlavi.

There is disagreement among scholars about the religion of the Arsacids. The cults of the old Iranian gods, including Ahura Mazda, were certainly worshipped in their times; but it cannot be easily assumed that they were Zoroastrian, since they tolerated Greek as well as Iranian cults, their bloody sacrifices would be repugnant to Zoroastrians and great temples flourished particularly dedicated to the worship of the ancient Iranian deities. It must be emphasized that in any case the religions of the common people must have been several and varied.

It is difficult to appreciate the position of written literature during the period, as there was a great oral tradition. However, there are a few notable exceptions such as the Pahlavi story, *Derakht-e Asurik* (Assyrian Tree), relating a debate between a goat and a palm tree, that is likely to date from the Parthian period, though its origins are in ancient Sumerian culture. Elusive as Arsacid literature is, it made an impact on other cultures. The legend of Tristan and Isolde, for example, was probably influenced by *Vis o Ramin* (Vis and Ramin), which has been rendered in Persian verse by the eleventh-century poet Fakhr al-Din As'ad Gorgani, and is normally traced back to the Arsacid period although it is no longer extant in the Parti-Pahlavi language.

More has survived of non-literary arts. Parthian art and architecture reflected the artistic eclecticism of the period. Most of the architectural remains lie in the west, and are influenced by the Achaemenid, Hellenistic and Mesopotamian forms, tempered by their own nomadic traditions. Some of the most important features of Sasanian and Islamic art, for example the *eyvan* (or *ivan*) and stucco decoration, have their origin in the Arsacid period.

Sasanian Persia (CE 224–651)

The Sasanians who rose from Persis (or 'Persia proper') and defeated the Arsacids ruled Persia for over four centuries and ran a large empire, though it was smaller than the Achaemenids'. During the Greek and Parthian periods Persis had managed to retain more of the traditional Persian character, and, unlike some of the other regions of the empire, Zoroastrianism had flourished in that region. The Sasanians, being Persian proper rather than Parthian, are often thought to have restored the Achaemenid empire. It is, however, telling that *Shahnameh*, the great ancient Persian epic that has been handed down by the Sasanians, makes no mention of the Achaemenids at all.

Shahnameh is the great epic, which includes tragedy as well as romance and recounts ancient Iranian myths and legends. It also includes a legendary history of the Sasanians. Rendered in verse by the great Persian poet Abolqasem Ferdowsi from the tenth to the eleventh century, *Shahnameh* is made up of three cycles, Pishdadiyan, Keyaniyan and Sasanian. The first cycle, beginning with the dawn of man and the kingdom of Pishdadiyan, is pure mythology. The next cycle describes the Iranian kingdom of Keyaniyan, the long story of a heroic age in which myth and legend combine to produce an ancient epic, the exploits of Rostam, Sohrab, Siyavosh, Esfandiyar and many other heroes and champions. The first two cycles of *Shahnameh* are centred on eastern Persia, whereas the third cycle is centred in the south and west. It mixes history with legend while providing an account of the history of the Sasanian monarchy, the last Persian dynasty before the Arab conquest.

Returning to Sasanian history: they faced periodic conflicts on three of their frontiers – west, east and north. In the west they faced the Byzantine Romans, the objects of their conflicts often being Armenia and western Mesopotamia. In the east they faced the intrusions and sometimes invasions of various Central Asian nomads, the (racially Iranian) Kushans followed by the Hephthalites, or White Huns, who were later supplanted by Turks. And in the north they had to contend with the continual raids of nomadic Huns, as well as the conflict over Armenia with Rome.

However, while the Sasanians' foreign conflicts and difficulties have been extensively discussed, since they have involved many wars, their domestic divisions have received less attention. For conflicts over succession and general disorder as a result of foreign or domestic weakness persisted under their rule, so that there were many more years of near anarchy or weak government than of stability and firm rule. Of the numerous Sasanian rulers, only four ably defended or extended the empire's frontiers and maintained powerful and stable governments at home: in the third century CE, Ardeshir Babakan, the founder of the empire, and his son Shapur I; in the fourth century, Shapur II; in the sixth century Chosroes (Persian, Khosrow) I.

The Sasanian ruler was, like previous Iranian rulers, regarded as omnipotent and, as one described himself, 'Companion of the stars and brother of the sun and moon'. His word was law. The grand vizier or chief administrator was the next most powerful in the land, more powerful than princes of the blood, who lived in constant danger of losing everything including his property and life on dismissal – a pattern that, for nobles and notables, remained the same throughout Iranian history.

The administration of the state was centralized along Achaemenid lines. A few vassal states remained, but the remaining provinces were run not by satraps but by governors-general or *marzban*s who played an important role, especially in frontier provinces, in keeping the peace and managing their region. While the administration was relatively centralized, the relationship between vassals, governors and grandees and the state greatly depended on the position and personality of the ruler. An able and powerful shah such as Shapur I (and after him, Shapur II) was able to assert the authority of the centre to the full, but often for decades the relationship would become loose and result in states of anarchy or semi-anarchy.

As noted above, the Sasanians formed the first Iranian state to have an official religion – Zoroastrianism – and since then, Iran has always had a state religion. Nevertheless, various other cults and faiths had open or secret currency including Judaism, Christianity and Buddhism. Christians were tolerated, even welcomed, for as long as they were persecuted by Rome. But once Christianity became the state religion in Rome, they were constantly persecuted, except for the Nestorian Christians, who were in turn persecuted as heretics by the official Church of Byzantine Rome. The Christians joined the Zoroastrians in the persecution of the Manichaeans and Mazdakites.

As mentioned above, Ardeshir Babakan was already ruler of Pars (Persia proper, the Iranian province on the Persian Gulf) when he rebelled against his overlord Artabanus (Ardavan), the Parthian emperor. Ardeshir, a grandson of the Zoroastrian high priest Sasan, then extended his authority to neighbouring provinces as well. Artabanus tried to stem the tide but was defeated and killed in battle in CE 224, and the Sasanian empire was thus founded.

Ardeshir's triumph led to the rebellion of other vassals and provinces who wished to become independent, with Roman support. At that point, direct conflict with Rome became inevitable and after a series of defeats Ardeshir made some territorial gains at the expense of Byzantium. It was Ardeshir who made Zoroastrianism the state religion.

Zoroaster is the English name of the prophet Zarathustra, who reformed the ancient Iranian cult and was the first prophet to teach a revealed monotheistic religion similar to the Abrahamic faiths. There is much uncertainty about the period in which he flourished, but according to recent studies he was born between 1400 and 1000 BCE. According to the Gathas, the seventeen hymns in verse which are his own works, Zoroaster was trained for priesthood, which he probably entered at fifteen. Based on Zoroastrian traditions, he was thirty when he received his call: he saw a shining divine being at the bank of a river who led him to the presence of Ahura Mazda flanked by six other radiant beings.

It was there and then that the prophet received his revelation. Zoroaster proclaimed Ahura Mazda as the one eternally existing god and supreme creator of all that is good, including all the beneficent divinities. Coexisting with Ahura Mazda, however, is the lord of darkness, Ahriman, the equally uncreated god and supreme lord of what is bad, of 'non-life', in contrast to Ahura Mazda who rules over all that is good, over 'life', and who will eventually triumph over Ahriman. Zoroaster assigned individual responsibility to human beings for clean living and care for others, summarized in the moral code 'good thoughts, good words, good deeds'. Zoroastrian cosmic history consists of three cycles, Creation (the original state of bliss), Mixed State (the present world in which good and evil exist side by side) and Separation (the final state of permanent bliss). All human beings irrespective of rank and gender will go to paradise (Old Persian, *pardis*, or garden) if they are worthy of it. The dead person is met on the Bridge of the Separator by three angels who weigh up his or her worldly deeds on a scale. If the scale tips towards the good deeds, the person will be sent to paradise; if bad deeds, to hell, and if they just balance, to purgatory, a neutral state of neither bliss nor torment, until the end of the world.

Zoroaster seems to have taught that a saviour would come after him who would lead the final war on evil and return peace, harmony and bliss to the world. This is Saoshyant, who Zoroastrians believe will be born of the sacred seed of the prophet himself which is miraculously preserved at the bottom of a lake. When the time comes, a virgin will bathe in the lake and become pregnant with the prophet's seed and give birth to a child who will thus become the saviour of humankind. The popular belief that Zoroastrians are fire-worshippers is due to a misunderstanding. Fire was sacred to them as the symbol of light. Consequently the Sasanians built fire temples everywhere. These were places where the faithful held their communal prayers and sang the sacred hymns in front of perpetual fires.

In CE 240, Ardeshir's son Shapur succeeded him. The war with Byzantium was going well and Persian territories were extending in the north and west. At one stage the Roman emperor Valerianus himself became a prisoner and died in captivity. A famous relief on the wall of Naqsh-e Rostam shows Shapur mounted while Valerianus is kneeling in front of his horse. Shapur too had to deal with the continuing menace of nomads on the eastern frontiers of the empire.

It was during Shapur's reign that Manichaeism made its first appearance. Its founder was Mani, a man of Iranian origin probably with a Jewish-Christian background, who advocated the new faith, a hybrid and highly mystical form of Zoroastrianism, Christianity and Buddhism. Shapur initially welcomed Mani, but pressure from Zoroastrians and Christians obliged him to banish him honourably to the eastern provinces and to neighbouring countries where, both by the force of his personality and teaching, he made a lasting impact among the population, who were in large part Buddhist. He was later allowed to return, but when he succeeded to the throne, Shapur's son Bahram ordered the execution of Mani and persecution of his followers, prompted both by his own fanaticism and by pressure from Zoroastrian and Christian leaders.

Shapur I's strong, able rule was again followed by a period of weakness, rebellion, palace coups and short-lived reigns. Between CE 272, the year of Shapur's death, and 309, the year of the accession of Shapur II, no fewer than six rulers reigned in Persia. The country was still in a state of anarchy when the chiefs agreed upon the succession of the boy king Shapur II, who was, fortunately, a strong and successful ruler.

After Shapur II reached majority, he led a campaign against the Kushans in the east – who had taken advantage of the turmoil and expanded their territory – in effect abolishing them as a state. Shapur was in the midst of trying to check similar Roman expansionism when the White Huns disturbed the eastern frontiers, which ended up with concessions from both sides. Returning to the conflict with Rome, he eventually succeeded in recovering the disputed territories, including Armenia. Next he put down his Arab vassals who had rebelled during the previous reign and brought chaos.

An important event under Shapur II was the conversion of the Emperor Constantine to Christianity, which made it the state religion in Rome. Armenia too was converted. From then on, the contest over Armenia acquired a whole new dimension, and the attitude of the Sasanians towards their Christian subjects underwent a basic change. Christians who had enjoyed relative freedom of worship before were persecuted under Shapur II and afterwards, except for the Nestorian Christians when they escaped from Roman persecution to Iran.

Shapur II died in CE 379 after ruling Persia with an iron fist for almost seventy years. Once again, this was followed by a century of turmoil and mediocrity. There were periodic provincial rebellions, palace coups and even the intervention of White Huns in Persia's internal affairs.

The Christian question took an unusual turn under Yazdgerd the Sinner (399–421), who was well disposed towards Christians. It was an important reason for his being unpopular with the notables and the priesthood, though they also accused him of ill temper and cruelty. As a result, he earned the title *bezehkar*, meaning 'sinner'. According to received history, which was written by his opponents, he not only killed those Zoroastrian priests who disagreed with his religious policies but also gave favourable treatment to Jews and Christians. Christianity was recognized as an official religion during his reign, and the Byzantine historian Agathias refers to him as a 'pro-Christian' king who was also 'friendly and peaceable'. His reign was a time of peace with Rome, and the Roman emperor asked Yazdgerd to become his son's guardian. According to legend, the King of Kings was in

Hyrcania (modern-day Gorgan) when he was kicked to death by a magical horse believed to have been sent by God to kill him in punishment of his sins. The most likely explanation is that he was murdered by the nobility and the story was invented later.

Yazdgerd's enemies put someone other than his son, Bahram V, on the throne, but the latter (421–38) managed to defeat the usurper and recover his throne with military aid from the Arab prince who had brought him up. In an ordeal, the crown was put between two hungry lions and Bahram managed to kill the lions and take it. He was also known as Wild Ass Bahram, apparently because of his love of hunting onagers (wild ass). According to legend, he went down in quicksand while chasing an onager; though, rather like his father, he may have been the victim of an assassination.

Bahram loved music, wine, women and the chase, and has been widely romanticized in classical Persian literature, the best example being Nezami's poem *Seven Beauties*. While wandering through the palace, Bahram discovers a locked room which contains a depiction of seven princesses; hence the name *Haft Peykar* (seven beauties). Each of the princesses is from one of the seven different climes (the traditional Zoroastrian, and later, Islamic division of the earth) and he falls in love with them. This happens before his father's death and his accession. When he becomes king, he searches for the seven princesses and wins them as his brides. He orders his architect to construct seven domes for his new brides. The architect tells him that each of the seven climes is ruled by one of the seven planets, and advises him to adorn each dome with the colour that is associated with that clime and planet. The princesses take up residence in the splendid pavilions. The king visits the princesses on successive days of the week; on Saturday the Indian princess, who is governed by Saturn, and so on. Each princess relates to the king a story matching the mood of her respective colour. These seven beautifully constructed and sensuous stories occupy about half of the whole poem. The rest of the story is occupied with the remainder of Bahram's life and times.

In CE 488, fifty years after Bahram's death, his descendant Qobad succeeded to the throne. He was deposed and imprisoned in 497, escaped jail and with the help of the White Huns regained his throne in 499. The reason for this palaver was his conversion to Mazdakism. Mazdakism had emerged after fifty years of famine, defeat and anarchy, which was not showing any sign of subsiding. Mazdak's was a religion, or heresy, the principal message of which was social and economic reform, and it attracted large numbers of supporters and activists. He advocated, and for a time succeeded in opening the state granaries to the people, and opening up some of the notables' harems, which led to the unlikely charge against him that he believed in wife-sharing. Qobad was converted but Mazdak's teachings threatened the social position of the priesthood and notables. The situation was comparable to Shapur I's early encouragement of Manichaeism, only much worse for Qobad.

Qobad moderated his support for Mazdak after regaining his throne, but religious and upper-class opposition remained strong. It was led by Qobad's third son Chosroes (Khosrow) whom the opposition had imposed as his father's heir designate. The show-down came in CE 524, when in an assembly organized by Chosroes and his men, ostensibly for conducting a debate between Mazdak and his opponents, they fell on the prophet and his supporters, beginning a tide of violence against Mazdakites all over the country.

On Qobad's death Chosroes I, Anushiravan (one with an immortal soul), succeeded to the Persian throne. He was further entitled the Just, a title that in Iranian socio-historical culture was fully justified not only because he destroyed Mazdakism but especially as, through sheer wisdom and extraordinary ability, he finally stamped out decades of famine, disorder, foreign defeat, economic decline and weak government. He was therefore deemed to have held the *farr* or Divine Grace more clearly than most other Sasanian rulers.

With Persia strong and stable, war with Rome was almost inevitable, although after thirty years of battling there was a return to the previous status quo. Between CE 558 and 561 Chosroes finally overthrew the Hephthalite (White Hun) kingdom in the east. At the same time the Persians were being pressed from behind by Central Asian Turks, who replaced the Huns as the new nomadic and semi-nomadic power on Persia's eastern frontiers. A change that would have far-reaching consequences both for the future of Iran and Europe when, centuries later, Turkish nomads began to pour into Iran and Asia Minor, eventually resulting in the foundation of the Ottoman empire.

Hormazd (Hormoz) IV replaced his father on his death in 579. Typically after an exceptionally firm rule, the country's basic stability and strength began to be lost and the underlying tendency towards chaos set in. This time the decline was for good, and several decades later it led to the defeat and dissolution of the Sasanian empire by Muslim Arabs. According to the *Shahnameh*, Hormazd killed all of his father's counsellors and secretaries upon succession apparently, as Sa'di later wrote, because he was afraid of them since he sensed they were afraid of him.

Conflict in the east and west continued without much success. There was domestic conflict and opposition when Bahram Chubin, an able general, rebelled and, in 590, with the support of the shah's son Chosroes and the latter's maternal uncles, killed Hormazd. Shortly afterwards, Bahram also deposed Chosroes and declared himself shah, though this time his rebellion did not prevail and he lost his life.

Chosroes II, later entitled *Aparviz* (modern Persian, *Parviz*), or Victorious, for a time superficially plastered over the crumbling structure of the Sasanian empire. Of all the rulers of ancient Persia, Chosroes II is the most romantically portrayed in classical

Persian literature for his adventurous love of Shirin, his Armenian wife, other women, wine, music and horses.

Nezami's great poem *Khosrow and Shirin* recounts the story of Khosrow's courtship of Princess Shirin, and the demise of Shirin's devoted lover Farhad, Khosrow's unequal rival. Khosrow endures long journeys, physical and spiritual, before returning to Shirin, his true love. There are other women, including Khosrow's other wife or concubine Shekar, Shirin's jealously of whom plays a role in strengthening her love for Khosrow. It is worth noting that, in Persian, *shirin* means sweet and *shekar*, sugar. There is much adventure but pure and selfless love is represented in the figure of Farhad, secretly in love with Shirin, who finally falls victim to the shah's jealous wrath.

Khosrow's twenty-seven-year warring with Byzantium, which were at first successful, ended in disastrous defeat, and the country was in ruins both materially and in spirit when, taking a leaf from his own book, the rebels, supported by his son Shiruyeh deposed, blinded and later killed him in CE 624. According to legend, Shirin committed suicide after the murder of Khosrow.

There followed about a dozen rulers, one after the other, most of whom were killed or blinded. In CE 632 a prince was put on the throne as Yazdgerd III by the notables, who in practice dominated him. Only four years later in 636 at Qadesyieh, a small Arab force defeated a mighty Persian army. Ctesiphon fell a couple of years later, and this was followed by the rout of Yazdgerd'a army at Nahavand in Persia proper. Yazdgerd escaped towards the east with a large retinue but nowhere were they prepared to let him stay, let alone provide support for him. Eventually he sought refuge with the governor of the city of Marv (now ruins in Turkmenistan), and in one way or another he led Yazdgerd to his death in 651.

One reason for the swift, easy victory of the Arab armies was their freshness, zeal and total faith in their revolutionary ideology.

But the fact that they broke the entire Persian empire so quickly must have been due to already existing dynastic struggles, chaos and the people's lack of interest in defending the regime that ruled over them. It also largely explains why the Arabs did not manage to conquer Byzantium, then or later.

Thus ended the eleven hundred years of ancient Persia. The Persians proper ruled the empire for half this period, the Achaemenid and Sasanian civilizations being separated by the Seleucid Hellenistic interlude and the Iranian Parthian empire. The rise and fall of the fortunes of each of these empires, and those who lived and ruled them, was based on absolute and arbitrary rule combined with frequent anarchy and disorder which gave rise to a society that was characteristically Iranian. They ruled vast territories inhabited by peoples of various racial and ethnic origins; they lived at war and in peace with Greece, Rome and the peoples of Central Asia and the Caucasus; they created or absorbed many cults and religions; and they gave rise to a complex culture, many of whose traces can be observed down to the present day.

2

Medieval Persia

Iranian history is marked by dramas of various dimensions. The greatest of these dramas were the Alexandrian Greek conquest of the Achaemenid empire, the Arab conquest of the Sasanian empire, the Mongol invasions and conquests of the thirteenth century and the Afghan rebellion of the early eighteenth century that brought down the Safavid empire. And if these events have one thing in common which makes them distinctly Iranian, it is the fact that they were all short, sharp and decisive, taking only a few years and meeting little resistance.

In the mid-seventh century, following the Arab conquest, ancient Persia came to an end and medieval Persia began. This was an extended period, stretching over eleven and a half centuries. Clearly, Iran in the eighteenth century was in many ways a different society from that of the seventh century, a fact that is equally true of the early feudal period compared with the late feudal period in Europe, also classically defined as medieval. But in terms of its basic sociological, technological, religious and cultural features, and compared with what went before and what came after it, the period is demonstrably distinct. Put briefly, it stretches from the end of the ancient period to the dawn of modernization in Iran in the early nineteenth century.

The Arabs and Islam

The advent of Islam in Arabia in the early seventh century CE ushered in a long, deep, widespread revolution in the lands extending from the Indus to Spain. Not only parts of the

Byzantine empire, but the whole of the Persian empire suc-
cumbed to the onslaught of Muslim Arabs within a short period
after the death of the Prophet Mohammad in CE 632.

Mohammad, the Prophet of Islam was born in Mecca, in the
Arabian Peninsula, around CE 570 into a notable family of the
Hashim clan of the great Quraysh tribe. However, he was
orphaned at an early age and grew up impoverished. On reaching
adulthood Mohammad became a merchant, travelling to lands
such as Syria and Palestine, and married one of his employers,
Khadija, believed to have been older than him.

The Prophet was forty when he received his first revelations
in Mecca, instructing him to call the community to the worship
of the one God. Mecca was a centre of trade and a place of pilgrimage, where pilgrims gathered every year in peace to exchange
goods and enjoy the festival, which involved worship, trade and
social intercourse. The cubic structure, the Ka'ba, at the very
heart of the city, was the object of pilgrimage and at the time
housed several idols worshipped by the peoples of Arabia.
Mohammad's message, 'Say there is no god but the one God', was
thus a direct threat to the old pluralistic faith. By CE 622, the
persecution of Muslims in Mecca had reached such a point that
Mohammad responded to sympathetic calls from Medina, to
which he and his followers migrated. This mass migration is
called *hijra* in Arabic and is the basis of the Islamic calendar in the
same way that the birth of Christ is the basis of the Christian
calendar.

Thenceforth a state of war existed between the Muslims and
Meccans. Muslims raided caravans bound for Mecca and the
conflict soon escalated until several battles eventually led to the
Muslims' triumphal return to Mecca in 630. Before his death in
632, Mohammad had united the whole of the Arabian Peninsula
as the *Umma*, or community of Muslims.

'Islam' means submission to the will of God. The Qur'an, its
holy scripture, contains the revelations of God to the Prophet

from his first investiture until his departure from this world. Abraham is seen as the first Muslim in the word's literal sense, the first person to become monotheist, the ancestor of the Arab (as well as Jewish) people, and the founder of the Ka'ba as the House of God. The Old and New Testaments are accepted as holy books of the Abrahamic tradition, with reservations about certain parts which contradict the teachings of the Qur'an. For example, the Qur'an rejects the divinity of Christ but accepts the virgin birth as a manifestation of God's will.

The main pillars of Islam shared by all the Muslim sects are Monotheism, Prophet-hood (Revelation) and Resurrection in the Day of Judgement, to which the Shi'a (followers of Imam Ali) add Divine Justice (*Adl*) and Divine Leadership of the Community (the Imamate). Muslims must say the ritual prayers five times a day, go on pilgrimage to Mecca (hajj) at least once if they can afford it, enjoin the good and forbid the bad, give alms to the needy, and so forth. They are not to drink alcohol, may not eat pork, are not to backbite, or practise incest.

There is no celibacy in Islam, and marriage is encouraged. Men may marry up to four wives, but must treat all of them fairly and evenly. Women have the right to inherit from their parents, siblings and other family members, but only half the amount inherited by the male heirs. Under the Prophet, hejab did not include the covering of the face and hands, and in fact women were quite active in the community. Men had the right of divorce, but women could ask for divorce on certain grounds.

What Muslims believe

Muslim beliefs in heaven, hell, angels and Satan are all in line with the Jewish, Christian and – in a different form – Zoroastrian traditions. They believe that God created the world in six days, and that Adam and Eve were expelled from the Garden of Eden because they ate the forbidden fruit, though in the Islamic version this is wheat, not an apple. Helping the community is a highly rewarded deed. 'Muslims are brethren; make peace among your brothers.' There are moral obligations to oneself, one's relatives, to society and to God. Human beings are judged at death, and their good and bad deeds are weighed up to see whether they should go to heaven or hell. There will be universal judgement at the resurrection. God is merciful, compassionate, loving and forgiving, but he is also the ultimate judge and arbiter of right and wrong, and will reward the righteous and punish wrongdoers.

Upon the Prophet Mohammad's death, conflict broke out over the succession. In a meeting of community leaders, a close companion of the Prophet, Abubakr (632–4), was elected his successor or caliph, that is, one who had replaced the Prophet's authority in both worldly and spiritual matters. The Prophet's own clan, Bani Hashim, were not pleased with this election, including Abbas, the Prophet's uncle (from whom the long line of Abbasid caliphs would later descend) and the party of Ali – Mohammad's cousin and son-in-law – who had not been present at the election meeting.

Abubakr was followed by Omar (Arabic, Umar, 634–44), also a leading but radical member of Mohammad's personal companions, during whose rule the Arab conquest of the Sasanian empire began. Next came Osman (Arabic, Uthman, 644–56) who, unlike the first two caliphs, was not ascetic and was suspected of favouritism and nepotism. The opposition to his rule finally led to a rebellion that cost him his life. He was succeeded by Ali, the Prophet's son-in-law.

Shi'ism

Shi'ism is the sect of Islam that was born out of the dispute over the succession of the Prophet, and which later developed other important differences to the majority sect of the Sunnis. The Shi'a believed (as they still do) that Ali was the rightful successor because, they held, the succession was not an elective matter but had been preordained by God and confirmed in public by the Prophet before his death, which the majority sect, the Sunnis, denied. Thus they regarded the first three caliphs as usurpers, and revered Ali not just as a caliph but the real and rightful leader of the Muslims from the start, the Imam who was sinless and infallible and – according to some interpretations – omniscient.

Shi'ism later divided into several subgroups, by far the most populous of which today is Twelver Shi'ism, Iran's state religion and the majority faith in Iraq. The Shi'as were a minority in Iran before the sixteenth century when it was made the state religion under Shah Ismail I, the founder of the Safavid dynasty.

There are various differences in matters of ritual, law, and so on between Sunnis and Shi'as, but the most fundamental difference is on the question of the Imamate. The Twelver Shi'as believe that the twelve Imams descending one after the other from Ali and the Prophet's daughter Fatima have been the rightful, preordained leaders of the Islamic community. None of them, except during Ali's short rule, ever ruled the Islamic world but this did not put in doubt their true righteousness in any way, and each in their time was regarded as spiritual leader of the Shi'a community. Four of these Imams have the greatest significance. The first is Ali, 'Lion of God' and 'Shah of Men'. Second is the Third Imam, Hoseyn, second son of Ali, who was martyred by the army of Umayyad Yazid in the plain of Karbala (see below). Third is the Sixth Imam, Ja'far al-Sadiq, who is the founder of the Twelver Shi'a school of law and jurisprudence. Fourth is the Twelfth Imam, Mohammad son of Hasan entitled Al-Mahdi (the Guided One), the Hidden Imam, 'Lord of the Time' and 'Guardian of the Age', who disappeared from sight and then went into 'the greater occultation', being present but hidden all through time as the leader of the Twelver Shi'as, and who would eventually rise as the Saviour and rid the world of injustice and corruption.

The Imam is sinless, infallible, possibly all-knowing and capable of working miracles, both alive and dead. His unquestioned obedience is the duty of all the faithful, who must follow, 'emulate', him in every way. All of the Imams are believed to have been martyred. Indeed, their martyrdom too had been preordained. Some extreme Shi'a and Sufi sects go so far as to regard the Imams as divine. There have certainly been some – known as the *Ali Allahi*s – who have worshipped Ali as such. The great majority of the Shi'a ulama do not go as far as that, but in practice the idea is close to the attitude of the common Shi'a believer.

During the absence of the Lord of the Time, the faithful pay their religious dues to the *mojtahed*s, who are doctors of Shi'a law and held as the Imam's deputies but not his representatives. They also put their problems to, and ask their questions regarding law and proper conduct, of the *mojtahed* whom they choose to 'emulate'. The great *mojtahed*s are called *marja'-e taqlid* or 'source of emulation', a position which has evolved since the mid-nineteenth century. The *mojtahed*s and *marja*'s have been addressed, respectively, as ayatollahs and grand ayatollahs since the early to mid-twentieth century. There is no organized church in Shi'ism, but there are Shi'a colleges, mosques and other institutions, which have been undergoing change since the Islamic Revolution.

Ismailis are Sevener Shi'as. They adhere to Ismail, eldest son of the sixth Imam and his descendants, whereas the Twelver Shi'as' seventh Imam is the younger son, Musa al-Kazim. Between the tenth and twelfth centuries the Ismailis founded the successful Fatimid caliphate in Egypt and Syria. Towards the end of their rule there was a schism over succession. One group regarded al-Musta'li as the rightful Imam, whereas the other group adhered to his elder brother, Imam Nizar, from whom the present Ismaili leader Aga Khan traces his descent. The seat of the Nizaris then moved from Egypt to Iran, where they established themselves in a number of mountain fortifications and waged war against Seljuk Turks who were orthodox Sunnis. There are few Ismailis now left in Iran, being mainly concentrated in Central Asia, Pakistan, East Africa and the West.

Arab caliphates (632–1258)

The Umayyads (661–750) formed a caliphate after the death of Ali. They ruled an empire from Damascus larger than the Achaemenids', stretching from Spain to Central Asia and north India. Theirs was a dynastic, arbitrary rule, styled to some extent on the Sasanian and Byzantine monarchies, although it still retained some of its original tribal roots. Unlike their early Abbasid successors they were not Iranophile, but nevertheless largely depended on Persian administrators, scribes, accountants and tax collectors in running their caliphate, especially in the east.

From the word go the Umayyads faced revolts. The campaign against them was nowhere more potent and effective than in Persia, and particularly Khorasan, where underground Abbasid propagandists – that is, followers of the House of Abbas, the Prophet's uncle – advocated the righteousness and legitimacy of 'the Prophet's family' in general and the House of Abbas in particular as successors of the Prophet.

The movement chose Mohammad, a great-grandson of Abbas, as their leader, and on his death at the hands of the Umayyads, it was his son Ibrahim who, in 745, sent the Khorasani Persian Abu Muslim as his personal representative to liberate Khorasan. Having succeeded, Abu Muslim then led his armies to the west, defeated the last Umayyad caliph in 749 and declared al-Saffah (Ibrahim's brother, who had been killed in the meantime) caliph.

The Persians

An early Arab historian described the Abbasids as 'Khorasani Persians'. This is obviously an exaggeration, for the simple reason that the Abbasids were Arabs, but the description indicates both the degree to which the Abbasid victory was owed to Persian support and the impact of Persian culture and peoples on their court, culture and government.

Ibn Khaldun, the great Arab historian and sociologist (before sociology was a recognized discipline) of the fourteenth century wrote that 'only the Persians are engaged in the task of preserving knowledge and writing systematic scholarly works. Thus the truth of the Prophet's statement becomes apparent, "If learning were suspended in the highest parts of heaven, the Persians would attain it."'

Shi'a, Manichaean and Buddhist Iranians played a major role in the rise of Sufism or Islamic mysticism, while at the same time the Persians excelled in many fields including science, medicine and philosophy. The ninth-century Al-Khwarazmi (Algoritmi), whose name is at the root of the modern term 'algorithm', and the eleventh-century Biruni (al-Biruni) were great mathematicians, astronomers and astrologers. The advance in medicine culminated in the careers of such great figures as Razi (Razes) and Ibn Sina (Avicenna), who flourished in the tenth and eleventh centuries. They were also great rationalist philosophers who continued and developed the application of Aristotelian and Neoplatonic philosophy to Islamic knowledge and learning. One such revolutionary theory came from Razi, who denied revelation and saw religion as a main cause of conflict and war.

Avicenna (980–1037) is generally regarded as the most important and influential polymath of the Islamic golden age. Born in the eastern city of Bokhara, now in Uzbekistan, he died in the ancient city of Hamadan, often trying to keep out of harm's way and sometimes serving local principalities as vizier. He has over four hundred works to his name on a wide range of subjects, of which about 240 are extant. A hundred and fifty of these are on philosophy, and forty of them on medicine. His most famous works are *The Book of Healing* (Al-Shafa'), a vast philosophical and scientific encyclopaedia, and *The Canon of Medicine* (Al-Qanun) which was a standard medical text at many medieval universities in Christendom as well as in the Islamic world. His corpus also includes writing on philosophy, astronomy, alchemy, geology, psychology, Islamic theology, logic, mathematics and physics as well as poetry.

Razi (865–925) was born and died in Reyy near Tehran, and was an outstanding philosopher, chemist, alchemist and physician, renowned for his philosophical rationalism and original contributions to science and medicine. Nezami Aruzi, the twelfth-century critic and poet tells the remarkable legend of how Razi treated a Samanid ruler. This Amir became paralysed in his legs, and no amount of treatment had the slightest effect. In the end, he sent for Razi, who lived far away in Reyy but agreed to come. When they reached the Oxus, Razi, who had never seen such a great river, refused to board the boat, saying that if he drowned wise men would blame him for having taken the risk. When it proved impossible to change his mind, he was forced to board the boat. However, his treatments also proved ineffective. In the end he said he had only one treatment left, but for this he and the Amir must be left alone in a bath. Once in the bath, he took the Amir's clothes off and gave him some soothing medicines. Then he suddenly began to abuse the Amir for his own forced crossing of the river and drew his sword as if he wanted to strike him with it. In absolute terror, the Amir stood up, passed out and later rose to be fully recovered. Razi then left the bath and, together with the slave who was waiting for him, left for home. Whether or not this legend is true, it certainly shows that the Iranians at the time knew not only of hysterical paralysis as a psychological illness, but also about the shock treatment as a possible cure for it.

The Iranian contribution to the early Islamic world – the caliphate that stretched from India to Spain – in matters of government and administration was just as impressive. Almost from the beginning, the administration of the caliphate had to depend largely on the Sasanian models of managing the realm and on Persian administrators to apply them. The Persian *divan*s or departments, whether of finance, the army or postal services, came into being much earlier than the office of vizier or chief minister, and they became even more extensive and influential when the early Abbasids adopted the Sasanian model of administration, government and court etiquette almost entirely, and appointed a vizier to head the administration.

It took the Persians two centuries, after the Arab conquest, to found Persian-speaking dynasties and produce written literature in Persian, although, as has been noted, they were otherwise very much engaged in the creation of the new international Islamic civilization. In CE 820 Ma'mun the Abbasid caliph gave Taher, son of Hoseyn, who had helped him gain power, the highly important governorship of Khorasan – the first Persian ever to hold the office – while Taher's son Abdollah replaced him in his former post as the chief tax collector of Iraq. Once in Khorasan, Taher's relations with Ma'mun began to cool off, reflected in the act of omitting Ma'mun's name from Friday prayers. What this might have led to we cannot know, since Taher died soon afterwards in 822.

Taher was succeeded by another of his sons, Talheh, who died in 828 and was replaced by his brother Abdollah as governor of Khorasan. From his capital Neyshabur he ruled a vast territory, which later stretched as far as Kerman and further east, to the borders of India. But he soon had to face an enemy who would spell doom for Taherid rule. This was Ya'qub son of Leyth the coppersmith (*Saffar*).

The Taherids had initially owed their power to the caliphate, and went on ruling in Khorasan as their nominal representatives and real allies. Ya'qub and his brothers who rose from Sistan (in the south-east of modern Iran) to establish the Saffarid rule, on the other hand, were common local people whose achievements they owed entirely to their own efforts. Ya'qub was a coppersmith. What made him give up his trade and become a bandit leader is not known, though according to legend, predating Robin Hood, he robbed the rich and helped the poor, until he established himself as a ruler in Sistan and overthrew the Taherids in 872. He led an army to Baghdad, intending to take it and overthrow the caliph but died on the way. He was succeeded by his brother Amr, who eventually came to terms with the caliph, but when he tried to conquer Transoxiana he faced the able and competent Samanid ruler Ismail who, in 900, finally defeated him and thus terminated the short span of Saffarid glory.

The Samanid ruler Ismail was son of Ahmad, whose earliest known ancestor Saman (hence Samanids) had claimed descent from Bahram Chubin, the colourful rebel general of Khosrow II (see Chapter 1). It was under the Samanids that Persian literature and culture began to flourish, the foundations of classical Persian literature were laid and Persian science experienced a period of splendour.

It was with Abu Abdollah Rudaki that new Persian poetry reached its early maturity. He belonged to the Samanid court that encouraged and promoted the new poetry and particularly appreciated Rudaki's works. He is thus normally regarded as the founder of classical Persian poetry. In addition to being a poet, he played the lyre and drank wine, both of which, according to his admirers, enhanced the quality of his poetry. Not much of his poetry has survived, but from what there is it is clear that he wrote charming lyrics and eloquent odes as well as shorter pieces. Aside from panegyrics (poetical praises of the great and good) he wrote lyrical, reflective and nature-descriptive poems employing rich imagery and metaphor. Towards the end of his life he wrote

the remarkable poem nostalgically describing the pleasures of the
past and lamenting the decline of old age. It opens with the following two couplets:

> Every one of my teeth consumed and then fell
> Teeth they were not, glowing lights, so to tell
> They were pure white silver, reef and pearl
> They were the Morning Star, drops of dripping rain

Towards the end of the tenth century, the fortunes of the
Samanids rapidly declined. They were constantly under pressure
from the Turkic tribes, who eventually defeated and killed the last
Samanid in 999.

While the Samanids flourished in eastern and north-eastern
Persia, two other dynasties were established in much of the rest
of the country, by far the greatest being that of the Buyids. It was
founded by the three sons of Buyeh the fisherman and soon
became an empire, which extended to Baghdad and turned the
Abbasid caliph into a pawn. The most glorious ruler of this
dynasty was Azod al-Dowleh, seated in Shiraz, who became the
senior Buyid in supreme command of the whole of Buyid land.
But his death in 983 typically led to a struggle for succession
which ultimately broke up the Buyid unity. The last Buyid of the
Persian hinterland ruled a small state from Reyy and was overthrown by the new – and typically short-term – power, Mahmud
of Ghazna.

Alptegin – once a Turkish slave soldier in the service of the
Samanids – managed to establish himself in Khorasan and, after
his successor's death in 956, his son-in-law established himself in
Ghazna and extended his rule over a considerable territory. His
death in 997 led to a struggle for succession out of which his
younger son Mahmud emerged victorious.

Mahmud was an able military leader as well as an empire-
builder. He was also an orthodox Sunni, dedicated both to the

persecution of Shi'ites and the destruction of Hindu temples. Religious intolerance and love of riches were his principal motives for attacking Indian territories to the east of his domain and looting Hindu temples further beyond. He overthrew the Buyids and extended his rule as far west as Isfahan. His eventual empire extended in the south-east into India, and covered much of central and northern Persia with Khorasan as its main homeland.

Mahmud was not just an incorrigible warrior but also a dedicated patron of literature and science. There were many leading poets and scientists at his court, including such stars as Farrokhi, the great poet, and Biruni, the great polymath. Ferdowsi dedicated his *Shahnameh* (the great epic poem) to Mahmud's name and wrote in his praise, although he had started writing the epic before Mahmud came to power. Ferdowsi does not seem to have spent any length of time at his court, and is believed to have been disappointed by Mahmud's reward on the completion of his poem.

Abolqasem Ferdowsi (940–1020) was born and died in Tus, and is regarded as one of the four great stars of Persian poetry. His epic *Shahnameh* is both a poem and a narrative account of ancient Iranian myths, legends and history. As described in Chapter 1, *Shahnameh* is made up of three cycles, the Pishdadiyan (the dawn of man), the Keyaniyan (the Iranian kingdom) and the Sasanian (an account of the history of the Sasanian monarchy). Rostam is the greatest hero of the epic, but there are others, including Siyavosh, Sohrab, and Esfandiyar.

The story of Rostam and his son Sohrab whom his father kills by mistake is the most moving tragedy of *Shahnameh*. In its opening verses, Ferdowsi issues a personal commentary:

It is a story which keeps the eyes well watered
It brings on Rostam the anger of the soft-hearted
If a whirlwind blows from the Ganges
It would bring down unripe oranges . . .

Why should the young person feel free of care?
Death after all is not just due to old age ...

Mahmud's death in 1030 led to a struggle for succession between two of his sons, Mohammad, who had been his favourite, and Mas'ud, the elder son who was then governor of Isfahan. The great contemporary historian Beyhaqi's account of these events is highly instructive in how chaos and conflict arose in Persia after the death of a great ruler, how quickly various parties shifted positions to be on the winning side and how the vanquished lost everything, often including their lives.

In 1035 Mas'ud was defeated by Seljuk Turks and made peace with them. But the peace did not last. In his second war with the Seljuk, Mas'ud was heavily and irreversibly defeated and withdrew from Khorasan. Thenceforth the Ghaznavids mainly retreated to their possessions in India, but they still maintained a link with Persia through their official use of the Persian language and patronage of Persian literature.

The Turks

Turks were already present in Iranian lands at this point, and even founded the Ghaznavid dynasty. But from the eleventh century on, they began to cross the Oxus river from Central Asia in large numbers and move westwards. They were led by the Seljuk of the Ghozz tribes, a move which eventually led to the creation of the Ottoman empire and modern Turkey. First they encountered the Ghaznavid empire, and having chased them out of Khorasan it was relatively straightforward to conquer the Iranian hinterlands, Iraq, Syria and Anatolia. They thus formed a vast empire but it did not last long and was gradually broken up.

The Seljuk (1037–1157) were the first Turks who led the way to massive Turkish migration from the east into Persia and beyond leading to lasting ethnic, linguistic and cultural impacts on these lands. They were headed by the brothers Toghrol Beg and Chaghri Beg. While the latter remained behind in Khorasan, Toghrol pushed westwards, captured Reyy which he made his capital, overran the scattered Buyid principalities, entered Baghdad in 1055, ended the Buyid rule in Iraq and was named sultan by the puppet caliph. Until then, apart from the Ghaznavid territories in the east, which were Sunni, Shi'ism had been the dominant power in much of the Muslim Middle East, with Buyid control of Iraq and much of Persia and Egypt and Syria in the hands of Ismaili Fatimids. The Seljuk's was an orthodox Sunni state.

In 1063, Toghrol died and was buried in a tower in Reyy which is still standing and bears his name. His dead brother Chaghri's son, Alp Arsalan succeeded to the sultanate. In his son Malekshah's short reign the Seljuk empire reached its apogee both in its vastness (surpassing even the Sasanian empire) and its prosperity and glory. The administration of the empire was in the hands of the illustrious Persian vizier Nezam al-Molk, who had posted his twelve sons to various provinces to ensure loyalty and efficiency. He founded a number of *madreseh*s (colleges), the most famous at Neyshabur and Baghdad, in the latter of which Mohammad al-Ghazali (the famous mystic and theologian) taught, and where Sa'di (the celebrated classical poet) later studied. His structural addition to the great Congressional Mosque of Isfahan is regarded as a most notable architectural achievement of the period. Another of the great vizier's protégés was Omar Khayyam, the poet and mathematician who played a leading role in calculating a precise solar calendar. Yet Nezam al-Molk did not escape the usual fate of Iranian viziers. He was dismissed at eighty and though killed by an assassin, Sultan Malekshah is likely to have known about the plot.

The Congressional Mosque is the largest, oldest and most majestic mosque in the city of Isfahan, which is renowned for its historic mosques and other buildings. Dating back to CE 800, this impressive structure was built in the four-*ivan* (an *ivan* is a vaulted open room) architectural style, placing four gates face to face. Construction under the Seljuk included the addition of two brick domed chambers, for which the mosque is renowned. The south dome was built in 1086–7 by Nezam al-Molk, and was larger than any dome known at the time. The north dome was constructed a year later by Nezam al-Molk's rival, Taj al-Molk. The dome was certainly built as a direct riposte to the earlier south dome, and successfully so, claiming its place as a masterpiece in Persian architecture for its structural clarity and geometric balance. *Ivan*s were also added in stages under the Seljuk, giving the mosque its current four-*ivan* form, a type which subsequently became prevalent in Iran and the rest of the Islamic world.

From the beginnings of the Seljuk conquests the administration of the state was left in the hands of the Persians, running a system which was broadly similar to the Ghaznavids and earlier periods, being based on *divan*s, secretaries, tax officials and the like, a system which in general served the country till the mid-nineteenth century when European influence introduced new forms. *Eqta'* (Arabic, *iqta'*) was a form of land assignment which had been in use since the Arab conquest, itself modelled after the assignment systems which had prevailed before Islam. The supreme example of this under the Seljuk was the case of Khwarazm. In 1077 Malekshah granted the *eqta'* of this eastern province to his favourite cup-bearer, Anushtegin, a humble servant. The assignment was later confirmed in Anushtegin's line, until one of his descendants claimed independence from the then sultan Sanjar.

Soleyman Ravandi, the classic historian of the Seljuk, casually relates a story about the Seljuk Sultan Mohammad which is worth a brief mention as it demonstrates vividly the unstable and frightening condition of state officials. Zia al-Molk Ahmad, the sultan's vizier, had offered 500,000 dinars for Amir the Seyyed, a very important and capable man (who was also a seyyed, or descendant of the Prophet Mohammad), to be put 'at his disposal' – presumably from a grudge or sheer rivalry – and the sultan had agreed. But Amir the Seyyed quickly saw the sultan, and offered him 800,000 dinars if he would put Zia al-Molk at his disposal instead. The sultan agreed, and sold his vizier for money.

The glorious days of the Seljuk empire had already passed by the death of Malekshah towards the end of the eleventh century, but Sanjar's sixty years of wise and relatively stable government in the east kept the Seljuk of Iran under an overlord till the mid-twelfth century. Sanjar's greatest sources of worry were the unruly Ghozz and the rebellious Atsez, descendant of the cup-bearer Anushtegin, who succeeded to the governorship of Khwarazm in 1127.

But the great catastrophe came in 1153, when Sanjar finally lost control of the Ghozz, who defeated him and took him into captivity, while at the same time setting Khorasan ablaze with slaughter and plunder. Sanjar managed to escape after three years, but being both old and broken he died shortly afterwards, and with him the great Seljuk sultanate of Iran came to an end.

The Ismailis

The Ismailis were the Sevener Shi'ites, described briefly above (page 35). From CE 909, their main branch had managed to establish its rule in Egypt and Syria, but was overthrown by Saladin in 1171. They were known as the Fatimid caliphate because of their claim to descend from the Prophet's daughter Fatima, a claim disputed by their opponents.

Perhaps the most brilliant period of Fatimid rule in Egypt was the long reign of Al-Mustansir (1035–94), which almost exactly coincided with the period of the rise of the Seljuk until the end of Malekshah's rule. It was during his time that the great Persian poet and thinker Naser Khosrow visited Cairo, was converted and returned to Khorasan as a prominent Ismaili missionary. The death of Mustansir led to schism due to the rival claims of his two sons, Musta'li and Nizar, which Musta'li won.

Before these events, Hasan Sabbah was already an astute and tireless campaigner for the Ismaili movement in Iran. He had managed by a brilliant strategy to get hold of the mountain fortress of Alamut near Qazvin. That was in 1090, but when a few years later the Musta'li–Nizar schism occurred, Sabbah went over to the Nizaris. From their impregnable positions in the mountain fortresses, Sabbah struck terror into the hearts of rulers, governors and other important orthodox Sunnis by sending Ismaili devotees to 'assassinate' them regardless of the great risk they ran of being captured and hideously killed.

To explain this, their enemies said that the assassins were shown extremely pleasant scenes while under heavy influence of hashish, pretending that it was a foretaste of paradise in the event of martyrdom. Hence the Ismailis' title of *hashashin* (literally heavy hashish users) from the corruption of which the European term 'assassin' was coined. Such a schooling is extremely unlikely. To understand the psychology of the assassins, it would be sufficient to be reminded of the Japanese kamikaze pilots and contemporary suicide bombers.

The twelfth century was a period when great strides were taken in Persian literature, both poetry and prose, seeing the rise of such stars as Nezami Ganjavi, Iran's master of classical romance. Art and architecture flourished and advanced in the Seljuk period, despite the recurring turmoil and instability. Seljuk art is known for combining Persian, Islamic and Central Asian elements and thus gaining distinction in the Islamic world. Architecture flourished, as did the arts of the book (whereby books were copied, illuminated, decorated, bound and sometimes illustrated), but few of the latter have survived from the period.

However an impressive legacy of Seljuk architecture, Sanjar's Mausoleum, still survives in Marv, now in Turkmenistan.

The Khwarazm-shahs

As noted above, Atsez, a descendant of Malekshah's favourite cup-bearer, to whom he had assigned the province of Khwarazm, rose in Sanjar's time and eventually declared independence from Seljuk domains as Khwarazm-shah. He died in 1156, shortly before Sanjar, following which the Khwarazm-shahs quickly grew from a provincial power into a major territorial state, rising above the fragmented Seljuk rulers. Yet much of the expansion took place under the last effective sultan of the Khwarazm-shahs, Ala' al-Din Mohammad (1200–20) who for a brief period became ruler of a vast empire and conquered practically the whole of central and eastern Persia.

Meantime Changiz (anglicized, Genghis) Khan had united the Mongols, conquered parts of China and extended his vast empire to the neighbourhood of the Khwarazm-shahs. He was, contrary to Mohammad, an accomplished military leader, an able administrator and an astute diplomat. It is likely he had had designs for expansion in the west, but the catastrophe when it came, and how, was largely of Mohammad's own making because he condoned the murder of several Muslim merchants who were Changiz's subjects, and rejected his demand for rectification with contempt. In 1219 the Mongols attacked Transoxiana. A year later, Mohammad died a fugitive on a small island off the coast of the Caspian Sea.

The Mongols

There were two Mongol invasions of Persian lands. The first one, led by Changiz Khan, began in 1219 and had subsided by his death in 1227. The second wave was led by Changiz's grandson Holagu Khan in 1253, which resulted in the foundation of the Mongol Ilkhan empire in Iran.

In 1256, Holagu led his forces into Iran with the aim of overthrowing the two centres of Islamic faith, the Ismailis in Iran and the Abbasids in Iraq, although his motive was military and political rather than religious. The Ismaili castles fell in 1256 and Baghdad was sacked in 1258. As the Ilkhan, Holagu was in possession of a vast empire consisting of Persia, Iraq and parts of Anatolia, centred in Azerbaijan, with Maragheh as the capital, though this was later moved to Tabriz. His Persian vizier was Nasir al-Din Tusi, the renowned scientist and philosopher.

The Mongol devastation was worse than any catastrophe that had befallen Iran before and since. There are more or less contemporary reports of the total destruction of cities and massacre of their inhabitants, some of them with populations of more than a million, by the forces of Changiz and, following him, Holagu. There may have been some exaggerations in these reports, but not a great deal. Holagu himself wrote to St Louis (Louis IX), king of France, that in his 1258 sack of Baghdad alone more than 250,000 people had been massacred.

The Ilkhans, Holagu and his descendants ruled Iran for about eighty years from 1260 to about 1340. The running of the realm was, as usual, in the hands of Persian viziers and administrators. Of the nine grand viziers of the Ilkhans, only one died a natural death. The military forces, on the other hand, were in the hands of the Mongols.

Ghazan Khan's rule (1295–1304), although no longer than nine years, is generally regarded as the apogee of the Ilkhan regime. He began with a significant amount of bloodletting, but also declared an important series of administrative and financial reforms. He showed awareness of the fact that perpetual plunder of the peasantry would mean long-term financial bankruptcy for the state, and set out to improve taxation and to moderate the abuses to which the people were subject from travelling officials, who used their food and services free of charge and often plundered them as well.

Such were Ghazan's edicts and intentions as detailed by his exceptionally able vizier Rashid al-Din in his *Complete* or *Universal History*. It is more difficult to know the extent to which the reforms were implemented, given that they required the cooperation of a large number of Mongol commanders and officials. Ghazan's early death without male issue led to the succession of his brother Oljaitu (1304–16), who is especially remembered for two things: his personal experiment with various religions, and his capture of Gilan for the first time, since up until that point in Iran natural barriers had made that province almost impregnable. He transferred the capital from Tabriz to Soltaniyeh, where he built a magnificent mausoleum, which still survives as the greatest architectural monument of the whole of the Mongol period. He was succeeded by his son Abu Sa'id (1316–35), whose early death, probably by poisoning, marked the end of the Ilkhan dynasty and the fragmentation of their empire.

Both Rumi and Sa'di flourished in the thirteenth century, Rumi in Konya and Sa'di in Shiraz. Rumi is regarded as the greatest Persian mystic poet of all time. He is the author of *Masnavi-e Ma'navi*, an extensive book of mystic poems in couplets which has been translated into many languages, and which brought its author universal fame and a great following. Rumi also wrote a large volume of Sufi lyrical poems. Sa'di is a most eloquent and accomplished sage as well as lover in the history of classical Persian poetry. His works were translated in Europe, and he was particularly admired by the eighteenth-century French *philosophes*, the men and women of the Enlightenment, to the extent that, in the nineteenth century, a leading French mathematician and a French president were named after him. Sa'di left his native Shiraz in the wake of the first Mongol invasion. When he returned thirty years later, about 1255, he celebrated

the peace – 'the leopards had given up leopard-like behaviour' –
little knowing that Holagu's troops were on their way. He wrote
two painful elegies, one in Persian and one in Arabic, on receiving the news of the sack of Baghdad: 'The sky would rightly
weep blood on the earth full / For the kingdom of Musta'sim,
Commander of the Faithful'.

Timur and his descendants

Born a Muslim near Samarqand (now in Uzbekistan) in 1336
and made lame in childhood, Amir Timur's (Tamerlane's) rise and
devastation of Persia and other lands compare with those of
Changiz, but were even more cruel than his role model. He
claimed descent from Changiz, but there are strong doubts
about the veracity of this claim. He was later known as *guregan*
or 'son-in-law' when he married two women who descended
from Changiz Khan. What emerges is that Timur did not have a
pattern of conquest, but attacked and then abandoned towns and
regions which he sometimes later reconquered. In Isfahan alone,
which had risen against his unbearable taxes, 70,000 people were
slaughtered. In 1405 he set out for the conquest of China, the
biggest prize, but died on the way and was buried in his beloved
Samarqand. There is a legend about Timur's meeting with Hafiz,
one of the greatest Persian poets of all time, which is colourful
but unlikely to be true. Hafiz has a famous poem, which begins
with the following couplet:

> If that Turk [= light-skinned boy] of Shiraz meets my wishes all
> I will grant Samarqand and Bokhara for his Hindu [= black] mole

According to the legend, Timur summoned Hafiz on entering
Shiraz and told him: I fought hard to conquer these great cities,
and a beggar like you claims to give them away for the mole of

his beloved? And the witty Hafiz replied: Sire, it is precisely because of such generosity that I am as poor as this.

Typically, the death of Timur led to civil war until his son Shahrokh took power and began a reign of relative peace and cultural achievements. Sadly, his death in 1447 was followed by further power struggles and royal bloodletting. Since the reign of Shahrokh, the Uzbeks had been trying to penetrate Transoxiana. They became the nightmare of the Timurid descendants of Shahrokh and eventually conquered the whole of Transoxiana, thus anticipating the modern Republic of Uzbekistan, which paradoxically holds Amir Timur as her greatest historical hero.

The last Timurid prince was Sultan Hoseyn Baiqara (1468–1506), who was overthrown by Uzbeks. It was under his benefi-cent direction that Herat achieved the zenith of its glory as a centre of art, literature and scholarship. And it was at Hoseyn's court that the poet Amir Ali Shir Nava'i rose to prominence, along with the miniature-painter Hoseyn Behzad and the poet Jami.

Persian poetry occupied a central place in the process of assimilation of the Timurid elite to the Perso-Islamic courtly culture. The most famous poet of the late Timurid era was Abdurrahman-Jami, the last great medieval Persian mystic poet. The Timurid ruler Baysonqor also commissioned a new edition of the Persian national epic *Shahnameh*, known as the *Shahnameh of Baysonqor*, and wrote an introduction to it. According to T. Lenz in the *Encyclopaedia Iranica*:

> It can be viewed as a specific reaction in the wake of Timur's death in 807/1405 to the new cultural demands facing Shahhrokh and his sons, a Turkic military elite no longer deriv-ing their power and influence solely from a charismatic steppe leader with a carefully cultivated linkage to Mongol aristocracy. Now centred in Khorasan, the ruling house regarded the increased assimilation and patronage of Persian culture as an

integral component of efforts to secure the legitimacy and authority of the dynasty within the context of the Islamic Iranian monarchical tradition, and the Baysanqor *Shahnameh*, as much a precious object as it is a manuscript to be read, powerfully symbolizes the Timurid conception of their own place in that tradition.

The golden age of Persian painting was ushered in during the reign of the Timurids. Indeed, it was in this and later periods that Chinese art and artists had a significant influence on Persian art. Apart from that, Timurid artists refined the Persian arts of the book, which combined paper, calligraphy, illumination, illustration and binding in a brilliant and colourful whole.

Persia united, divided and reunited

The Safavids descended from Sheykh Safi al-Din of Ardabil (1252–1334) who was a Sunni Sufi leader, probably of Kurdish descent, although the late fifteenth-century Safavid movement that eventually captured secular power had an unmistakably Turkmen character (the Turkmen are a Turkic people who are now concentrated in the Republic of Turkmenistan). Contrary to their own claim, it is no longer believed that they have descended from the Seventh Shi'ite Imam Musa al-Kazim. After the death of Safi al-Din, the Safavid Sufi order grew steadily and came into contact and conflict with the White Sheep empire, ruled by a confederation of Turkmen tribes. Ismail, the twelve-year-old Safavid warrior defeated them in 1501, and became the first Shah of Persia since the Arab invasion of Iran in the seventh century.

The Safavids restored the old Persian empire by reuniting virtually the whole of the Iranian lands as 'The Guarded Domains of Iran'. Ismail was the leader of a fanatical Sufi order, and both he and his military devotees, the Qezelbash or Redheads tribe, so called because of their red headdress, saw him as a divine being rather than an Iranian nationalist leader. He imposed Shi'ism as Iran's state religion.

Once the conversion to Shi'ism had been made, it became clear that there were few Shi'ite ulama in the country to continue the task of conversion and to spread the knowledge and practice of the new doctrine, its rites and culture. To fill the gap, a continuing stream of Shi'a ulama, teachers and jurists began to be imported from the Shi'ite Jabal Amel, a mountainous region of southern Lebanon.

From their inception, the Safavids had to face two formidable Sunni enemies on their western and eastern fronts: the Ottomans and the Uzbeks. In 1514, the Ottoman Sultan Salim led a large army east to meet Ismail. The battle was fought in Chaldiran, in eastern Anatolia, and despite Ismail's great display of bravery his army was routed. Many historians believed that the cause of the Ottoman victory at Chaldiran was that the Safavids did not possess firearms, especially field artillery. This is a myth: the likeliest reason for Ismail's heavy defeat is that his army was outnumbered by about one to three.

Ismail died in 1524, ten years after Chaldiran, when he was barely thirty-seven. The myth of his invincibility having been broken at Chaldiran, he spent many of his remaining years drinking and debauching in the company of 'rosy-cheeked' youths. He certainly did not lead his army again into battle.

However, his youthful achievements should not be overshadowed. He had led a revolution and founded an empire, which, after experiencing the vicissitudes of time, would end up with the physical and cultural boundaries of modern Iran. He was as intelligent perhaps as he was cruel; as valiant, charming and charismatic as he was brutal, whose bloodthirstiness one contemporary observer compared to Nero's.

Ismail's son, Tahmasp I, was only ten years old when he succeeded his father in 1524 amid turmoil. That circumstance was enough to result in conflict and faction-fighting among the Qezelbash, the military backbone of the regime, which might even have led to the collapse of the dynasty. It took Tahmasp nine years before he could assert his absolute power and stamp out domestic chaos. And though, till the end of Tahmasp's natural life, Iran experienced many foreign wars and domestic conflicts, relative order prevailed in the land.

His death in 1576 was followed by total disarray until 1588, when his grandson Abbas I overthrew Tahmasp's son (and his own father) and captured the throne. Had it not been for Abbas, Safavid Persia might well have come to an end by the close of the sixteenth century. In the twelve years since the death of Shah Tahmasp, domestic chaos, strife, rebellion and civil war had left little or no central authority. The country's external weakness was a direct consequence of her internal discord and anarchy. The Ottomans had occupied much Persian territory in the northwest and west, including most of Azerbaijan. In the east, the Uzbeks had helped themselves to large territories in Khorasan and Sistan, and were poised to occupy the whole of that province. The long-term task of achieving domestic peace and stability required a significant reduction in the power and influence of the Qezelbash chiefs. That could be best achieved by creating a countervailing military power which would be permanently available and directly under the shah's own command.

Shah Abbas set about systematically organizing a standing army from the Caucasian *gholam*s, the Georgian, Armenian and Circassian military slaves who had been brought from wars in the Caucasus. The process had begun in an unplanned and embryonic manner under Tahmasp, but under Abbas it was consciously planned and extensively organized. He also took further measures to break the traditional power of the Qezelbash.

Abbas knew that he could not win a war on two fronts, and that the enemy in the east was the less formidable adversary. In 1590 he reached a humiliating agreement with the Ottoman Turks whereby he ceded to them the large Safavid territories they already occupied.

The temporary peace in the west made it possible to take on the Uzbeks, and by 1602–3 the Uzbeks had been sufficiently driven out of Persian territory for the shah to turn his attention back to the Ottomans. In 1603 Abbas marched to Tabriz and took it from its Ottoman garrison. By 1607 Iran had regained all the territory that it had owned in 1555. Turkish attempts at peace negotiations did not succeed, and in 1623 Abbas invaded Iraq and took the city of Baghdad. By Abbas' death in 1629, Persia had once again reached the borders that had been established by Shah Ismail at the peak of his reign.

Abbas encouraged domestic and international trade directly as well as through the construction of extensive infrastructures such as roads and caravanserais. Carpet-weaving, which had begun to develop into a major industry under Tahmasp I, received a further boost under Abbas such that the Persian carpet reached the peak of its development during the Safavid period. Miniature-painting, calligraphy, the arts of the book and ceramic and metallic arts also developed and flourished under Abbas and his descendants. As part of Abbas' policy of economic development, the shah transferred thousands of industrious Armenians from the northern city of Jolfa to the southern suburb of his new capital Isfahan, which thenceforth was called New Jolfa or Jolfa of Isfahan.

The change of capital from Qazvin to Isfahan enabled the shah to apply some of his energies to the conversion of his seat of government into a great world city. Rather than demolishing and rebuilding the old city, standard practice in Iranian history, the shah built a new city by its side which, through the Chahar Bagh or central parkway, extended to the Zayandeh Rud river.

Much of Shah Abbas' Isfahan has been destroyed, beginning with the Afghan invasion and devastation of the early eighteenth century. Fortunately the great Naqsh-e Jahan ('Image of the World') Square has survived, and still houses the magnificent Shah (or Blue) Mosque, the royal court of Aliqapu (the Exalted Porte) and the small but beautiful Mosque of Sheykh Lotfollah.

The Shah Mosque is an excellent example of the architecture of Islamic Iran. It is one of the recognized masterpieces of architecture in Iran and the world, and is registered, along with the Naqsh-e Jahan Square, as a UNESCO World Heritage Site. Construction of the mosque began in 1611, and its splendour is due chiefly to the beauty of its seven-colour mosaic tiles and calligraphic inscriptions. Its portal measures 27 metres high, and on top of it are two minarets 42 metres tall. Surrounded with four *ivan*s (portals) and arcades, all the walls are ornamented with seven-colour mosaic tile. The most magnificent *ivan* of the mosque, the one facing the Qibla (direction for prayer), is 33 metres high, and behind it is a space which is roofed with the largest dome in the city at 52 metres. The dome is double layered, and the acoustic properties and reflections at the central point under the dome is a point of interest for many visitors. There are two seminaries at the south-west and south-east sections of the mosque. It is one of the treasures featured on the popular BBC television series *Around the World in 80 Treasures* presented by architecture historian Dan Cruickshank.

Other visual arts flourished under Shah Abbas and some of his descendants, even more so than under his grandfather Tahmasp I: painting, calligraphy and *tazhib* (ornamentations around each manuscript page) reached their peak in the work of Mir Emad al-Hasani, the great calligrapher of the reign of Shah Abbas II.

For all his positive achievements, Shah Abbas was a cruel and brutal ruler. He blinded his half-blind father after deposing him.

He killed his eldest son on suspicion (wrongly) of plotting against him, and blinded two of his sons for similar reasons, one of whom committed suicide as a result. All this was of course due to the fact that royal legitimacy in Iran lacked a firm legal basis and could therefore be snatched via a palace coup just as Abbas himself had done. In order to reduce the threat even further, he established the policy of immuring royal males in the harem, the enclosed women's quarters, so that they would be ignorant of the outside world and cut off from would-be plotters. It is not difficult to imagine what effect this had on the future Safavid shahs who emerged from the harem to rule the country. Still, Jean Chardin, the French jeweller who spent several years in Iran under Shah Abbas and ended his years in England, and who understood the nature of Iranian state and society as few other Europeans ever did, wrote in full knowledge of Abbas' positive as well as negative sides: 'When this great prince ceased to live, Persia ceased to prosper.' Such are the ironies of Iranian history.

There were four other Safavid shahs between the death of Abbas I in 1629 and the conquest of Isfahan by the Ghalzeh Afghan tribe in 1722. But this was not a case of steady descent; indeed it is only after the death of the able Abbas II in 1666 that 'decline and fall' would become an apt description. Abbas II's son Shah Soleyman had emerged from the harem at eighteen to rule a vast empire, and, like his grandfather Shah Safi, displayed all the symptoms of such an upbringing: drinking, debauching and killing military chiefs and heads of the bureaucracy. It was from later in his reign that the power of the ulama began to rise and persecution of religious minorities – not just Christians and Jews but equally Sunni Muslims and Sufis – was introduced.

Soleyman was followed by his son Soltan Hoseyn, who, despite suffering a similar upbringing in the harem, emerged with quite a different character. He was pious and good-natured – though that did not exclude promiscuity and drinking – but he intensified the persecution of religious minorities, in particular angering the Sunnis in Afghanistan who were eventually forced to obtain *fatva*s (binding religious edicts) from their ulama that they should not suffer Shi'a rule. Being already in revolt, the Ghalzeh Afghans overran the Persian hinterland typically over a short period and in 1722 triumphantly entered Isfahan. The pathetic Soltan Hoseyn personally delivered the crown to their chief Mahmud.

The eighteenth century was a dark period of Iranian history. Apart from two decades of relative peace under Karim Khan Zand later in the century in parts of the country, it was a period when not only did it often look as if the country would be dismembered as badly as she had been before, but death and destruction took so long that in some ways life for the people of the country was as bad as it was in the Mongol period.

While Isfahan was still under siege by the Afghans, Tahmasp Mirza, Soltan Hoseyn's third son, managed to escape from the city and after receiving the news of his father's abdication, declared himself shah as Tahmasp II in Qazvin, although he was spending more time on wine and sex than on mobilizing resistance to the Afghans. Meanwhile the Russians and Ottomans took advantage of the situation and occupied extensive parts of Iran in the north, west and north-west. Mahmud, who had crowned himself shah in Isfahan, had at first tried to rule even-handedly but soon began mass slaughter and was himself killed in a coup against him by his cousin Ashraf, who proclaimed himself shah in April 1725 and in time killed the unfortunate Soltan Hoseyn.

Tahmasp II's two most important generals were Fath'ali Khan, chief of the Qajar tribal confederation and, his bitter rival, Nader Qoli, a Sunni military genius, who joined the shah's forces at the head of his 2,000 Afshar tribal troops. The competition between the Afshar warrior and the Qajar chief led to the execution of the latter on Tahmasp's order. By 1736, Nader had defeated the Afghan Ashraf, driven the Russians and Turks out of

Iranian territories, deposed Tahmasp II and been crowned as Nader Shah.

Nader was forty-seven, and had he then settled down to a long period of reconstruction he would have been worthy of much of the praise that nationalist Iranian governments and historians levelled at him in the twentieth century. Instead, he embarked on a career of ceaseless domestic and foreign strife and conquest, imposed insufferable taxes on the people, massacred, killed and blinded groups and individuals including his own son, until he was assassinated by his generals in 1747 and died a universally feared and hated man.

Persia fell from Nader's organized chaos into lawlessness and disintegration until Karim Khan Zand, who had been a commander in Nader's army managed to bring most of it under his own rule, while a grandson of Nader ruled in Khorasan and the Afghans returned to Afghanistan. Still, Karim Khan had to deal with recurring Qajar revolts, mainly led by Mohammad Hasan Khan (son of the aforementioned general Fath'ali Khan) who was eventually killed in battle. Karim Khan was an agreeable ruler and the two decades of his regime brought relative peace and security to the parts of the country under his control, although some of his military chiefs, notably his half-brother Zaki Khan, behaved with memorable barbarity towards those vanquished in civil wars.

A number of buildings and monuments are left in Shiraz from Karim Khan's time, of which the imposing royal citadel, the Mosque of Vakil and the Bazaar of Vakil are the most notable. He also built public utility buildings such as caravanserais and renovated others, including important Shi'ite shrines. Karim Khan's death in 1779 was followed by turmoil and a scramble for succession and fratricide of the first order until the accession of the dashing but young and inexperienced Lotf'ali Khan, who was captured and killed by Aqa Mohammad Khan Qajar in 1794.

The Qajars were a confederation of tribes originally of the Central Asian Turkmens, and an important contingent in the Qezelbash Safavid military elite. As mentioned above, one of their chiefs, Mohammad Hasan Khan, was a pretender to the throne and was killed in war. His son Aqa Mohammad, castrated by an enemy as a child, was a hostage at Karim Khan's court when the latter died, and he managed to run away.

Aqa Mohammad then began concerted military campaigns, first subduing the north and later the south and the south-east. By 1785 he had conquered much of the Persian hinterland. He made Tehran his capital in 1786, mainly for strategic reasons, and eventually managed to subdue the whole of the country.

Aqa Mohammad Khan subdued his opponents both within the Qajar territories and across the country with efficiency, ruthlessness and cruelty, but was nevertheless welcomed for bringing peace and stability. Thus the Qajar Khan managed to reunite the country and put down widespread marauding and pillage. He also began, by sheer military force and administrative ability, the process of making the roads safer, the peasants less open to regular looting, towns more immune from chaos and normal productive and commercial activities less hazardous, which was to continue under his nephew and successor. He put down all claimants to autonomous power and recaptured Khorasan from its blind ruler, Shahrokh (a grandson of Nader Shah), whom he tortured so savagely to reveal the hiding place of his treasures that he died, even though he gave up the treasures in the end.

Aqa Mohammad Khan's last great military campaign was in Georgia, which had in effect slipped out of Persian dependency since the death of Nader. The campaign ended in the massacre, in 1795, of the people of Tiflis (Tbilisi) after the town had been captured and 15,000 souls taken into slavery. Aqa Mohammad Khan was crowned in Tehran the next year, and was killed by three of his slaves in June 1797 while he was still campaigning in the Caucasus. The three were later found and cut into small pieces. Aqa Mohammad Khan was succeeded by his nephew, Fath'ali Shah.

This brought to an end the eleven and a half centuries of medieval Persia. Only in the last three centuries of the period was the country reunited, although that unity was almost lost in the eighteenth century. In the nineteenth century, increasing contact with Europe brought Iran into the modern period.

3

The dilemma
of modernization
and the revolution
for law

It can be argued that Iran entered the modern era from the accession of Fath'ali Shah in 1797, although it took another century before movements for modernization began to attract popular appeal. Iran's encounters with modernity began in the early nineteenth century with her perennial military conflicts with Russia, which also led to closer contacts with Britain and – to a lesser extent – other European powers. She was thus introduced to modern techniques of warfare, modern technology, and later, in the latter half of the nineteenth century, to European systems of law and governance which she tried to adopt without much success, although she was inevitably affected by the actions and reactions involved in the process. Nevertheless, seen by contemporary observers, whether Iranian or non-Iranian, both the state and society were still almost as traditional as they had been in previous centuries: around ninety per cent of the population was still rural (both settled and nomadic), the productive technology was still traditional and the people, most of them Shi'a, were deeply religious. Baba Khan, crowned as Fath'ali Shah, was a son of Aqa Mohammad Khan's deceased brother.

Aqa Mohammad Khan's and Fath'ali Shah's achievements in state building had had no match since the Safavids. Despite being a fierce and relentless warrior, Aqa Mohammad Khan had aspired to build a kingdom and a dynasty comparable to the Safavids'. Following his death, Fath'ali Shah went on to revive ancient traditions of court splendour and protocol. He was pleasure-seeking, unheroic and avaricious, but it was partly due to fundamental changes in global and regional circumstances that his reign was not a glorious one.

Fath'ali Shah's reign saw the appearance and rivalry of two powerful European empires, British and Russian, in Iran and the inauguration of the Great Imperial Game, which was to continue in various forms for the next 150 years.

Fath'ali Shah, 1798. (Source: via Wikimedia Commons)

THE GREAT GAME

The Great Game was a term for the strategic rivalry and conflict between Britain and Russia for supremacy in Iran and Central Asia. The original Great Game period is generally regarded as running approximately from the Russo-Persian treaty of 1813 to the Anglo-Russian Convention or 1907. The second, less intensive phase followed from the end of World War I until after World War II when the Anglo-Iranian Oil Company was nationalized. Both empires were competing for material and geopolitical advantages in the region, with Britain being particularly anxious about the potential Russian threat to British India in the nineteenth century.

The Russo–Persian wars first broke out in 1804. Initially British involvement was intended to contain Napoleon's overtures to Iran for a possible alliance. With Napoleon out of the way and British power emerging in the Persian Gulf, British policy focused on the maintenance of the status quo in order to forestall Russian expansion southwards, which instability in Iran would have encouraged. Britain was also anxious to seal off Afghanistan from Iranian rule, which in Britain's view might facilitate Russian advance towards India.

There had been brushes with the Russian empire since Peter the Great (1682–1725; see Chapter 2), but they did not thwart Russian ambitions for annexing the Caucasus. Aqa Mohammad Khan managed to keep Georgia by ruthless action, but late in 1799 Russian troops entered Tiflis (Tbilisi), abolished the Georgian principality and annexed the territory. The Iranians were alarmed and began to woo Britain and France for support. But these countries were themselves involved in conflict, sometimes with and sometimes against Russia. Various French and British missions came, but with the decline of the French it was Britain which became Iran's countervailing power to Russia.

The Russo–Persian wars

In 1802, Prince Tsitsianov became Russian commissioner for the Caucasus, and his deliberate encroachments on Iranian territory led to the war in 1804, which lasted until the Iranians sued for peace via British mediation and signed the Golestan Treaty in 1813. Most of the Caucasus was ceded to Russia, and only the Russians could keep a fleet in the Caspian Sea. The Golestan Treaty humiliated the shah and his heir-designate Abbas Mirza, governor-general of Azerbaijan, who had led the Persian armies against the Russians and had personally conducted the negotiations.

Abbas Mirza's rival brothers and other detractors tried to blame him for the defeat. But that was not the end of the affair. Russian encroaching along the new, uncertain Russo–Iranian border continued, and severely persecuted Muslims poured down across the border, asking the ulama to intervene. And so they did, with great vigour. It is not clear if Abbas Mirza himself was in favour of the renewal of war but, in 1826, he renewed hostilities. On the other hand, his maternal uncle Allahyar Khan Asef al-Dowleh was in favour of war, and led one of the Iranian forces into the Caucasus. Helped by British officers, Abbas Mirza had organized a new army along European lines.

The campaign ended in greater disaster than before. Peace negotiations led to the signing of the Treaty of Turkmanchai in 1828, which resulted in the secession of the whole of the Caucasus to Russia and the payment of an indemnity of twenty million roubles. The capitulation agreement gave Russia extra-territorial rights in Iran for the voluntary repatriation and legal protection of its subjects as well as former subjects of the Russian empire. As Abbas Mirza was the heir-designate, in compensation to him and with the support of Fath'ali Shah, Russia guaranteed succession to the throne in the line of the prince. This was a further setback for Persian sovereignty; but it was consistent with the historical tradition that rulers could not guarantee the succession of their heir-designates. In time, capitulation rights were also granted to Britain. All in all, the decline of Persia as an independent state can be traced from 1828 and the signing of the Turkmanchai Treaty.

Fath'ali Shah's death in 1834 ended a reign that had seen Iran's first encounter with and responses to the consequences of modernization and industrialization in Europe. Never before had Iranian rulers faced a power it looked as if they could never match, either in open conflict or through peaceful diplomacy. At first they regarded the problem at its most obvious level – the difference in military technology, structure and organization. Hence Abbas Mirza's well-intentioned rush to raise his New Army. The success of the Russian and British armies was seen to lie in their order, discipline and efficiency. The problem facing Abbas Mirza was that, unlike the Europeans, the Iranian military system was inherently disorderly, undisciplined and inefficient. That was a key reason why his New Army proved to be no match for the Russians in the 1826–28 war.

The Russian humiliation of the Persians reached its anticlimax in 1829 in the massacre of Alexander Griboyedov and his entourage. A very promising Russian writer, Griboyedov arrived in Tehran as minister plenipotentiary (diplomatic representative below the rank of ambassador). His immediate task was the implementation of the Treaty of Turkmanchai, but the mission had behaved badly on the way as regards people's property and wives. Once in Tehran, the defection to Russia of an Armenian eunuch at the royal court (who had previously converted to Islam), and the compulsory removal to the Russian embassy of two Armenian wives of Asef al-Dowleh, led to strong popular reaction. A large mob gathered outside the Russian legation demanding the release of the eunuch and the two women. Gaining entry to the buildings, they proceeded to massacre the Russian mission. After the violence had subsided, the shah sent a high-level delegation to St Petersburg to offer fabulous gifts and profuse apologies for the incident. Nicholas I obliged and the matter was relegated 'to eternal oblivion'.

At home, Fath'ali Shah's reign was one of the most peaceful and stable since the fall of the Safavids. His court's splendour and strict protocol was such that it impressed even some of his important English visitors. He patronized poetry and painting, in part because of his appreciation of literature and the arts and in part to satisfy his vanity by having himself praised in portraits, works of art and panegyrics.

Fath'ali Shah himself was a poet, and has a published *Divan* (collected poetical works). There is an anecdote that once, in a poetry-reading session at the court, the shah read one of his own works and asked Poet Laureate Saba what he thought of it. Saba's response not being sufficiently complimentary, the shah ordered that he be held in the royal stables for a while. On another occasion, long afterwards, the shah once again asked Saba for his opinion of a poem which he had just recited, whereupon the Poet Laureate rose and began to walk towards the door. Puzzled, the shah asked him what he was doing. 'Sire, I am going to the royal stables,' the poet replied.

The rise of the ulama

Fath'ali Shah also patronized religious institutions, and his reign saw the rise of the autonomous power of Shi'a ulama. The fact that Shi'a theory regarded only the sinless Imam's rule as wholly legitimate was also consistent with the more ancient Iranian tradition of regarding state power theoretically as illegitimate. Nevertheless a modus operandi normally existed between rulers and clerics. The ulama's relationship with the people was two-sided: they posed as the leaders of the people, and in their turn, those who could afford it – notably the bazaar community – paid them their religious dues and gave them support whenever they confronted the state. The novelty in the nineteenth century was that the ulama enjoyed a degree of autonomous power that they had never experienced before.

The origins of the rise of ulama power are not easy to discern. On the theoretical plane, the triumph of the Osuli Shi'a school over the Akhbari school was certainly instrumental. The Akhbaris maintained that the principal source of guidance was the tradition of sinless Imams, as received through *akhbar*, the traditional body of knowledge on their thoughts and actions. The Osulis, by contrast, advocated the necessity of rational interpretations of the religious law by the ulama, and the emulation by the faithful of such interpretations and pronouncements issued by a recognized *mojtahed* (doctor of Shi'a law). Thus, the Osuli position placed the ulama in a pivotal position, providing them with legitimate authority to pronounce opinions which might even conflict with decisions of the state. It was recognized that one *mojtahed*'s opinion may be different from, sometimes conflicting with, another *mojtahed*'s. Each was regarded as valid, meaning that followers of different *mojtahed*s could hold opposing views within the Shi'a community.

On the ground, there were a number of causes. In part it was a practical consequence of the virtual autonomy of the Shi'a cities under the Ottomans, where the *hawzeh* (seminary) of Najaf, an Osuli stronghold, grew powerful as a result of the decline of Isfahan, itself being a consequence of the long period of chaos in the eighteenth century. In part it was a product of Aqa Mohammad Khan's and Fath'ali Shah's deference to religious institutions and dignitaries and need for their patronage, not suspecting that this would lead to the creation of a rival authority to the state. From Mohammad Shah (Fath'ali Shah's successor) onwards, the ulama's power had become too entrenched to be dislodged, and all that the various rulers and governments could do was to try and contain their power, usually by favours and ultimately by force.

The ulama's ascent culminated in their leadership of the Tobacco Revolt of 1890–2 – a conflict that we shall look at in more depth later – the triumph of which raised their authority to a level previously unknown.

Civil war and interregnum

Fath'ali Shah's death in 1834 was followed by the familiar struggle for succession. Early in 1834 he had appointed as heir-designate Mohammad Mirza, the eldest son of Abbas Mirza who had died the year before, partly in recognition of Abbas Mirza's services and untimely death, and partly in keeping with the Treaty of Turkmanchai. The revolt of Alishah Zel al-Soltan, Mohammad's uncle and governor of Tehran, was peacefully settled, and that of Fath'ali Shah's senior son Hosyen'ali Mirza, governor-general of Fars, aided by his full brother Hasan'ali Mirza, governor-general of Isfahan, led to their defeat in a civil war. Apart from that, the mere news of the shah's death led to pockets of rebellion around the country, the worst of which shook the western regions for some time.

In putting down these revolts and 'seditious' risings after the shah's death, the able but unpopular chief minister, Qa'em-Maqam, played a very important role. But it did nothing to stop the new shah from feeling threatened by him and having him put to death, despite the fact that he was generally a mild and meek ruler and inclined towards Sufism.

The fourteen years (1834–48) of Mohammad Shah's rule may almost be described as an interregnum in so far as it was a weak and undistinguished episode between the reigns of his grandfather Fath'ali Shah and his son Naser al-Din Shah. It was volatile as far as court intrigue, foreign relations and provincial chaos were concerned, but otherwise almost static. There was a shift of emphasis in foreign relations to greater reliance on Russia

than Britain, now that Russian territorial ambitions towards
Persia had been satisfied. Russia encouraged Iran to reach an
entente with Kabul and Qandahar and assert her traditional sovereignty over Herat, but Britain was determined to thwart these
ambitions. Mohammad Shah's siege of Herat in 1837 was abandoned in the following year as a result of intense British pressure.
In addition to influencing foreign policy, the envoys of both
powers were regularly involved in the usual court intrigues, not
least regarding the question of succession.

Naser al-Din Mirza, the shah's eldest son, was governor-
general of Azebaijan and the heir-designate. Hajji Mirza Aghasi,
who had succeeded Qae'm-Maqam as chief minister, courted

Naser al-Din Shah, 1889. (Source: Jungmann & Schorn, Hofphotographen
Baden-Baden, Cabinet Photography, via Wikimedia Commons)

the shah's favourite son, Abbas Mirza, the little boy whom the shah had both named after his father and given the latter's title of prince regent. As chief minister, the Hajji was bound to be unpopular. But his most powerful detractor at court was the shah's first wife and mother of Naser al-Din Mirza, who, among other things, resented the favours shown to the boy Abbas Mirza by another wife.

By the time of Mohammad Shah's succession, the ulama had acquired a large degree of independent authority. However, both Mohammad Shah and Hajji Mirza Aghasi were Sufis. And although theirs was a firm, religious form of Sufism, inevitably there was some shift in the state patronage from the ulama and colleges to the Sufis and their establishments, although the Sufis could not compete with the ulama in power or following.

The strongest, longest example of state–ulama conflict found expression in the attitude and behaviour of the extremely rich and powerful *mojtahed* Seyyed Mohammad Baqer Shafti of Isfahan. By 1830 he had become the virtual ruler of the province, running the city with the aid of the ruffian community. It was a glaring example of disarray in the midst of arbitrary rule. The chaos subsided and the Seyyed's rule ended only upon the appointment to Isfahan's governor-generalship of the tough, ruthless Manuchehr Khan Gorji, the Armenian eunuch who, in 1834, had stamped out the war of succession, when Mohammad Shah came to power, with exemplary severity. The Seyyed himself was left unmolested, a fact that bore witness to the exceptional position of the ulama vis-à-vis the state.

Mohammad Shah's rule also saw the rise of the Babi movement. Sheykh Ahmad Ahsa'i was the founder of the Shi'a Sheykhi sect. He preached that although the twelfth Imam was hidden from the material world, his essence was always present in a living person, the *Bab* or door between him and the Shi'a community. Sheykh Ahmad was succeeded by Seyyed Kazem Rashti who advanced similar views. After the latter's death in December

1843, the Sheykhi movement split along three lines. But it was only one of them, the Babi movement, which was destined to attract significant popular support, that led to confrontation both with the ulama and the state which finally resulted in a completely new religion: the Baha'i faith.

THE BABI MOVEMENT

The Babi movement was led by Seyyed Ali Mohammad Shirazi, known as the Bab, who later said that he himself was the Hidden Imam. The Bab appealed to relatively large numbers of people, for various reasons: anti-state feelings, grievances against the ulama, desiring social change and the Bab's own charisma. This popularity caused concern both to ulama and state, although it also attracted sympathy and support from some members of the ulama, including a few *mojta-heds*. As a result of the outbreak of cholera, the Bab left Shiraz for Isfahan. Manuchehr Khan Gorji, who, as noted, was now governor-general of Isfahan, took the Bab under his own protection. However, Manuchehr Khan died about six months later, and the Bab was seized and orders came for him to be sent to Tehran. But he never reached Tehran as Haji Mirza Agasi diverted him to be imprisoned in the fort of Maku and later Chihriq. From there, he was sent off to Azerbaijan, the seat of Naser al-Din Mirza, the youthful heir-designate. Here, according to a letter sent by the prince to his father, the Bab was questioned in front of three leading Tabriz ulama and severely flogged. In the wake of the Babi revolt in three different regions of the country, he was brought back to Tabriz in 1850 and executed.

The new reign

The premature death of the lethargic and mystical Mohammad Shah and the inevitable fall of his lacklustre vizier, Hajji Mirza Aghasi, followed by the succession of the young and dashing Naser al-Din Mirza with the chancellorship of Amir Kabir heralded a hopeful new age, but not for long. The shah's death once again threw the centre into uproar. Hajji Mirza Aghasi managed to escape by the skin of his teeth, being allowed safe passage to Iraq but forfeiting his immense fortune as a matter of course.

The triumphant march from Tabriz of Naser al-Din Mirza, organized by Amir Kabir with British and Russian support, ended the disorder in Tehran and inaugurated the long and eventful reign of the new shah. Between 1848 and 1852, Amir Kabir ruled the country in the shah's name. The shah was young, intelligent and promising. Over time, he became vain and pleasure-seeking, but still hoped to make the country stronger through basic administrative reform, institution-building and modernization. Still later, he lost heart in reform and progress and was resigned to a life of hunting and lusting after money and women. Despite this later decline, he was able, authoritative and self-respecting at home as well as abroad; and he managed to hold the country in one piece to an extent that, in the circumstances, an average ruler would have been unable to do.

Amir Kabir's reforms

Amir Kabir was brilliant as a civil and military administrator, in certain respects comparable with Reza Khan in the twentieth century. He was highly educated and enjoyed great imagination, but lacked wide support and facilities for state-building and modernization. He depended almost entirely on his own ability and the good will of the shah, while making powerful enemies among the elite and the ulama as well as large segments of the public. Being the most powerful man in the land, the normal opposition of Iranian society to the state was directed against him while he was in power. It was not until after his fall and destruction that he was turned into a hero, lauded for the very reforms for which he was, just years before, reviled – a retrospective honour not uncommon in Iranian society.

Amir Kabir's vision in so far as it may be discerned from his actions was to stamp out actual or potential revolts with an iron fist and centralize the state. Thus, in 1850, he not only crushed Hasan Khan Salar's continuing rebellion in Khorasan, but also suppressed with great severity the revolt of the Bab's followers in Mazandaran, Zanjan and Fars. He set out to reduce all autonomous power, be it of the provincial magnates, of the ulama, of the court nobility and of dignitaries and officials. They in time gathered around the shah's mother, who was leading a deadly campaign against Amir Kabir. According to a rumour repeated as fact by a future prime minister, Mokhber al-Saltaneh (Mehdi Qoli Hedayat), he in turn was trying to persuade the shah to get rid of his mother by a contrived accident.

Amir Kabir tried to continue Abbas Mirza's military reforms with greater vigour and intensity. The Dar al-Fonun College, which was opened after his demise, had been planned along the lines of the renowned French *écoles polytechniques*, where European teachers (many of them Austrian) taught military, medical and other sciences as well as modern languages. The impact of Amir Kabir's reforms was felt mainly in the short run and for as long as he was at the helm. They could not have long-term, cumulative effects in a fundamental way so long as they were applied in a short-term, arbitrary state and society. Whether or not he was aware of the necessity of reforming the arbitrary nature of power and introducing government based in law it is impossible to know. He certainly did not have the chance to take any steps in that direction – a task much greater and more essential than all of his reforms put together – before he was sacked and executed as a result of a court intrigue in 1852.

Shortly after the dismissal and killing of Amir Kabir, a group of Tehran Babis made an unsuccessful attempt on the shah's life. The result was a hideous backlash, the like of which, in the words of the renowned twentieth-century historian Ahmad Kasravi, had never been seen in Tehran before. Scores of Babi leaders and activists were handed over to various groups of people, who killed them using extremely cruel methods such as making holes in their bodies and filling them with lighted candles. This was followed by the exile of members of the movement to Ottoman territory, where conflict between the two leading figures, the brothers Mirza Hoseyn'ali Baha' ullah and Mirza Yahya Sobh-e Azal led to schism and split, the Baha'is founding a completely new religion and emerging as the main body of the movement. The Azalis were a minority, actively supporting the Constitutional Revolution and dwindling into insignificance by the 1920s.

Anglo–Russian rivalry

The Russian and British rivalry and interference in Iranian affairs continued and intensified as the century advanced. Towards the end of the century, almost all important state decisions had to have the approval of at least one of the two great powers. This rivalry between the powers almost certainly saved Iran from direct colonization by either of them. On the other hand, it was no longer a fully independent country.

The Russian and British influence had at least one positive result in tempering certain features of arbitrary rule. For example, without their support, Mohammad Shah's accession would have involved more conflict and chaos, and Naser al-Din Shah's would have been less smooth than it was. Their strong protest against the killing of Amir Kabir (which the British foreign secretary described as an uncivilized act) introduced a new means of stopping the arbitrary killing of nobles and notables, although it did not go so far as to save their property from confiscation.

Thenceforth, consideration of European opinion became an important factor regarding such decisions. This can be seen in action when, decades after Amir Kabir's demise, the governor-general of Fars bastinadoed (beat the soles of the feet of) Qavam al-Molk, one of the most powerful magnates and grandees of Fars, threw him in jail and asked the shah to 'sell' Qavam to him for money. The governor-general's failure to 'buy Qavam', wrote Etemad al-Saltaneh (the secretary and diarist who saw the shah almost every day), was at least in part because of probable adverse European opinion: 'this is not like the age of Fath'ali Shah to be possible to buy and sell the magnates and notables; the Europeans would make a fuss'. Amin al-Dowleh writes in his memoirs quite independently that Fath'ali Shah 'even used to sell court officials and state dignitaries to each other'.

Mirza Aqa Khan Nuri, who replaced Amir Kabir, survived longer in office and was, just like most other officials, a survivalist, but still when he fell in 1858 he might well have lost his life had it not been for the shah's sensitivity towards European opinion. He lost all of his property nevertheless, and was banished to the edge of the Lut desert.

The loss of Herat in 1857 was also an indirect cause of the fall of Mirza Aqa Khan. The young shah had wished to pursue Iran's long-standing claim to sovereignty over Herat and score a heroic point in the process. The military expedition was successful and Herat fell to the shah's forces. The British were alarmed because of their belief that this would, or at least could, open the gateway for the Russians towards India, given that Herat's strategic location made it virtually the only passable route for a large army to cross the Afghan lands into the subcontinent. They landed troops in southern Iran in a bid to force the shah to withdraw from Herat. The Iranians withdrew, and in the peace treaty that was negotiated in Paris through the good offices of Napoleon III, Iran gave up her claim on Herat and perforce the rest of Afghan lands, this being the origin of the international recognition of Afghanistan as an independent state.

The Herat campaign was a monumental failure for the shah. It became clear that the half-hearted attempts for a partial acquisition of European technology and science were far from adequate for modernization. Besides, the fall and execution of Amir Kabir at a clap of the hands had demonstrated that the existing system of government was still as old as the hills. For the first time in Iranian history they struck upon the most ancient and fundamental problem of the state and society, that is, arbitrary rule (*estebdad*), the most crucial difference between Iran and Europe, where lawful government and orderly society had been the rule rather than the exception.

The discovery of law

Young Malkam Khan, son of an Armenian convert to Islam, who had spent many years as a student in Paris, became the chief theorist of constitutional and responsible government. In around 1860 Malkam submitted his long and comprehensive statutory frame to Naser al-Din Shah, apparently at the shah's own bidding, shortly after the collapse of the siege of Herat. This was the first constitutional frame ever written in Iranian history. Its most striking feature is the distinction Malkam makes between absolute monarchy and arbitrary rule: 'organized and orderly absolute monarchies', giving the examples of Russia and Austria; and 'disorganized and disorderly absolute monarchies' (or *estebdad*, which literally means arbitrary rule). What was needed for Iran, according to Malkam, was an *orderly* absolute monarchy, that is, one based in law: an absolute monarchy in which the crown laid down the law and where it was observed as well as executed by an organized, disciplined and responsible administration.

There then followed a comprehensive draft constitution, which required the entirety of state and religious law to be organized and written by a legislative council. This is a large and elaborate document, although all its articles follow from the basic precepts and principles outlined above. It took another decade for the shah to take any steps at all towards the fulfilment of some of these ideas, but even then it was soon abandoned.

It was also with the shah's knowledge that Malkam and a few other advanced men of note set up the *Farmush-khaneh* (House of Oblivion). This was modelled after European Masonic Lodges both in its name and in its aura of secrecy although, contrary to popular belief, it was not an official Masonic Lodge. It was the first modern society for political discourse, and its deliberate though superficial resemblance to Freemasonry is owed both to Freemasonry's important role in the French Revolution and to the mystique with which it was held even in Europe, which in Iran amounted to no less than real magical powers.

In a country where suspicion and conspiracy in matters of the state had been an ancient preoccupation, this was bound to alarm many a powerful person and social group, not least some of the ulama, especially given that its trimmings appeared to be foreign and Christian. The shah himself might have been concerned at the danger of licentious ideas being discussed behind his back, but pressure from others must also have been instrumental in his order to the secret society to disband. He went further than that and, in 1862, dispatched Malkam to the Persian embassy in Istanbul, though this was partly intended to silence his enemies. There he joined the staff of the Iranian ambassador Hajj Mirza Hoseyn Khan Moshir al-Dowleh, who was to lead the shah's second reformist ministry after Amir Kabir.

THE TELEGRAPH

In the meantime, the coming of the telegraph to Iran, the single most important technical advancement in nineteenth-century Iran, had increased the central government's grip on the provinces in that information could now be received and orders dispatched incredibly cheaply and quickly. Ironically, it was later to prove to be an equally effective instrument for organizing countrywide protest and revolution. The Indo-European Telegraph Department, a branch of the

British Government of India, based in London, managed a series of telegraph lines in Iran. To begin with, Charles Wood, the Secretary of State for India, entered negotiations with Iran's ambassador in London, Mirza Ja'far Khan, in early 1861. Then, on 17 December 1862 Edward Backhouse Eastwick, Britain's chargé d'affaires in Tehran, won agreement from the shah. The resulting Anglo-Iranian Telegraph Agreement, signed by Queen Victoria on 6 February 1863, called on Iran to build a line stretching from Khanaqin (across the Ottoman frontier from the Iranian town of Qasr-e Shirin) through Tehran and onward to Bushehr, supervised by a British engineer, Patrick Stewart.

The administrative system under Naser al-Din Shah was relatively decentralized, as before, but the shah was still the ultimate arbiter and decision-taker, and had the power to enforce his decisions far and wide through governors, financial auditors and other officials within the existing military, financial and social constraints.

The army continued to decline in men, equipment, discipline and leadership through lethargy and neglect. In later years, the only relatively disciplined and effective force was the Cossack Brigade, which was commanded and run by Russian officers. The Persian Cossacks were a gift of the tsar to the shah as his personal guards – an outcome of his second visit to Europe in 1878 – and in time became an instrument of Russian policy in the country.

Another experiment with reform

Moshir al-Dowleh, Iran's ambassador to the Ottomans, was a maternal cousin of the shah, although his grandfather had been a public bath assistant in Qazvin – an example of the unusually high degree of social mobility in Iranian society. Having been impressed with the modern European developments and Ottoman reforms of the state administration, Moshir al-Dowleh wished to promote both political and technological reform in Iran. He had accompanied the shah on his visit to Ottoman Iraq, when he had impressed him both with the idea of progress and with his own personal ability. Following that, in 1871 Malkam's erstwhile reform theories received a chance of being tested in a moderate and pragmatic though no less important form when the shah finally agreed to the formation of a cabinet run by ministers with fairly well-defined duties, having decision-making powers as well as individual and collective responsibility. Moshir al-Dowleh, now entitled Sepahsalar, was made, like Amir Kabir, chief minister as well as head of the army, and led Iran's first ever cabinet government. Malkam, who had been with him in Istanbul, was Sepahsalar's principal advisor in matters regarding administrative reform and economic development.

At first, the shah gave the reforms full support, but this later waned and the opponents of reform were as effective as ever. The ulama were unhappy since they saw such an administration as a threat to their own authority, especially as it was in a crypto-European form and had avowedly modernizing aims. There were others in government and among the notables who felt threatened by the programme of a reformist administration. In a pattern typical of Iranian history, various otherwise conflicting elements combined to achieve a negative objective: the eventual downfall of Moshir al-Dowleh and his reforms.

In order to shake up the economy and society from their state of backwardness, Moshir al-Dowleh hoped for substantial and far-reaching investment projects and convinced the shah to grant a concession to Baron Julius de Reuter, founder of the news agency, to provide the necessary capital, technology and skill. Reactions were sharp and strong when in 1872 the Reuter concession was finally approved. The ulama attacked the decision, as did all the opponents of Sepahsalar's government. The Russians opposed the scheme because it gave sweeping opportunity for exploration, exploitation and construction, including a railway network, to a British subject. Sepahsalar hoped to have Britain's backing for the Reuter concession but, strange as it may look, the British government was not forthcoming, perhaps not wanting to offend the Russians over a scheme in which they were not involved. No powerful party being in favour of the scheme, it collapsed and the concession was cancelled, in compensation for which the British-owned Imperial Bank of Persia was later established through another concession.

But Sepahsalar and Malkam had not given up. In 1873, they persuaded a willing and curious shah to go on his first tour of Europe, hoping that the spectacle of modern society would strengthen his resolve to continue with modernization and reform. It did not work. The shah went on the tour from Russia to England, and was much impressed with European industrial and social developments. He was accompanied by Sepahsalar and a large retinue, but as soon as they arrived back in Rasht, he sacked the hapless Sepahsalar. For all his hopes of legal reform, the man had to take sanctuary in the stables in fear of his life, although the shah later showed that his decision had been largely due to pressure from all sides.

That, at any rate, was the end of any serious reform from above, although the shah did return to the issue of government by law after his third and final visit to Europe. Sepahsalar was made governor-general of Khorasan where he died shortly after, rumours spreading that he had been poisoned on the shah's orders. The fact that the shah appropriated the dead man's estate was more or less routine and irrespective of his sentiments towards him.

The last phase

In the remaining twenty-three years of his life, the shah contented himself with maintaining his own authority at home, managing foreign relations as best he could and pursuing his favourite pastimes of hunting and women, to which extensive European tours were now added, once again in 1878 and a third time in 1889. He watched over the country's decline, although he still toyed with the idea of introducing law and responsible government to the country. On his return from his third European visit, he revisited the question of government by law instead of fiat, and ordered state luminaries to set up a council. He told them:

> All the order and progress which we observed in Europe in our recent visit is due to the existence of law. Therefore, we too have made up our mind to introduce a law and act according to it.

Nothing came of it. Power was still arbitrary, but government was decentralized, state interference in the lives of ordinary people limited and many decisions were reached through a bargaining process.

The shah's last important vizier was the young Mirza Ali Asghar Khan Amin al-Soltan, who was only twenty-six when he first became chief minister. Later, given the high honorific of Atabak, he was an intelligent, able and educated man, on whom the shah became increasingly dependent for running the administration and dealing with foreign envoys. Cunning and duplicitous, he was very good at building up support at court and among the notables, and dealing with Russia and Britain in a self-serving and pragmatic way.

The Tobacco Revolt

Perhaps Amin al-Soltan's greatest feat of survivalist performance was when he switched sides from Britain before the Tobacco Revolt of 1890–2 to Russia afterwards. Throughout the 1880s, various trading concessions were granted to Russian and, especially, British companies. The concession policy reached its climax, then anticlimax, when in 1890 the shah granted a concession to the British firm Talbot for the monopoly of production, sale and export of Iranian tobacco. Its scope was more limited than the ill-fated Reuter concession, but, unlike Reuter's, it was of little or no consequence for economic development, only for lining the shah's and ministers' pockets with royalties and commissions. The Russians were naturally opposed to it. So were tobacco merchants, who were joined by other merchant guilds. The ulama were drawn in, because of their role as 'leaders of the people', and because of fear of growing European domination. In turn, their opposition encouraged other urban groups.

The fact that the Talbot concession covered domestic trade and production as well was particularly alarming. Most of the ulama accepted the call of the protesters for support, and this came to its climax when a *fatva* (religious edict) attributed to Hajj Mirza Hasan Shirazi, the senior *marja'* ('source of emulation'), who lived in Samerra, Iraq was published, which simply read:

> As from today, consumption of tobacco and smoking the waterpipe is forbidden and tantamount to waging war against the Imam of the Time.

The people responded with full vigour and boycotted the use of tobacco. This was a blow to the shah and his chief minister Amin al-Soltan in particular. The shah tried to save part of the deal by offering to withdraw the concession for domestic trade, as he wrote to Mirza Hasan Ashtiyani, the leading Tehran *mojtahed*. However Ashtiyani and the public were insisting on the cancellation of the entire concession, and the conflict peaked in the bloodshed that followed public demonstrations outside the royal compound. Finally, the shah cancelled the concession.

The tobacco concession was obviously against the economic interests of merchants and traders, who were more active than any other social class in the revolt. Yet the matter went well beyond that, since it provided an important focus for all the discontented groups, reformist or otherwise. Most of the ulama supported the cause, which incidentally gave it a religious aspect, especially as it was against a concession given to non-Muslim foreigners.

It was almost an unprecedented event in Iranian history. For the first time the public had revolted peacefully, and for a clear and well-defined purpose. Also for the first time, the arbitrary state had given in to a public demand, rather than either suppressing it or being overthrown violently by the opposition. It was possibly the nearest thing to the European practice of politics that had ever been experienced in Iranian history. It can now be seen as a dress rehearsal for the Constitutional Revolution fifteen years later. The shah acted with tact and forbearance when the chips were down, but he gained little. Not only did the hoped-for royalties not materialize, but the shah had to pay a £500,000 cancellation fee facilitated by the Imperial Bank of Persia. It was the beginning of politics in Iran, though it took another century for it to grow some roots.

Apart from Shirazi and Ashtiyani, two figures played important roles in the campaign, albeit less directly: Malkam Khan and Seyyed Jamal al-Din Asadabadi, known outside Iran as Al-Afghani. Malkam, who was Persian minister (head of the diplomatic legation below the rank of ambassador) in London during the shah's visit there in 1889, was sacked over a conflict that was fomented by his enemy Amin al-Soltan regarding the sale of a lottery concession. Malkam cashed the £40,000 royalties in dispute and moved into open opposition, commencing the publication of the newspaper *Qanun* (Law). The paper advocated the establishment of government by law as opposed to arbitrary rule, and became very popular among the reformist elite via secret circulation.

Jamal al-Din, a charismatic and enigmatic ulama type, posed in Sunni countries as well as in the West as a Sunni in order to be acceptable to the Sunni ulama and intellectuals – hence his pretence to be an Afghan from Kabul. He advocated Muslim unity as well as technological and institutional advancement along European lines. He travelled far and wide, impressing both reforming Muslim thinkers such as Muhammad 'Abduh of Egypt and European intellectuals such as Ernest Renan. He had been to various courts, including the Ottoman Porte, and had been invited by Naser al-Din Shah to Tehran. His first visit did not bear any fruit, and on his second visit the shah saw him as a subversive element and had him arrested and expelled from the country with indignity. It cost the shah his life. Whether or not Mirza Reza Kermani, the Seyyed's devoted disciple, was instructed by him to assassinate the shah, his strongest motive in so doing was to avenge the shah's ill treatment of his mentor. That was in 1896.

Naser al-Din Shah was an arbitrary ruler just like all Persian rulers in Iranian history, but by no means one of the worst. It may even be argued that, allowing for the steady decline in the country's position in the nineteenth century, he was personally the best ruler that Iran had had since Karim Khan. He managed to keep the peace at home and did not cede much important territory except for Herat, which it was beyond his power to regain. He carried out some construction and development, notably in Tehran, including a remapping of the city, building various gates, the collection of rubbish and the installation of street lighting. His two most interesting additions to the palace complex were Shams al-Emareh, which has survived, and Tekyeh-ye Dowlat, designed mainly for official religious congregations and services and which, while perfectly sound, was demolished (or 'pickaxed') in 1946 to enable the building of the Bank Melli bazaar branch on the site.

The economy

First it must be pointed out that in the nineteenth century the Iranian economy was not integrated, such that one can speak of a national economy: most regions were nearly self-sufficient, and while one region could be doing badly, another could be faring better. With that caveat, three phases may be distinguished for study: 1800–50, 1850–70 and 1870–1900. As noted before, the first half of the nineteenth century was a period of relative stability compared with the chaotic eighteenth century. Heavy taxation and extortion – 'the fleecing of the flock' – was no different from normal periods of arbitrary rule, but it was a definite improvement on the previous state of affairs. The period 1850–70 was probably the happiest economic phase of the nineteenth century, compared to 1800–50 and 1870–1900. There is noticeable deterioration in the last phase, when foreign debts accumulated, the balance of payments deficit kept rising and there was a sustained and accelerating decline in the value of money.

There is a general consensus that the population grew from around six to seven million at the beginning of the century, to about eight to nine million at its close. The nomadic population remained fairly constant throughout the century, roughly at two and a half million, since the process of re-nomadization had ceased due to greater security. This would mean that the settled population grew by about two million, or thirty per cent, over the whole of the nineteenth century, implying a very modest average annual growth rate, which was nevertheless quite significant for its time.

Taxes consisted mainly of the land tax, the poll tax, various other taxes on productive activities and customs duties, but land tax was by far the biggest source of central and provincial revenues, to which must be added both regular and irregular extortion and the official plunder of output and property.

Other non-fiscal methods of raising revenues – such as sales of trade concessions to foreigners, sales of public offices and direct foreign loans – became more significant in the last decades of the century, though this does not imply an easing-off of taxes on the agricultural sector. The rate of land tax was different according to the productivity of the land, and it generally increased by about one-third in the last decades, mainly because of a further rise in fleecing and exploitation, since land tax was mostly collected in kind, and its rate cannot have been raised simply in response to rampant inflation.

There were inflationary pressures throughout the century, but they became much greater between 1870 and 1900. The causes of inflation were the official and unofficial debasement of the currency, the dramatic fall in the international price of silver – on which the Iranian currency was based – and the structural balance of payments deficit, all three of which were most acute in the last three decades. The increasing balance of payments deficit was due to the growing gap between imports and exports. The favourable tariff treaties of no more than five per cent imposed by the European powers played an important role in increasing imports, largely for minority consumption. The growth in exports fell far short of imports, and hence the balance of trade went on deteriorating.

Domestic handmade commodities such as textile materials, being generally more expensive as well as less fashionable than European machine-made products, experienced a relative decline in demand in the home market and an absolute decline in the foreign (export) markets. On the other hand, much of the growth of Iranian exports was due to shifts from secondary (industrial) to primary (agricultural) products, and particularly to the two main cash crops, opium and cotton. The figures indicate that, in the 1850s, the share of primary products in total exports was less than twenty per cent, but in the 1880s it had risen to sixty per cent, with a corresponding decline in the export of secondary products.

The rise in cash-crop production was largely at the expense of food production, and this raised food prices further (in addition to other inflationary factors), thus pushing the bare subsistence of the vast majority of the people to still lower limits.

It is clear from the above that the large increase in the volume of trade was first due to increasing European imports, and second, to shifts from food crops, such as corn, to cash crops, such as opium and cotton, for export to European countries. It was not due to the growth, much less the development, of the Iranian economy, which might possibly have led to greater saving and investment and a rise in employment and income, though it did enrich foreign trade merchants, swelling the wealth and import-ance of the most successful among them, men such as Amin al-Zarb and Malek al-Tojjar.

Barring the telegraph, which had an important impact by making correspondence cheaper and quicker, and resulting in greater socio-economic integration, there was no significant technical progress in the economic sense of the term in either industry or agriculture. The 'technical progress' to which political historians usually point largely refers to the minority consump-tion of the products of modern European technology. Likewise, there was no significant increase in the accumulation of financial capital and rise in the stock of physical capital.

The growth of foreign trade was the main force behind the concentration as well as centralization of financial capital; trade with Europe benefited the big merchants, and by swelling their personal fortunes it increased their potential political power at the expense of the state. European trade also played an import-ant role in weakening the arbitrary system in a number of indi-rect ways. First, the growing role of the imperial powers exposed the weaknesses of the Iranian state and robbed it of traditional public belief in its omnipotence, thus prompting Naser al-Din Shah to tell Etemad al-Saltaneh that 'the people's eyes and ears had not yet been opened' under Fath'ali Shah. Second, their payments for various concessions and privileges to the shah and state officials helped weaken the structure of arbitrary rule from within. Third, greater specialization in the production and export of raw materials, the relative decline of manufacturing, the use of the telegraph as a modern means of communication, the endemic rise in inflation, the crippling deficit in foreign payments and the resulting accumulation of foreign debt all led to a structural disequilibrium in the economy which the traditional state apparatus could not comprehend, let alone cope with. The chaos that followed the death of Naser al-Din Shah led to the further deterioration of the economy.

Literature and the arts

The rise of the Qajar monarchy nearly coincided with the emergence of the reversion to classical genres and styles in Persian literature, and more especially poetry, in the nineteenth century. This came after three centuries of the so-called Indian style of poetry. So-called, not just because the best poets in these genres were Iranian, not Indian, but particularly because the style or standard of these poets were not the same, and even worse, uniformly 'decadent' (as their nineteenth-century detractors called them). However, it is true that by the late eighteenth century Persian poetry had fallen into a sorry state, as had virtually every other component of Iranian civilization.

That, at any rate, is how a reversion to the classics (tenth to sixteenth centuries) was justified. Nineteenth-century poets and their works were certainly better than their eighteenth-century counterparts, and they did salvage Persian poetry from the sorry state towards which it had declined. They sometimes wrote *qasideh*s (long odes) that even an expert might take for a classical one if it was presented blind to him or her. Fathollah Khan Sheybani – that unhappy poet – is a shining example of those who imitated the classics almost perfectly. And just as they had harshly and hastily castigated their predecessors, they themselves were rejected with contempt by the modern literary critics of the twentieth century. It is true that there were virtually no major innovations in nineteenth-century Persian poetry, but this is a far cry from the pronouncements of its latter-day critics.

Take Qa'em-Maqam and Qa'ani Shirazi, for example. In different ways, they wrote some of the best pieces of the period, better than poems by some of the classic medieval exponents. Qa'em-Maqam's style was less distinctly pro-classical compared to many of the other poets of the century. Qa'ani Shirazi was eloquent and humorous, with a rich as well as clear expression, and was extremely good with words and use of language. He was not innovative in any major way, but the flavour of his poetry, and his sheer facility with language, reminiscent of Sa'di, cannot be easily found even among the old *qasideh* writers. His *qasideh* eulogising Amir Kabir is a sheer joy to read, opening with the couplet: 'Is a heavenly breeze blowing at the mountains / That the fragrance of musk is in the air of the meadows?'

Yaghma, however, was an angry poet, not unlike Aref and Eshqi in the early twentieth century, betraying a wounded ego, although he was a better poet than both. He was a major poet of the period, writing *qasideh*s, love lyrics and lampoons equally well.

Neshat-e Isfahani and Foroughi Bastami were better at lyrical poetry. Foroughi's, rather like the twelfth-century Sana'i Ghaznavi, inclined towards mysticism in later life, although the mystical poet of the century par excellence was Hajj Mullah Hadi Sabzevari, who is better known as a mystic thinker. Another remarkable mystic poet of the century was Tahereh Qazvini, known as Qorrat al-'Ain. Many of her lyrics are in the style of Rumi, passionate as well as musical, but, if possible, even more passionate than his. A few of them are just a little less fiery, reminding the reader more of Hafiz, some of whose lyrics she used as models for her own.

Sorush-e Isfahani was a leading *qasideh* writer under Naser al-Din Shah, and often used eleventh-century *qasideh*s as his model. He even wrote a *qasideh* hailing too soon the ill-fated conquest of Herat. It goes without saying that there were hundreds more local, provincial and metropolitan poets, which included members of the royal family. Fath'ali Shah himself wrote poetry. His son Malek Iraj was a poet and man of letters, and his son Gholamhoseyn Mirza became a court poet and fathered one of the major poets of all time, Iraj Mirza, who should best be viewed as a poet of the constitutional age.

Calligraphy, lacquer work and especially Western-style painting grew both in quantity and quality. The greatest painters of the century were Mohammad Khan Kamal al-Molk, Abol-Hassan Khan Sani' al-Molk and Mahmud Khan Malek al-Sho'ara (all of them from Kashan), of whom Mohammad Khan Kamal al-Molk became especially famous, but recent critical opinion puts greater value on the works of the latter two. Mirza Gholamreza Isfahani was perhaps the best calligraphic artist of the period, original and innovative. Printing, though still limited, became more widespread than before, and newspapers, virtually all of them official and semi-official, came into circulation.

The great change

The death of Naser al-Din Shah was followed by increasing turmoil both at the centre of Iran and in the provinces. Mozaffar al-Din, his son and successor, was well meaning but weak and easily manipulated by his entourage. Revolutions normally occur when the state is weak, even though revolutionary ideas and agendas may have been fomented and advanced over a period of time. At any rate, weakness of the state always ran the risk of rebellion in Iranian history. The aim of traditional Iranian rebellions was to overthrow an 'unjust' ruler and replace him with a 'just' one, since otherwise arbitrary government was regarded as a natural, therefore both a necessary and inevitable phenomenon.

This time, the window of Europe had offered a view of the very attractive alternative of lawful government as well as orderly society. It was such that Prince Zel al-Soltan, the shah's elder brother, who was not at all noted for democratic sentiments, said after visiting Paris: 'Although they say there is freedom and republic [in France], and there is absolute licence, this is not the case. In this country it looks as if everyone … has the book of law under his arm and in his mind, and knows that there is no escaping from the claws of the law.' Chaos had always been the natural alternative to arbitrary rule, just as arbitrary rule had been the only alternative to chaos. Now it looked as if there was a magic wand that was certain to rid the country of its traditional habits, arbitrary rule and chaos at a stroke.

Chaos

The end of the nineteenth century was a moment of great weakness for the Qajar state, due to a century of decline and the death of an able and authoritative shah. In his diaries for the years 1897–1905, the contemporary historian Malek al-Movarrekhin details the growing chaos. There are loud complaints of governors-general confiscating private property and raping women, as also of nomadic people attacking and looting villages and taking their inhabitants into slavery.

To give but two typical examples of a long list of chaotic events, in August 1899 Aziz Mirza, a ruffian as well as Qajar nobleman causes a great public mischief, and the governor of Tehran orders the soles of his feet to be beaten with a stick in his presence. While being beaten, the offender pulls a revolver from his pocket and fires at the governor, but misses. The governor reports the incident to the shah and the latter orders them to cut

off Aziz Mirza's hand. This causes unrest among the large community of other young nobles. The shah sacks the governor and
orders him to pay pecuniary compensation to the mutilated man.
He also orders the expulsion from town of the officer who
arrested him. In April 1903, Ein al-Dowleh, Tehran's governor
(who became chief minister later in the same year) receives a
regular bribe of about one thousand *toman* a day from the bakers
and butchers. Both bread and meat are short, and expensive.
Some women stop the shah's and the governor's carriages and
complain. The governor orders them to be beaten.

Such was representative history for the lower orders. At a
higher level, there was an equally cumulative sense of turmoil.
Atabak (Amin al-Soltan) took two large government loans from
the Russians during the five years up to 1903 that he ran the
government after the reformist chief minister Amin al-Dowleh.
The loans were partly used to finance the shah's costly and waste-
ful tours in Europe, and were believed by many to have been
wholly squandered that way. Another source of complaint was
the conduct of the recently employed Belgian customs officers.
They were led by Joseph Naus as director of customs who was
later made minister of customs. Both Iranian and British traders
resented his discrimination in favour of the Russians, and the
Iranian merchants' anger turned into hatred, not least for Atabak,
who was seen by many as little more than a Russian agent.

At the same time there was 'a deadly competition' between
Ein al-Dowleh and Amin al-Soltan, even after the latter was
sacked and replaced by the former. On the other hand, given the
highly decentralized nature of the Shi'a institutions, both vigor-
ous competition and destructive conflict among the ulama was a
familiar tradition. After the death of Ashtiyani, who had been the
most prominent *mojtahed* in Tehran, both Sheykh Fazlollah Nuri
and Seyyed Abdollah Behbahani wished to be recognized as
the chief *mojtahed* in the city. Nuri and his friends tended to support Ein al-Dowleh, while Behbahani's circle, as well as Seyyed

Mohammad Tabataba'i (another leading Tehran *mojtahed*), opposed him, and Behbahani was close to his rival Amin al-Soltan. Thus the personal rivalry between Nuri and Behbahani began to take shape along political lines, although Nuri acted in concert with other ulama at the crucial moments before the campaign for the constitution bore fruit.

The revolution for law

Two international events played important psychological roles in strengthening the cause of constitutionalism. First came the defeat of Russia in the Russo–Japanese war of 1904–5. Iranian constitutionalists literally believed that 'Japan defeated Russia because the former was a constitutionalist regime, the latter a despotic one'. The ensuing outbreak of the 1905 revolution in Russia was even more potent, both in providing a model from the dreaded big bear itself, and by spreading radical ideas and campaign methods, especially among modern intellectuals, who included many still in religious attire. Young radicals, democrats and social democrats, particularly in Tehran, Tabriz, Gilan and Mashhad, began to form associations and launch campaigns for radical revolutionary programmes. All they needed was a trigger.

The first explosion came with the increase in the price of sugar. The governor of Tehran, Ala al-Dowleh, blamed the sugar merchants and had the soles of the feet of a few of them heavily beaten. The event led to the departure of many ulama, students, merchants and shopkeepers to a sit-in, or *bast*, at the shrine of Hazrat-e Abdol'zim near Tehran, in a traditional demonstration of great anger against the government. The *bast* was financed by various sources, especially merchants and traders, but also by some important enemies of Ein al-Dowleh who otherwise cared little for lawful government. They even included Mohammad Ali Mirza, the heir-designate and enemy of Ein al-Dowleh, who was later to fight hard against constitutionalism. This demonstrates in a particularly clear and unambiguous way the discordant and intrigue-ridden nature of the arbitrary state, where – contrary to the European tradition – some of the biggest pillars of the regime were apparently supporting those that wished to bring it down, precisely because of the absence of European-style class structure and cohesion.

Contrary to Marxist analyses of the revolution, it was not just the merchants and shopkeepers but the whole of urban society which rose not against the landlords but against the state. Religious dignitaries who, in terms of rank and influence, were even higher than cardinal archbishops, tribal leaders and provisional khans who ruled their own territories more powerfully than the average European duke, joined the movement, along with state officials, the high mandarins who were running the government apparatus.

Likewise, the revolution's triumph did not result in a bourgeois government, democratic or dictatorial. It led rapidly to the onset of traditional Iranian chaos in new forms. Clearly, then, this was a revolution that displayed all the features of the traditional Iranian revolt, the important exception being that it aimed for law and against arbitrary rule rather than against mere injustice, and it used modern European forms and devices in trying to achieve it.

By January 1906, the protesters had returned from their *bast* to Tehran on the shah's agreement to meet their demands, including the central issue of instituting independent judicial courts. The triumphal return of the *bast*is strengthened the cause of the opponents of the chief minister and the campaigners for constitution. Ein al-Dowleh resorted to familiar tactics: stalling, bribery and intimidation. But the point – both long and short – had been reached that such tactics would not work. Tabataba'i, who was perhaps the most revered leader of the movement in Tehran, wrote to the shah himself, and in his letter he spoke of the need for a Majlis, as they called the parliament. But the shah never saw the letter. Intimidation led to violence and bloodshed, especially when the leaders replied to Ein al-Dowleh's message that, not only must there be a parliament, but that he himself must step down. Following this letter, the ulama, together with many of their adherents, 'migrated', this time not to the Abdol'zim shrine but to Qom.

With still no action from the shah's camp, public agitation in Tehran spread further and resulted in thousands of people led by prominent merchants taking *bast* in the British legation compound. At the same time, heir-designate Mohammad Ali Mirza, seated in Tabriz (who, as noted, opposed the chief minister) encouraged Tabriz's religious dignitaries to appeal to the shah, attacking 'arbitrary' and 'traitorous' ministers and supporting the cause of the ulama of Tehran. The pressure was such that the shah, who personally had no stomach at all for the prolongation of the conflict, agreed both to the demand for a constitution and the dismissal of the chief minister.

This was August 1905, and the constitution, which was hurriedly written to ensure it would be in time to be signed by the shah and the heir-designate (since there were rumours that the shah was unwell), was signed late in December. Five days later, the shah died and was succeeded by his son, whom certainly the younger, more radical and modernist intellectuals of the movement both disliked and distrusted: Mohammad Ali Mirza's campaign against Ein al-Dowleh was not widely known, but, as governor-general of Azerbaijan, he had shown his dislike for constitutionalism in that province.

The first and foremost task of the parliament (Majlis) was the preparation and approval of the constitution that was later endorsed by the shah and Mohammad Ali Mirza. Many future Iranian politicians found their way to the Majlis, including Vosuq al-Dowleh, Hassan Taqizadeh, members of the Hedayat clan and others.

Shah versus parliament

The Majlis soon came into increasingly destructive conflict, both with the new shah and with Sheykh Fazlollah Nuri. He had, haphazardly, collaborated with the constitutionalists up to this point, but became increasingly critical of what he and his followers saw as Europeanizing outlooks and legislation. There was also serious conflict between moderate and radical constitutionalists, but this did not come to light fully until 1909 after the shah and Nuri had been defeated. The conflict escalated until the shah staged a coup against the Majlis in June 1908, which was supported by Nuri and his group.

From the outset in 1907, Mohammad Ali Shah and his close advisors, if not hoping to turn back the clock completely, wished to retain as much executive power as possible. The Majlis in general did not trust the shah, and insisted on exercising many of the executive functions as well. It saw itself as 'The House of the People', as opposed to the state. In other words, although a constitution had apparently removed the traditional basic antagonism between society and state, it still survived in actual attitudes and relationships. Historically, when the state was beaten, the society became free from the state's constraints, with the usual disastrous consequences. Now, for the first time, laws had been established to define and regulate the relationship between the state and the people. But neither the state – or what was left of it – nor society had sufficiently absorbed the fundamental novelty of the situation. They were both still trying to eliminate each other as a political force, and hold the reins of power exclusively.

Apart from that, the constitution itself had granted so much power to the legislature at the expense of the executive, which would have made it difficult even now, in the early twenty-first century, to govern Britain, despite the fact that it is one of the most governable societies in the world. And yet there were no properly functioning parliamentary parties, which might have negotiated with each other and the shah in an attempt to manage the conflicts. Finally, the revolutionary radicals – who were especially influential in some of the official and unofficial 'associations' – were not in any mood for compromise. Not only did they insist on almost unlimited people power, but at the same time they were impatient to apply European modernization as extensively and as quickly as their dreams would allow.

This was the sharpest end of the conflict in so far as the religious traditionalists were concerned. It certainly is true that Nuri was engaged in an intractable personal rivalry with Behbahani, but his fears and forebodings, along with those of other *mojtahed*, were not just limited to narrow, private self-interest, but included the rise of modernism as well. In any case, they tried to make a public case for their opposition by advocating constitutionalism based on Islamic law. Eventually they sided with the shah against constitutional government.

Apart from that, the radical wings of the two sides – roughly, the shah and his cohorts and the radical constitutionalists – were not given to negotiation, and characteristically wished to eliminate each other politically and, even in some cases, physically. The new chief minister Amin al-Soltan tried to forge a compromise but neither side wanted one, and his assassination by the Democrats relieved the Royalists from doing the same.

Perhaps the fate of Naser al-Molk's cabinet demonstrates the problem of the more compromise-seeking parties in a less ambiguous way. Amin al-Soltan's assassination in August 1907 led after a while to the creation of Naser al-Molk's cabinet, which was largely made up of politically moderate, sophisticated and (unlike Amin al-Soltan) financially honest constitutionalists such as the brothers Moshir al-Dowleh and Mo'tamen al-Molk, and brothers Sani' al-Dowleh and Mokhber al-Saltaneh. It lasted only a few weeks, while the shah was preparing his first open assault on the Majlis, and the radical newspapers *Ruh al-Qodos* and

Mosavat, even *Sur Esrafil*, were busy publishing invectives against the person of the shah and his mother.

In mid–December 1907, prompted by the royal court and its associates, large numbers of ruffians took to the streets shouting slogans against constitutional government. At the same time as the mob set up tents in Artillery Square, the shah summoned, beat up, dismissed and arrested his ministers, threatening to kill Naser al-Molk, who was saved by the intervention of the British legation on the condition that he would leave Iran, which he duly did next morning.

As things turned out, the shah was not quite ready to go the whole way against the Majlis. But in retrospect, it is clear that Naser al-Molk's ministry was the last chance for a compromise, if a compromise would have been at all possible in a situation where most of those concerned did not want one.

The failure of the coup against the parliament

The shah was more determined and better prepared next time round, although he launched his attack on the constitutionalists after an unsuccessful attempt on his life. This was the coup of June 1908, in which the shah's Cossack Brigade bombarded the Majlis, attacked and looted the homes of constitutionalists and their sympathizers and arrested a large number of younger leaders and activists, including some Qajar noblemen, which led to the execution of a number of them. These were dastardly acts by a deceitful, arbitrary ruler. But the part of the radical constitutionalists in helping him bring about the situation was not lost on an old constitutionalist leader with such impeccable credentials as Abdorrahim Talebof, who wrote to the young and fiery Ali Akbar Dehkhoda in exile condemning zealous and excessive behaviour by idealists and unruly alike.

The coup led to numbness at first, but slowly the people of Tabriz began to rise up and eventually took over their town and, through heroic resistance led by the legendary folk leader Sattar Khan, held the revolutionary fort until other provinces also began to move against the shah's unlawful government. The government laid siege to Tabriz, and almost brought it to its knees by blocking food supplies. At one stage, there was a real scare that Russian troops would go to the help of the government forces on the excuse of protecting European lives. The threat was there most of the time, but when in the end the Russians arrived, in April 1909, they went to relieve the town from certain famine and forced the government to lift the siege, because by then both Russia and Britain had formed the view that the shah must compromise with the constitutionalists.

On 31 August 1907 the Anglo-Russian Convention, subsequently known as the 1907 agreement, was signed in St Petersburg. This had been actively canvassed and brokered by the French, anticipating the 'triple entente' between the three countries when World War I broke out. It divided Iran into three Russian and British spheres of influence and a neutral zone, although it made the usual, but largely spurious, professions of safeguarding Iran's independence and integrity. This was a deliberate comedown by Britain from her position in Iran, in anticipation of a European war in which it would be allied with Russia. Yet, while it visibly reduced the level of official British sympathy for the constitutionalists, Sir Edward Grey, the foreign secretary, played a role in discouraging the Russians from overt intervention on the shah's behalf. In the end, the two great powers publicly demanded that he restore a form of constitutional government and try for compromise.

It is difficult to know whether it would have been possible for the opposition to sell to the people a peaceful settlement with Mohammad Ali when, in April 1909, he began to sue for peace. It is highly instructive that, of all the people, Taqizadeh, then tribune of the radical revolutionaries, expressed profound regret, in his old age, to his close friend and disciple Iraj Afshar for his total rejection of the shah's offer of a return to constitutional regime short of his deposition. For, in the meantime, the constitutionalists had gathered their forces and were poised to launch an attack on Tehran.

The forces of Gilan, led by the great landlords Sepahsalar and Fathollah Khan Akbar, included a notable contingent of militiamen from southern Caucasus – especially Baku – almost all of whom were radical democrats or social democrats. The forces of Isfahan were made up largely, but not entirely, of Bakhtiari riflemen, led by their khans headed by Sardar As'ad. Earlier, and in As'ad's absence in Europe, his brother Samsam al-Saltaneh had already captured Isfahan.

The battles of July 1909, outside and inside Tehran, happily did not take long, nor did they occasion heavy casualties. The shah was deposed and allowed to cross the border to Russia, being succeeded by his ten-year-old son Ahmad. Generally, harsh and vindictive measures were not taken against the shah's party, save for a couple of executions, including that of Sheykh Fazlollah Nuri. This would not have been possible without the approval of Behbahani and Tabataba'i in Tehran, and the great ulama in Najaf, the latter of whom had publicly condemned him as a *mofsed*, or guilty of a capital crime under Islamic law. At first Nuri had advocated constitutional government based entirely on *shari'a* law, but after the shah's coup had denounced constitutionalism as well.

Nuri and his supporters interpreted the constitutionalists' notion of political liberty as sheer licence. In leaflets they were putting out from the shrine of Hazrat-e Abdol'zim, where Nuri had taken *bast* against the Majlis, they described the constitutionalists as free-thinkers, Babis, nihilists, anarchists and socialists, and as advocates of licentious and irreligious agendas. On the other hand, the ulama of Najaf – Khorasani, Mazandarani and

Tehrani – supported the Majlis against the claims both of the shah and of Nuri, and after the coup threw all their weight behind the movement. It is difficult to see how the constitutionalist movement might have succeeded the way it did if the Najaf ulama had wavered in their support or, indeed, doubted the legitimacy of constitutionalism. Walter Smart, a young British diplomat was astonished at the fact that large numbers of the clergy in quality as well as quantity actively supported the revolution, since it was very difficult from the European standpoint to imagine religious pontiffs fighting the state on behalf of the people.

It took only a few months for the traditional disorder after the fall of the state to begin to emerge in what was now no longer arbitrary rule. That encouraged the deposed Mohammad Ali to try his luck again by leading an army from Russia into north-east Iran, but he was ultimately beaten and driven back into Russia. The next major drama was staged when the young American Morgan Shuster, employed as Iranian treasurer general with wide powers, clashed with the Russians over the confiscation of a property which they claimed to be collateral for a debt owed to the Russian Loan Bank. The Majlis and street crowds strongly backed Shuster, contrary to the government's best advice, and eventually had to relent in the face of Russian threats to move their troops in the north and occupy Tehran. It was another example of idealism and disunity ending in disaster, since Shuster had to be dismissed and the parliament shut down shortly before the end of its natural term. This came in December 1911, which is now normally regarded as the end of the Constitutional Revolution.

By the time World War I broke out, nine ministries had been formed in less than five years.

At the same time, the young Ahmad Shah had come of age and the third round of parliamentary elections was held. The new parliament and most Iranians were pro-German, while

Russian and British forces were present in the north and south of the country. The government declared neutrality, but the Turks sent troops into Azerbaijan to face the occupying Russian forces in that province. The outbreak of the war had exacerbated the post-revolutionary chaos, so that by the end of the war in 1918 many more ministries had come and gone. In November 1915 the Russians moved their considerable troops in Qazvin towards Tehran in an act of intimidation. This resulted in the 'migration' of the majority of parliamentary deputies to Qom, then Kashan, then Isfahan and eventually Kermanshah, where, in 1916, the alternative 'Provisional Government of the Migrants' was declared. This alternative government, which included both leading Democrats such as Soleyman Mirza Eskandari, and leading moderates, notably the *mojtahed* politician Seyyed Hasan Modarres, declared war on the entente and was financially supported by Germany, which already had active agents, most notably the legendary Wilhelm Wassmuss, in the southern and western parts of the country.

The failure of the 1919 agreement

The Russian Revolution of 1917 brought much relief to Iran after a century of imperial interference and intimidation. But it was followed by severe famine and the Spanish flu pandemic which, combined, took a high toll of around two million, mostly of the Iranian poor. When the war ended, the country was truly on its knees and in serious danger of disintegration. In August 1918 Vosuq al-Dowleh, an able and astute politician, formed a cabinet with active British support. Britain, emerging from the war as the sole power in the Middle East, and the foreign secretary, Lord Curzon, who had a special interest in Iran and long before had published the book *Persia and the Persian Question*, entered the ill-fated 1919 agreement with Iran. This would make

Iran a client state of Britain to the exclusion of all other great powers – the US, Russia and France. All of these powers, and perforce Iranians themselves, incorrectly but incorrigibly believed that Vosuq and his two close cabinet allies had 'sold' the country to become a British protectorate.

Meanwhile the Bolsheviks won the civil war in Russia and, having taken over the newly independent Russian Azerbaijan north of Gilan, crossed the border and helped to form a coalition government of Iranian Bolsheviks and the popular *Jangali* (Forest) forces led by Mirza Kuchik Khan, which, in May 1920, declared the Socialist Republic of Gilan in Rasht. British troops had been ordered to retreat to Qazvin in the event of a Russian invasion and this spelt doom for Vosuq's cabinet, which resigned a few weeks later.

The 1921 coup

Disorder reigned, the country was broke, its sole functioning military consisted of the Iranian Cossacks mainly led by Russian officers and now financed by Britain and the 1919 agreement, which might possibly have resulted in stability and recovery was, despite Curzon's hope against hope, already a dead letter. Moshir al-Dowleh succeeded Vosuq for only a few months, and through the sheer force of popularity managed to put an end to Sheykh Mohammad Khiyabani's revolt in Azerbaijan and split the socialist republic in Gilan by persuading Kuchik to end his coalition with the Bolsheviks.

However, when General Ironside, the tough new commander of the British North Persia Rifle Force (Norperforce) stationed in Qazvin managed to take indirect command of the Cossack Division, which had been beaten by the Gilan forces and settled near Qazvin, Moshir resigned in protest and was succeeded by an ineffectual politician. Through the autumn and early winter of

1920–1, Tehran was in constant dread of the onslaught of the Gilan socialist forces, when, as it was certain, Norperforce would be withdrawn by the British War Office in the spring. Ironside, the British diplomats and all but one British officer in Iran who had seen the ruinous results of Curzon's policy, together with Seyyed Zia al-Din, a young and able journalist–politician who led his Committee of Iron, concluded that the remedy was a military coup.

They chose Colonel Reza Khan to lead the Cossacks from Qazvin to Tehran, made sure that the gendarmerie (paramilitary rural police) and civilian police would not put up a resistance, and reassured the shah that no harm was meant to him. Reza Khan's forces entered Tehran on 21 February 1921 and Seyyed Zia became prime minister through a coup which was in defiance of Curzon's policy, and in which the British government had had no hand. It took just a hundred days for Reza Khan to topple Zia's government and, with the shah's support, send him into exile. Within a couple of years countrywide chaos, which had looked as if it would never subside, came to an end.

Unsurprisingly, however, it was to be replaced not long afterwards with arbitrary rule in a modern form.

4

Iran under the Pahlavis

Reza Shah and Mohammad Reza Shah Pahlavi, father and son, ruled Iran between 1926 and 1979. During their reign Iran witnessed all seasons, including modernization, dictatorship, arbitrary rule, chaos, foreign invasion and revolution. It was also a period in which the Pahlavis' nationalist ideology clashed with democratic ideals, communist ideology and – ultimately – Islamist ideology.

Dictatorship (1921–30)

Reza Khan was an intelligent, hard-working, forthright and ruthless soldier, with an astonishingly powerful memory and a high degree of self-confidence that, with success, turned to arrogance. He was both an ideological nationalist and a pure pragmatist, who would use whatever methods he thought necessary to achieve personal and national goals.

There is political vested interest among Reza Khan's detractors and his admirers in portraying his background, on the one hand as being mean and even base, and on the other, as that of a thriving middle-class family of the time. Wherever the truth lies, his literacy and knowledge of the world improved significantly with informal education over time, to such a degree that when he proclaimed himself shah in 1926, the move was accepted and indeed welcomed by many members of the modern upper and

Modern Iran

middle classes. Yet certain deeply rooted cultural limitations remained with him all his life.

Reza Khan believed, and even told a group of notables in 1924 when he was prime minister, that he had been brought to power by Britain, no doubt thinking that Ironside and the others had helped his coup on the order of the British government. This reinforced the conspiracy theory held by many Iranians that foreign powers, and especially the British, were behind sometimes even the most unlikely events in the country.

Highly intelligent and astute, Reza Khan was quick to learn and to adapt. He enjoyed an unshakable self-belief which at first served him well, but which with easy success later became self-delusion. According to Mokhber al-Saltaneh (Mehdiqoli Hedayat) – his longest-serving prime minister – he once said to the cabinet that 'every country has a certain type of regime. Ours is a one-person regime.' He was a nationalist of the new cut, inspired by the Aryanist and Pan-Persian ideology which had first been formulated in the latter half of the nineteenth century but began to gather real force only after World War I and in the wake of the hated 1919 agreement.

NATIONALISM

Since the middle period of Naser al-Din Shah's reign, modern concepts of nationhood and nationalism had begun to emerge among a very small elite. These were men among whom two leading intellectuals, Fath'ali Akhundzadeh and Mirza Aqa Khan Kermani – in two successive generations – were probably quintessential examples. The emerging modern nationalists believed in Iran's superiority, not only on account of its real and imagined ancient glories, but even more so because, as an Aryan people, it belonged to the Western European race which had created the great social and scientific civilization that was contemporary Europe. The frustration, not to say depression, of fervent nationalist intellectuals was the greater because of the glaring contrast between Iran's real contemporary backwardness and Europe's modern achievements, which they believed their country had failed to realize, mainly – if not solely – because of Arabs (later also Turks) and Islam. This new ideology of modern Iranian nationalism was greatly to influence the official attitude and policy in the Pahlavi era, and even dominate the psyche of many Iranian intellectuals who were opposed to the Pahlavi regime.

By 1921, and increasingly thereafter, many members of the modern upper and middle classes were converted to Aryanist and Pan-Persian nationalism. Led by politicians such as Abdolhoseyn Teymurtash and Ali Akbar Davar and supported by a younger intellectual elite, they almost openly advocated the use of dictatorial powers to establish a unified army, stamp out chaos, build a modern nation state, reassert national sovereignty, force the nomadic tribes into settled life, separate religion from politics, extend modern secular education, promote modern industry, impose a uniform dress code, order compulsory unveiling for women and stipulate the Persian language for the linguistic minorities, all of which they naively believed would turn Iran into a Western European version of society within a short space of time. What they did not anticipate was the likelihood of the dictatorship turning the clock back to arbitrary rule (*estebdad*) after Reza Khan became shah and, in time, turning against themselves.

Reza Khan had begun to emerge as the country's military dictator by June 1921 when Seyyed Zia was dismissed and driven out of the country. Nevertheless it took more than five years of power struggles before Reza Khan could defeat all opposition and establish his own dynasty. He had virtually a free hand in organizing the new army by uniting the old Cossack and gendarmerie forces under one command, expanding them and equipping them with improved weaponry. Chaos in most provinces was put down even before Reza Khan became shah, once again demonstrating the ease with which prolonged and seemingly never-ending periods of turmoil could be brought to an end by the existence of will at the centre. The matter was so urgent that in October 1925, in their speeches in the Majlis against the motion for making Reza Khan head of state, both Taqizadeh and Mohammad Mosaddeq praised his success in stamping out disorder.

Reza Khan becomes Reza Shah

Reza Khan and his supporters at first tried to remove the Qajar dynasty and declare a republic with himself as president. This met with severe resistance by both the Majlis opposition, who openly feared that he would then bid to become shah, and by the ulama, who associated a republican regime with pure secularism. The general public, as opposed to the modern elite, were also against it. In 1925, the republican campaign having collapsed in 1924, Reza Khan and his supporters managed to bring down the Qajar dynasty and replace it with Reza Khan's own, something that had probably been intended from the beginning. For this they had to call a constituent assembly solely to elect and establish Reza Khan's dynasty. The elections for this assembly, which met in December 1925, had been manipulated, but it did represent the commanding heights of the society, including many khans and provincial magnates, some prominent religious leaders, former leaders and figures of the Constitutional Revolution.

Seyyed Hasan Modarres, leader of the parliamentary opposition, offered a compromise for a certain degree of power-sharing upon Reza Shah's accession in 1926, which the shah at first accepted but which, before the year was out, he reneged on. By 1928 the shah had arrested, co-opted or chased out of politics all opposition.

Return to arbitrary rule (1930–41)

In 1929 the shah arrested his minister of finance and ardent supporter Firuz Mirza Firuz on trumped-up charges. This event heralded the beginning of the change of the dictatorship to arbitrary rule by fiat, since dictatorships, though not democratic, are normally constrained by law and involve elite participation in decision-taking, whereas arbitrary rule is not bound by a legal framework outside its own will and involves no power-sharing at all.

AN IRANIAN MUSTAFA KEMAL ATATURK?

Reza Shah has often been compared to Mustafa Kemal Ataturk, the founder of modern Turkey, whom he both admired and tried to emulate. The comparison is understandable but misleading. Ataturk was a modern dictator who strove to modernize Turkish politics along with his nationalist and modernist drive, in other words creating a secular nation state and modernizing the economy and society, allowing for limited participation and consultation in political decision-making. He was not an arbitrary ruler like the traditional Ottoman sultans and caliphs, he was not financially corrupt and – unlike Reza Shah – neither he nor his army and bureaucracy liberally took other peoples' lives and property. The fact that Reza Shah's regime had been established after a revolution for law and against arbitrary rule was the most important reason behind his later unpopularity, to some extent even behind the incorrect charge of his being an agent of Britain, which until recent times Iranians almost universally believed.

Indeed it was in 1929, the year of Firuz's arrest and disgrace, that the Secretary of the American legation in Tehran wrote to the Department of State that 'it may be doubted whether a nation is benefited by such a disregard for law and justice . . . Unless the people can feel confidence in the legal establishment of their country, they will have no confidence in their Shah and his reforms, and no lasting good will be accomplished.'

From then onwards none of the shah's supporters, including ministers, military commanders, provincial governors and journalists, was immune from sudden arrest, murder in jail, banishment and disgrace. By 1938, Abdolhoseyn Teymurtash, the strong and able minister of the royal court, the noted finance minister Firuz Mirza Firuz, the capable and faithful justice minister Ali Akbar Davar, the learned Mohammad Ali Foroughi, the shah's staunch supporter and servant even as prime minister and many others like them had been murdered, driven to suicide, imprisoned, banished, exiled and dismissed in disgrace. This is not to mention, of course, the remnants of the old and totally pacified members of the opposition such as Modarres and Mosaddeq.

Meanwhile, the modernization drive had led to significant social, economic and cultural changes, which were to continue until the shah's abdication in 1941. There was expansion in modern education, with more modern schools and institutes of higher education; in industry and services, with the construction of roads and railways; in the centralization and concentration of the army and bureaucracy; in reform of the judicial system; in the forced removal of chadors and scarves; and in the introduction of modern banking. It is worth emphasizing that much of this transformation affected only a small percentage of economic and cultural activities, since around eighty-five per cent of the population were illiterate as well as landless peasants and large numbers of urban people were common labourers. Nevertheless, it opened the way to modern developments, which, despite social and political upheavals, still continue today.

Reform of the army

The reorganization and rapid expansion of the army was Reza Khan's first priority. By 1926 when he became shah, he had 40,000 soldiers and a small air force at his command. In 1941, the army had grown threefold to more than 120,000. To finance his ambitious plans for the expansion of the army he began to use any means, legal and illegal. In 1928 the budget of the ministry of war was 122 million rials; by 1941, it had increased almost fivefold to 593 million rials.

Almost all the oil revenues, which accounted for thirteen per cent of total government receipts, as well as a third of the government's annual budget, were spent on the military, and the shah also used other means, including confiscation of private wealth and property, to augment the army's finances.

The army was effective as a domestic force, notably in disarming and forcing the nomads to settle, but proved useless in the wake of the Allied invasion of 1941, mainly because even some of the least significant decisions had to be personally approved by the shah. The same happened in the revolution of 1979, when the army felt impelled to declare neutrality in the absence of Reza Khan's son, Mohammad Reza Shah, from the country.

Reza Khan's 1923 conscription bill met with little opposition in the fourth Majlis, drawing support even from the opposition leader Modarres, but in 1928, the attempt at its full implementation led to resistance, though not bloodshed: the ulama, landlords, peasants, nomads and the bazaar were for fairly obvious reasons opposed to it. According to Amin Banani 'the annual visits of the draft boards to the village and tribal areas were generally a dreaded occasion', and 'fear of recruiting commissions was an important factor in the major tribal revolts of 1929'. The family of every army officer was assigned one or more conscripts at home, who they used as common domestic servants without pay.

It follows from the tribal policy that the state was highly centralized everywhere, with governors-general and governors sent to the provincial capitals and towns from Tehran, nearly all of them Persian speakers, in the non-Persian-speaking provinces as well. Each province had a standing army division; the police and gendarmerie's headquarters were in Tehran. All higher civil and military appointments including cabinet members were made by the shah.

SEDENTARIZATION

After the early 1920s when the chaos had been put down, the principal aim of the military campaigns against the nomads was to disarm the tribes for the first time in history. Beyond this, however, was the deeply resented and feared policy of forced sedentarization of the nomads, since the shah and the nationalist ideologists saw nomadic life and culture as evidence of backwardness, and felt highly embarrassed by it towards the Europeans. They were also jealous of any autonomous power, even if it was unarmed. Sedentarization could never be justified on rational grounds as it led to a great deal of death, destruction and hardship, and a sharp decline in the country's livestock production comparable to the effects of Stalin's forced collectivization of Soviet agriculture in the same period. According to Kaveh Bayat, a prominent modern Iranian historian, 'this programme of forced sedentarization . . . took a very brutal and, in some cases, genocidal form. In a short period of time the tribal life of Iran was transformed . . . through coercive and violent methods that virtually wiped out a large segment of the tribal population of Iran'. After the shah's abdication in 1941, almost all settled nomads returned to nomadic life, and the bitterness of their treatment in that period was to have serious consequences for their long-term relations with the state.

Judicial and educational reforms

The indefatigable justice minister Ali Akbar Davar made great reforms to the judiciary, which was almost a faithful copy of the

French system with suitable adjustments in the case of certain criminal and civil laws to the requirements of *shari'a* law. It was done with efficiency and dedication, though it could not serve more than five per cent of the population because the great majority were poor and illiterate, and the new system was expensive and complicated.

Various modern schools and university colleges had been founded between the mid-nineteenth and early twentieth centuries, but post-Constitutional chaos had prevented any rapid expansion, just as in the case of judicial reform. This was now remedied by the expansion of both primary and secondary schools, including some for girls, which had had only few precedents, the establishment of a coeducational modern university and teacher-training college. In the 1920s and 1930s, several hundred state students were sent abroad for university education, mainly to France, Belgium and Germany.

It was an elitist educational policy, favouring the children of the upper and middle classes, although the fees were nominal and it was open to all who had the means. History and literature glorified ancient Persia, denigrated Arabs and Turks, ignored the numerous Iranian ethnic groups which included Turks and Arabs, and pretended that Persian was the only language spoken in Iran.

Some of this was probably difficult to avoid while Aryanist and pan-Persian zeal and the glorification – in fact mythologization – of the ancient past was widespread among the policymakers. The most important criticisms that can be levelled at the educational policy is that it was a very high-cost project, and that it did not address the country's needs for the growth of literacy. By the time Reza Shah abdicated in 1941, ninety per cent of Iranians, including the great majority of the rural community, were illiterate. Nevertheless, according to recent studies, the total number of students increased sevenfold from 1922–3 to 1941–2.

Oil and the economy

Economic policy, like its political counterpart, was highly centralist and state-dominated. The bazaar – the close-knit merchant and trading community – in particular was unhappy because much of domestic and foreign trade was in the hands of the state. Landlords and peasants were also discontented because, through its monopoly, the state bought their products below market price; landlords were further disenchanted since the shah confiscated or bought at nominal prices their choicest estates, which also increased their sense of insecurity. Tariffs were high and were viewed as a source of revenue rather than as a means of protecting the domestic market. The tax on tea and sugar was forbiddingly high and hit the masses hard, since these (plus bread) were their staple foods. The proceeds were spent entirely on the construction of trans-Iranian railways, at the then colossal cost of $150 million, for which there was no economic justification whatsoever, but which was seen by the shah and the elite as proof that Iran had now become 'civilized'.

Investment was made, mainly by the state, in modern industry and technology, largely in light industries such as textiles and sugar-beet mills, which led to higher industrial employment and the familiarization of skilled labour with modern techniques. However, there was no strategy of industrialization as such which would create an interrelated industrial network. The state had begun to buy a modern steel mill from Germany, but was halted by the war's intrusion into Iran. Meanwhile a national bank had been founded with German technical advice, and a couple of other banks – all of them state-owned – came into being in the 1930s. Hardly anything was done to improve the lot of the peasantry, who made up about eighty-five per cent of the population.

The Anglo-Persian (later Anglo-Iranian) Oil Company had the concession for the exploitation of the country's oil resources in the south-west, sold to William D'Arcy at the turn of the century, fifty-one per cent of which was now owned by the British government. It was by far the biggest single employer and source of foreign exchange in the country. In the 1920s Iranians entered negotiations with the Anglo-Iranian Oil Company in order to improve Iran's meagre share of the proceeds. The negotiations dragged on, and no agreement was reached until 1932 when the company declared that Iran's share of the revenues was as little as a quarter of the previous year. In retaliation, the shah ordered the government to cancel the D'Arcy concession and Britain complained to the League of Nations, which led to negotiations in Tehran and the signing of the 1933 agreement. In some ways it was better for Iran than the previous agreement, except that, under pressure from the company's chairman, Sir John Cadman, the shah reluctantly agreed to the extension of the term of the contract by a further thirty years. This was clearly not in Iran's interest, and Taqizadeh, who as minister of finance signed the agreement ex officio, said in detail in parliament in 1947 that neither he nor even the shah had been happy about it, but that when the shah gave in he had had no choice but to sign it.

Dress code and forced unveiling

The official imposition of new dress codes, and even the forced removal of *hejab*, was based on another cherished nationalist modernist ideology. The law of December 1928 made it compulsory for all Iranian men to wear European dress (short jackets and trousers) and the 'Pahlavi hat', which was a variation on the French kepi. However, in 1935 the shah suddenly issued the decree that all men must wear the European *chapeau* or bowler hat, which most of them had never even seen. Unarmed protesters in Mashhad took sanctuary in the historic mosque adjacent to the shrine of Imam Reza, where, contrary to the traditional customs of taking *bast*, they were gunned down by police and soldiers. The shrine's trustee (appointed by the shah himself), who had apparently tried to act as an intermediary, was blamed and summarily executed. He was related to Prime Minister Foroughi, but the latter's attempt at interceding with the shah led to his own downfall in disgrace. Shortly afterwards the shah told a sceptical Mokhber al-Saltaneh (Mehdiqoli Hedayat), the former prime minister, that the compulsory change of hat was intended to stop the Europeans from 'ridiculing us'.

The shah's sudden decree for the removal of the women's *hejab* which followed a few months later in January 1936 was not openly resisted, coming so soon after the events in Mashhad over the European hat, but it left scars much deeper even than Reza Shah's tribal policy. Criticisms of *hejab* by modern intellectuals went back to the turn of the twentieth century, and entered the realm of wider public discussion at least from the end of World War I among the modern middle and upper classes. Iraj, the leading satirical poet, wrote against *hejab* and blind marriage arrangements, and emphasized that the covering of hands and faces by women was contrary to the teaching of the Qur'an. Around 1918, the nationalist poet Eshqi wrote the long poem entitled *The Black Shroud* which ended with the verse: 'As long as women live in shrouds / Half of the Iranian people are not alive.'

Women activists and self-help organizers began to campaign for women's rights. The women's journal *Alam-e Nesvan* ('Women's World', 1920–34) which had been the longest-running journal of its kind over the period was shut down by the government, along with many other women's journals, before the official banning of the *hejab* was enacted. The shah would not tolerate any independent journal or organization even if they fully supported his regime. They were replaced by the official *Kanun-e Banuan* ('Ladies' Centre').

All the anti-*hejab* campaigners were opposed to the face veil, which some women had already abandoned in the 1920s. The more radical of them also opposed the chador. But they were not against scarves, and hardly any of them believed that all women should be forced to remove their veils, as opposed to voluntary unveiling protected by the law.

The new government decree meant that even scarves were banned. As Mokhber al-Saltaneh (Mehdiqoli Hedayat) wrote in his memoirs: 'The police were ordered to pull the scarves off women's heads. The scarves were torn off or, if valuable, confiscated. The struggle between women and the police continued for some time.' Compulsory unveiling was received very badly by the large majority of women. In Europe it would have been tantamount to a decree declaring that women must go out topless. Some women remained at home for as long as the shah was in power and the ban was in force, and had to go out through the rooftops of neighbouring houses to go to the public baths. In 1936, orders were given for government departments and the municipalities to oblige their members, employees and local middle-class residents to attend social functions in the company of their wives. Some men took temporary wives to accompany them to parties. A few men and women committed suicide. Not surprisingly, the ulama also received the decree very badly: not only were the processions of *Ashura*, commemorating the martyrs of Karbela, banned, but also religious congregations meeting in homes or in mosques.

Foreign policy and the Allied invasion (1926–40)

Foreign policy largely followed the traditional methods of balancing Britain and Russia, except that Reza Shah was an incorrigible Anglophobe, and with the rise of Nazi Germany Iran steadily got closer to that nation both politically and economically. By the late 1930s Iranian trade with Germany had increased enormously at the expense of both Britain (apart from oil) and the Soviet Union.

When the war broke out, Iran declared neutrality but the shah, the military and much of the rest of society were pro-German. Naturally this worried Britain, especially as regards the Royal Navy's oil supply. On 22 June 1941 Germany attacked Russia, and this radically altered the situation, since as long as the Soviet Union was collaborating with Germany, Britain could not exercise real power over Iran.

During July and August of that year, Britain and Russia jointly put increasing pressure on Iran to expel about two thousand German residents whom they described as agents of Germany's war machine. Reza Shah, not quite taking notice of the great change after the German attack on Russia, and not wishing to displease the Germans, took the matter lightly. The result was the Anglo-Russian invasion of 25 August. Reza Shah made the moderate and highly respectable Forughi, whom he had previously disgraced, prime minister. Forughi persuaded him to abdicate and managed with some difficulty to arrange the accession of Mohammad Reza Shah. Reza Shah was sent first to Mauritius, then to Johannesburg, where he died in 1944.

'Constitutional' chaos (1941–51)

True to Iranian form, the fall of the arbitrary state quickly resulted in chaos both at the centre and in the provinces, just as it had done in 1909 when Mohammad Ali Shah had been deposed. Things would have been far worse if the occupying forces had not in effect set a limit to how far it could go. The thirteenth Majlis was still in session, divided as it now was between short-term factions. A British diplomat in Tehran remarked that in 'the chaotic conditions inevitable in the sudden changeover from pure despotism (*estebdad*) to an alleged constitutional and democratic regime, there was a general scramble for the fruits, though not for the responsibilities, of privilege and office'. It is telling that between 1941 and 1951, no annual budget could be passed by the Majlis because of special interests and personal stakes, while the executive branch of the government was virtually a pawn on their chessboard.

There were almost continuous incidents of disorder up and down the country. Some of these were large and historic, such as the major revolts in Azerbaijan, Kurdistan and the south. Some were less spectacular but made up for it in frequency, becoming a matter of monthly or weekly, if not daily, occurrence. After the fall of Reza Shah, there would certainly have been some trouble in a couple of provinces in reaction to his centralist and pan-Persian policies. Yet it would have been much easier and quicker to deal with if destructive conflict had not been prevalent in the centre itself.

One notable example of the background of destructive conflict in the centre and at the highest level of politics occurred between the shah and Ahmad Qavam, whom the shah both feared and despised, during the latter's short premiership between August 1942 and March 1943. Their bitter conflict eventually led to the bread riots of 8 and 9 December, when the mob occupied the Majlis, looted the shops and ransacked Qavam's house and set fire to it. Most domestic politicians and foreign diplomats had little doubt that the shah had had a direct hand in the riots.

Apart from safeguarding oil supplies, the biggest help to the Allies' war effort was the so-called Persian Corridor, using the trans-Iranian railways as well as roads to supply some five million tons of war materials both to the Soviet Union and to British forces in the Middle East. Having declared non-interference in the country's domestic affairs, the Allies nevertheless made important demands on the country which Iranian governments had little choice but to meet as long as Allied troops remained in Iran. The rial (Iran's currency) was devalued by more than a hundred per cent. This meant that Allied purchases of Iranian goods and services cost them less than half price, and Iranian import of their products cost Iran more than twice as much as previously. The Iranian government was obliged to print money in order to extend credit to the Allies for their expenditures in Iran, to be paid back after the war ended. These policies led to rampant inflation and scarcity of goods, especially bread, but just avoided a famine.

Historians usually divide the period of Mohammad Reza Shah's rule into two parts: 1941–53, the period of turmoil and democratic experiments which ended with the 1953 coup; and the period 1953–79, which they normally describe as the period of the shah's dictatorship ending with the revolution of February 1979. In fact, this second period should also be divided into two parts, with the cut-off point in 1963. In the first twelve years of his reign (1941–53), Mohammad Reza Shah was a constitutional monarch; in the next decade (1953–63) he was a dictator; but for the remainder of his reign until the revolution he was an absolute and arbitrary ruler.

Political movements in the 1940s

Despite the atmosphere of instability it generated, Reza Shah's abdication in 1941 and the restoration of political freedoms led to the emergence of a number of more or less effective political movements. The Tudeh party was founded shortly after Reza Shah's abdication. Later developments turned it into an authentic Communist party, but for most of the 1940s it was similar to the European popular anti-fascist fronts, made up of various leftist and democratic tendencies with a broadly reformist programme. The Tudeh party was led mainly by Marxist intellectuals many of whom – known as the Fifty-three – had been released from jail after Reza Shah's abdication.

The party pledged itself to constitutional monarchy and par-liamentary government. It was clearly inclined towards the Soviet Union, but at the time Russia was popular even in the West. Many if not most of its original members left the party at three successive stages as it became more and more radicalized, and later turned it into an authentic Communist party: at the revolt of Azerbaijan in 1945–6; at the party split of January 1948; and after the banning of the party in February 1949, when it went underground and, in all but name, became a standard Stalinist party of its time, even including internal assassinations. In the elections of 1943 for the fourteenth Majlis – the first to be held since Reza Shah's abdication – the party managed to send eight (out of a total of 136) deputies to parliament. At the time, it was the only well-organized political party with a clear outlook and popular support. It had the backing of the trade unions, which emerged with the party's active encouragement and which were effectively controlled by it.

Alongside the emergence of the Tudeh party as the main voice of intellectuals and the modern educated elite, a religious movement began to grow and spread which was to anticipate the religious and Islamist movements of the 1960s and beyond. This was at once a response to Reza Shah's anti-religious policies, the Tudeh party and other activities which the religious leaders and their community found repugnant or dangerous. The Fada'iyan-e Islam was a small but highly vociferous and militant political group. Other Islamist organizations came into being in the 1940s which focused their activities against the Baha'i community, 'materialism' and Ahmad Kasravi, a severe critic of Shi'ism as well as the Baha'i faith, who had nevertheless impacted the Shi'a activists' new religious outlook by prompting them to respond to his criticisms.

None of these organizations aimed at establishing an Islamist state; some of them even received support from the royal court and political magnates as antidotes to Tudeh and communism. One of the most active of these newfangled organizations was The Islamic Propaganda Society, which in some respects anticipated the Hojjatiyeh anti-Baha'i movement of the 1950s and beyond.

The Society for Islamic Instruction was founded in 1943 to spread formal religious instruction 'without intervening in current politics', and by 1947 it had set up sixty-one Islamic schools. Other religious societies also came into being in the capital as well as in various provincial centres. Alongside the religious organizations there appeared a number of Islamic journals, which, with different degrees of emphasis, advanced religious ideas and political views.

Among the secular political groupings and factions that came into being after Reza Shah's abdication, three of the most important were the Iran party, Seyyed Zia's National Will and Qavam's Democrat party. The Iran party, with liberal and social-democrat leanings, was largely manned and led by European-educated younger technocrats and university teachers. They were later to join the National Front, and some of them, notably Shapour Bakhtiar, the shah's last prime minister during the revolution of 1979, later became world-famous.

Seyyed Zia's National Will was formed after he returned from exile in 1943. It was a conservative-leaning, pro-British grouping whose existence depended entirely on its founder and his ambition to form a government. The Seyyed was elected to the fourteenth Majlis for Yazd; Mosaddeq, who was elected the first deputy for Tehran, unsuccessfully opposed his letter of credence for his role in the 1921 coup. Seyyed Zia was still hopeful until the mid-1950s, but later gave up his efforts and concentrated instead on his chicken-farming business, although little was left of his party after Qavam put him in jail in 1946.

MOHAMMAD MOSADDEQ

Mohammad Mosaddeq (1882–1967) was born into a privileged family, his mother being a Qajar princess and his father a mandarin. In 1908, after a period of government service, he went to Switzerland where he obtained a doctorate in law from the University of Neuchâtel. During World War I he taught at the Tehran School of Politics and Law and served as deputy finance minister, and in the early 1920s he was governor-general of the Fars province, minister of finance, governor-general of the Azerbaijan province and foreign minister, before becoming a parliamentary deputy and opposing the change of dynasty. He was later jailed by Reza Shah for no clear reason, but was released through the intervention of the then Prince Mohammad Reza and put under house arrest until the shah's abdication in 1941. He came back into politics as the first deputy for Tehran in the fourteenth Majlis, but having unsuccessfully campaigned in the fifteenth Majlis elections, he declared his 'political retirement' until, in 1949, he was persuaded to return to politics. From 1950–1 he led the movement for the nationalization of Iranian oil – shortly to be known as the Popular Movement of Iran – and was elected prime minster in April 1951. The oil dispute having dragged on and remained unsettled, his government was overthrown in August 1953 by a combination of foreign and domestic forces. He was jailed and banished for the rest of his life, and died in 1967 as the most popular Iranian of his time.

The Azerbaijan revolt

Qavam was a strong personality and an independent politician, pragmatic but not unprincipled. He was prepared to deal with the great powers as they came, but was not a client of any of them. He formed his second ministry of the 1940s in January 1946, with Soviet support, in the wake of the revolt in the Azerbaijan province of Iran. There were many strands to the revolt in Azerbaijan. The Azerbaijanis had been oppressed and humiliated under Reza Shah. They aspired to a dignified status; and, as everywhere in the northern provinces of Iran, they were influenced by leftist ideas and demanded social and economic reform. The Soviet Union supported the reconstituted Azerbaijan Democrat party, led by an old communist, Ja'far Pishevari, and hoped to fish in troubled waters. The Soviet army was still occupying the province and the access areas to it, making it impossible for the Iranian central army to move up to the province when the Democrats declared autonomy in December 1945.

There was not much love lost between Pishevari and the Tudeh leaders, however under Soviet pressure the Tudeh uncritically backed the Azerbaijan revolt. Throughout 1946, the initial sympathy of many in Tehran for the Azerbaijan Democrats began to melt away as fears grew of a plan to separate the province from Iran and join it to the Soviet Azerbaijan. The rebellion in Kurdistan and the formation of the Kurdish 'Republic' of Mahabad in January 1946, also with Soviet support, struck fear in Tehran even among those who had sympathy for the Kurds' and Azerbaijanis' legitimate grievances.

The shah had reluctantly agreed to Qavam's premiership because he had the ability to deal with the situation and was acceptable to the Russians. Qavam's negotiations with the Soviets eventually succeeded: the Soviets would withdraw their troops; the Iranian government would try to settle the Azerbaijan crisis amicably; the Iranian government would grant a concession for north Iran oil to the Soviet Union subject to the approval of the Majlis, which at the time was in recess. In March 1946 America issued strong notes of protest to the Soviet Union for its refusal to remove its troops from Azerbaijan, although there are doubts about President Truman's later claim that he had actually issued an ultimatum to the Soviets on the issue.

In the meantime Qavam formed his Democrat party, which was intended to compete with the Tudeh party by putting forward a programme of social reform not much less radical than theirs. It was the prelude to the canny Qavam's invitation to the Tudeh party for a short-lived coalition government. It lasted for just three months, during which time there was a rebellion by southern tribes led by Naser Khan Qashqa'i, which was intended to counter the Tudeh and the Azerbaijan Democrats.

There was a peaceful settlement with the southern rebels shortly before the coalition with the Tudeh collapsed, following which Qavam sent troops to the Azerbaijan province ostensibly to ensure the freedom of the impending Majlis elections. Russia having abandoned Pishevari's government, and the Soviet troops having already departed, the Azerbaijan resistance collapsed in December 1946 – a year after the revolt – and most of its civilian and military leaders and officers crossed the border into the Soviet Union. The central army meted out severe punishment to resistance fighters and many non-combatants alike, Azerbaijani as well as Kurdish, whose 'republic' likewise fell to pieces.

The ensuing fifteenth Majlis elections were manipulated by Qavam's party, resulting in the overwhelming electoral victory of his Democrat party and his return to office. Encouraged by the shah, many of the party leaders eventually turned against him but before his government fell in December 1947, Qavam took the bill for the Soviet concession of north Iran oil to the Majlis in October. He was almost certain that it would be defeated, as in fact it was, adding to Soviet and Tudeh anger and delighting the Anglo-American powers.

Soviet demand for north Iranian oil dated back to 1944 when, following earlier approaches by British and American companies, the Soviets demanded a concession for Iran's northern provinces. The conservatives resisted this demand and the Tudeh vociferously supported it, which resulted in some internal party criticism. Eventually, Mosaddeq submitted a bill to the Majlis which forbade the granting of any foreign concession without the approval of the Majlis, and which was passed by an overwhelming majority. That was the reason why Qavam's subsequent proposal in 1947 had had to be submitted to the Majlis. In his speech for his bill, Mosaddeq had incidentally attacked the 1933 oil agreement which had extended the D'Arcy concession for thirty years, and the attitude and behaviour of the Anglo-Iranian Oil Company in Iran. Following two abortive cabinets after Qavam, it fell to Mohammad Sae'd's second premiership of 1948–9 to try and renegotiate the 1933 agreement to obtain better terms for Iran.

Mohammad Reza Shah was anxious to curb the influence of the Tudeh party, extend his own power and reduce parliamentary chaos. The opportunity for banning the Tudeh party and amending the constitution to enable the shah to dissolve the Majlis arose after an abortive attempt on the shah's life on 4 February 1949. Nureddin Kiyanuri, a Tudeh leader later to become its first secretary under the Islamic Republic, was involved in the assassination plot, but the party as a whole did not have prior knowledge of it.

The constituent assembly to amend the constitution met in the following April. It provided for the establishment of an upper house or senate, half of whose members would be appointed by the shah and the other half by an electoral college; more important than that, it empowered the shah to dismiss parliament. Qavam, Ayatollah Kashani (a leading political cleric) and Mosaddeq objected, although the mere constitutional amendments did little to change the situation.

AYATOLLAH SEYYED ABOLQASEM KASHANI

Ayatollah Seyyed Abolqasem Kashani (1882–1962) was born into a notable clerical family of Kashan. He went to the Shi'ite seminary in Najaf, Iraq, where he qualified as a *mojtahed* during World War I. After the war he joined the anti-British campaign in Iraq and, in fear of arrest, fled to Tehran in 1921. In 1925 he became a member of the constituent assembly that established the Pahlavi dynasty. During World War II he was interned by the Allies for fear of his possible opposition to their occupation of Iran. In 1949, and in the wake of an unsuccessful attempt on the shah's life, he was exiled to Lebanon on suspicion of having been privy to the plot, but was allowed to return to Iran during the campaign for the nationalization of Iranian oil when he lent full support to the National Front. But later in 1953, he turned against Mosaddeq's government and briefly supported the August coup against him. This did not last for long and in 1955 he spent a short spell in jail, but he was no longer a popular political figure. He died in 1962.

To recap, Qavam was still prime minister when the Majlis instructed the government to open negotiations with the Anglo-Iranian Oil Company after rejecting the Soviet Union's demand for the north Iran oil concession. A deal, known as the Gass-Golsha'iyan or the supplemental agreement, was eventually negotiated under Mohammad Sa'ed, which moderately improved Iran's annual revenues. But the opposition saw this as too little, too late. In the meantime, Taqizadeh had announced in a Majlis speech that he had signed the 1933 agreement under duress, which had seriously put the legality of the agreement in doubt.

In October 1949 the National Front, a broad political formation of liberal democrats and nationalists led by Mosaddeq, was formed. Elections for the sixteenth Majlis had been largely rigged by the government in the provinces, and now battle lines were drawn for the Tehran elections. Mozaffar Baqa'i and Hoseyn Makki, who had led the opposition to the supplemental agreement in the previous Majlis, had brought Mosaddeq out from his self-declared 'political retirement' to lead the campaign for free elections and against the supplemental agreement.

They and seventeen other protesters took *bast* at the royal palace against ballot-rigging. Three days later they left, and announced the formation of the National Front on 23 October. On the same day, the Tudeh party's official newspaper described its leaders as agents of imperialism as well as of the royal court. New elections were held, and seven Front leaders and Ayatollah Kashani, who was still in Beirut in exile, found their way to the Majlis. Shortly afterwards, General Ali Razmara, the forceful chief of staff, became prime minister. In the meantime, an ad hoc oil committee of the Majlis chaired by Mosaddeq had been set up to deal with the oil question. The National Front faction was small but they enjoyed wide popular support.

Razmara was an exceptionally able general and an astute politician. As prime minister, he pushed the supplemental agreement bill and had friendly relations with the British embassy; he attracted America's support as a strong leader who would save Iran from communism; he also made a commercial treaty with the Soviet Union, and had secret relations with the banned Tudeh party. The Anglo-Iranian Oil Company eventually offered Razmara a fifty-fifty deal, with each party receiving fifty per cent of the net proceeds, after it became clear that the Majlis would not approve the supplemental agreement. For unknown reasons he did not make this offer public before he was assassinated in the Royal Mosque on 7 March 1951.

Razamara's self-confessed assassin was a member of the Fada'iyan-e Islam; though from the start it was believed that the shah had had a hand in his assassination. Whatever the truth, there is evidence that the shah did not receive the news of the general's death with regret, since he firmly believed that Razmara had been planning a military coup.

Shortly after Razmara's assassination the Majlis unanimously passed Mosaddeq's oil bill, nationalizing Iran's entire oil industry, the only political force which publicly opposed it at the time being the Tudeh party, since it saw the bill as a plot to replace Britain with America and was still mindful of the Soviet claim to north Iranian oil. Hoseyn Ala's caretaker government lasted only two months, and Mosaddeq became prime minister on 29 April 1951.

Oil nationalization (1951–3)

While the shah and the conservatives saw themselves as the natural clients or allies of Britain and later America, and the Tudeh the natural allies of the Soviet Union, Mosaddeq pursued a non-aligned foreign policy which, since the early 1940s, he had described as the policy of 'passive balance'. He saw the nationalization of Iranian oil as a necessary step towards the achievement of full independence and democracy. The strongest motive behind oil nationalization was thus political rather than economic, and that is why the movement was shortly to become known as the Popular Movement of Iran. He was willing to compensate the Anglo-Iranian Oil Company on similar terms to the recent nationalization of private industries in Britain, but the Anglo-Iranian demanded either a new concession with better terms for Iran, or full compensation, to include the profit they would have made if they had continued until 1990.

From the start Britain was unhappy with a Mosaddeq government, trying to bring him down via a Majlis vote of no confidence. Still, in the summer of 1951 they sent a negotiating team headed by government minister Richard Stokes, but no agreement was reached. There followed Iran's repossession of the oil operations in September 1951, leading to the boycott of Iranian oil by the main international companies – known as the Seven Sisters – backed by the Royal Navy in the Persian Gulf and beyond. Thus Iran's principal source of public revenue and foreign exchange was cut off, while it had to pay the labour and maintenance costs of an idle industry.

Britain's complaint to international bodies led to Mosaddeq's defence at the UN General Assembly, who referred the case to the International Court, which Iran eventually won in July 1952. While he was in the United States, meeting both President Truman and Secretary of State Acheson, he agreed to a compromise solution, but Anthony Eden, the British foreign secretary, turned it down.

At the same time, the World Bank offered to mediate by restoring and operating the production and export of Iranian oil for two years. This would have considerably reduced the scale of confrontation between Britain and Iran and might well have led to a permanent settlement of the dispute. Mosaddeq was receptive at first, but some of his influential advisors were against it, knowing that their Tudeh and rightist opponents would call it a sell-out. The World Bank's attempt having failed, the government embarked on a policy of 'non-oil economics' (running the economy and the country without the oil revenues), which in the circumstances it managed well by adopting realistic, albeit unpopular, policies; but clearly it could only be a short-term measure.

The Anglo-Iranian oil dispute and domestic political strife, added to the loss of oil revenues, made it almost impossible for the government to take the major reformist decisions demanded by some of their supporters – notably Khalil Maleki, leader of the socialist Third Force party – over issues such as land reform and the enfranchisement of women. The religious establishment's open hostility resulted in shelving the plan for giving the vote to women. Regarding rural reform, late in 1952 a law was passed, based on the model of one that Qavam had previously ratified, that obliged landlords to give ten per cent of their share of the output to the peasants and another ten per cent to a rural development fund, though the government did not last long enough to see it through.

The British embassy continued its attempts to replace Mosaddeq with another government, and having decided that Seyyed Zia was too unpopular for the task, they focused their gaze on Qavam. In July 1952, the conflict between the shah and Mosaddeq regarding which of the two should appoint the minister of war led to Mosaddeq's resignation. There followed

Qavam's ill-fated and short-lived ministry, the people's revolt against it and Mosaddeq's reinstatement on the day the International Court voted in favour of Iran's position that, contrary to the British argument, it had no jurisdiction in the dispute. Not long afterwards there began a rift in the Popular Movement for both political and personal reasons. It was led by Ayatollah Kashani and Mozaffar Baqa'i, who had been two of the most important figures in the movement. Meanwhile, political turmoil went on as before, the law being passive towards the licentious behaviour of the press and unauthorized public meetings, let alone riots, as well as plots to bring down the government by illegal means.

Serious internal dispute was now added to the foreign conflict. And precisely for that reason, the Popular Movement would not have succeeded without a settlement of the oil dispute which would have been tolerable to Britain and America. That is why some of the less idealistic of Mosaddeq's advisors – for example, Mohammad Soruri and Khalil Maleki – believed that he should settle for something less than ideal, so as to save the movement and his own government. On the other hand, many more of his advisors were afraid of cries of 'sell-out' the minute he began to reach such a settlement.

There was another brush with the shah in late February of 1953 which, once again, Mosaddeq 'won'. It happened when the shah declared his intention of leaving the country, which led to unsuccessful anti-Mosaddeq riots with the aim of bringing down his government. Meanwhile, in November 1952 the British and American intelligence services had begun to discuss the possibility of instigating a coup against Mosaddeq by organizing and financing his domestic opposition, and they reached a definite agreement in April 1953. It was in the same month that Mosaddeq's opposition kidnapped and murdered the chief prefect of the police, for which both General Zahedi (who was involved in the preparation for the coming coup) and Mozaffar Baqa'i, among others, were officially charged.

The 1953 coup

With no end in sight to the debilitating non-oil economy and no prospect of the settlement of the oil dispute, the unhappiness of increasing numbers of middle-class people about the turmoil in the streets and the revolt of almost half of the Popular Movement deputies, Mosaddeq decided to hold a referendum to close the seventeenth Majlis and hold new elections, ignoring the opposition of some of his best advisors such as Gholamhoseyn Sadiqi, the deputy prime minister and Khalil Maleki, leader of the pro-Mosaddeq Third Force party.

This played straight into the hands of his domestic and foreign opposition to put the coup plan into operation by obtaining from the shah a dismissal notice for Mosaddeq and a notice of appointment to premiership for General Zahedi. But before the commander of the royal guard could deliver the dismissal notice to Mosaddeq at one a.m. on 16 August 1953, the plot was discovered, the leading generals involved were arrested and the shah left the country. There followed two days of anti-shah demonstrations and rioting, some of which, according to publicly available CIA documents, was organized or augmented by the Anglo-American operators on site in order to frighten the public into an anti-Mosaddeq reaction. In view of the resulting sense of lawlessness and acute insecurity of the public come 18 August, the government banned public meetings and demonstrations the very next day.

Taking advantage of the situation, the anti-Mosaddeq coup operators, including such powerful religious personalities as Aytollah Behbahani, managed to bring out a considerable number of people from the city's slums and persuade parts of the army as well as the city police to join them. The Fada'iyan, Baqa'i's Toilers party and Kashani-supported Majma'-e Mosalaman-e Mojahed – making around one thousand individuals in all – also took part in the coup. Mosaddeq did not call for help while his home was being attacked. The coup-makers captured

Tehran's radio station in the afternoon, and by early evening it was all over. Thus the shah, who had gone to Rome via Baghdad thinking that all was lost, returned to Tehran in triumph.

Dictatorship (1953–63)

The decade following the 1953 coup was characterized by a dictatorship comparable to the decade that had followed Reza Khan's coup in 1921. The coup did not result straight away in personal and arbitrary rule, although within a couple of years – certainly after his dismissal of Zahedi – the shah had become by far the most powerful player in the country. Apart from its foreign sponsors, the coup had been the product of a coalition of social and political forces. Therefore, all the shah's allies shared in the power – although at a decreasing rate – until the White Revolution and the revolt of 1963 when the shah inaugurated his final phase, the period of absolute and arbitrary rule.

Three phases may be distinguished during the shah's dictatorship. The period from 1953–5 was one of consolidation of power and the elimination of both the Popular Movement and the Tudeh party from politics. The years 1955–60 saw a concentration of power and a rising economic boom which ended in bust. This period was followed by power struggles between 1960 and 1963, which the shah won.

From 1953–5 Mosaddeq was tried and convicted in two military courts and sentenced to three years in solitary confinement, and was later forced to live on his rural estate until his death in 1967. The Popular Movement parties were banned and their leaders and activists jailed for some time, except for foreign minister Fatemi who was executed. There were attacks against the Tudeh party, and the discovery and destruction of its military network of more than 450–600 army officers dealt it a devastating blow, ending with the execution of scores of its members. But let it be emphasized that, although Tudeh and Mosaddeqites were eliminated from politics, political and religious establishments still had a share in power and made up the shah's support and social base.

Relations with Britain were restored in 1954, and an agreement with a consortium of British, American, Dutch and French oil companies settled the oil dispute on a fifty-fifty basis for a period of twenty-five years. Following that, and in his first move to consolidate his own power, the shah dismissed Zahedi in April 1955 and sent him into honourable exile. The conflict between the shah and Abolhasan Ebtehaj (the country's first and most able technocrat, who later founded his own private bank) was further proof of the concentration of power. Ebtehaj was the exceptionally able and honest head of the Plan Organization, then the chief agency for economic development, and was dedicated to financial integrity and the use of oil revenues for development projects rather than military expansion. Having failed to persuade the shah to back him on these views, he resigned in 1959 and between 1961 and 1962 spent a term in jail.

Meanwhile the shah, who at the time advocated the ideology of 'positive nationalism' (implying that Mosaddeq had been a 'negative nationalist'), had launched a two-party system. The Melliyun (purported to mean Nationalist) party was headed by prime minister Eqbal; the Mardom (People's) party was led by the shah's closest confidant and minister of the interior, Asadollah Alam. But it was no more than a window-dressing exercise.

The religious establishment had been behind the new regime, as it had played a significant role in the coup and its legitimization, and the shah's good relations with them peaked during the official anti-Baha'i campaign in 1955. The Fada'iyan-e Islam's newspaper *Nabard-e Mellat* was elated; yet they made an unsuccessful attempt on prime minister Hoseyn Ala's life the following November, angered by his decision to join the

Baghdad pact (later, the Central Treaty Organization). Five of them, including their leader Navvab Safavi, were arrested, tried and executed, but the religious establishment did not rally to their support.

After the 1953 coup, British influence in Iranian politics began to assume second place to that of America. Within a relatively short period, a client–patron relationship was built up between Iran and the United States. American aid was crucial in the first two years before oil revenues could once again become a significant source of state revenue and foreign exchange. It was to continue throughout the 1950s in the form of financial and military grants and later, public loans.

Iran dropped its policy of neutrality and non-alliance. In 1955, with strong US support, it joined a military pact with Britain, Turkey, Iraq and Pakistan, first described as the Baghdad pact, later the Central Treaty Organization (CENTO) after the 1958 coup in Iraq when that country left the pact. In 1957, the CIA sent a five-man advisory team to Tehran, which over the course of the next four years helped organize and train an internal secret service which became known as SAVAK.

The Soviet Union did not at first react as sourly as might have been expected to the American-sponsored coup of 1953, the suppression of the Tudeh party and Iran's alliance with the West. But they became increasingly concerned about America's influence, and its use of Iranian military facilities for intelligence-gathering and the establishment of air bases along the Soviet border with Iran. However, their concern turned into public indignation and anti-shah propaganda in 1959, when the shah entered a mutual defence pact with the United States at the same time as he had been negotiating with the Soviet Union for a non-aggression treaty. Beginning in 1963 there was to be a thaw in the two countries' relations, following the decline of the Cold War and the shah's victory in the domestic power struggles of 1960–3.

Economic planning and policies

The flow of oil and foreign aid brought the economy out of the stagnant state of non-oil economics, with increasing consumption and imports benefiting mainly the upper and middle classes. In 1955 the Plan Organization was charged with the preparation and execution of the Second Seven Year Plan (1955–62) for economic development, since the first plan had fallen by the wayside due to the oil dispute and loss of oil revenues.

Total expenditure for the period came to about 70 billion rials. Forty-eight per cent of this was spent on infrastructure: transport, telecommunications, public utilities, for example; twenty-two per cent was spent on agricultural projects, fourteen per cent on regional development, eight per cent on industry and mines and 7.7 per cent on unanticipated costs. Thus industry very much took a back seat, in accordance with prevailing attitudes towards 'Third World' development at the time.

Meanwhile, following Ala's caretaker cabinet, Manuchehr Eqbal's government (1955–60) followed an economic policy of high-consumption expenditure and liberal imports. Cheap money in the hands of the upper classes and speculators led to a thriving movement in urban land speculation, bidding up urban land and property prices and putting pressure on the housing market. In 1955, the country's balance of payments including oil was $11 million, and excluding oil, -$37 million; in 1960 the figures had fallen respectively to $219 million and -$583 million. There followed almost three years of economic depression and political power struggles, from which the shah emerged triumphant.

Amini's government (1961–2)

In 1960, the shah faced serious problems in both the domestic and international spheres. There was runaway inflation, and the consumer boom was about to go bust. In 1958 he had foiled a suspected coup by General Qarani, the army intelligence chief. The American embassy had been aware of Qarani's activities, and Ali Amini, then Iranian ambassador to Washington, was dismissed on suspicion of being involved in his plot. In 1960, Senator John F. Kennedy, a severe critic of corruption and waste of American aid in Iran and other countries, had been elected president. The Soviet Union was still angry, conducting a scathing radio propaganda campaign against the shah and the royal family.

The shah's declaration that the upcoming elections for the twentieth Majlis would be free was largely to appease Kennedy, just as the shah's move to liberalization of 1977 was mainly a response to the election of President Carter. Amini, the second National Front and other peaceful opposition groups began to organize, but the elections were rigged nevertheless. What broke the camel's back was the teachers' strike of April 1961, when, in the course of a massive but peaceful demonstration, a teacher was shot dead by the police. The shah sent for Amini, whom he believed was America's candidate for the premiership. Amini accepted the offer on the condition that the shah, using his powers under the 1949 constitutional amendments, would dismiss parliament, knowing that the Majlis was packed with landlords and the shah's appointees who could bring him down at any moment and would certainly not support his proposed land reform policy.

The shah both disliked and feared Amini who, though loyal, was independent and capable and wanted to trim some of the shah's dictatorial powers. The shah was also afraid that Amini's moderately liberal approach, added to his land reform policy, could help him steal the show both with the public and with America. The pro-shah and anti-reformist elements began to campaign against Amini. And to Amini's chagrin, the second National Front also led a relentless campaign against him on the pretext that he should immediately call 'free elections'.

In January 1962, the Land Reform Law for abolishing the landlord system and giving land to peasants – described as the first stage of the reform – was passed and ultimately affected 14,000 villages, or thirty per cent of the total (excluding hamlets), or 520,000 peasant households. The logic behind Amini's land reform programme was to create a wider and more secure base for the regime and enable and encourage public participation in economic and social development. He believed that a comprehensive land reform, with compensation to the landlords, would win the support of the peasantry and make agricultural development possible, while it would both persuade former landlords to invest (or lend to others to invest) in the urban sector, and encourage the bourgeoisie to invest in modern industry.

By July 1962 when Amini fell he had no political force to depend on: the shah, the landlords, the second National Front and the Tudeh supporters were all against him. In a recent visit to America, the shah had been reassured that he could dismiss Amini if he so wished. He was replaced by the shah's close confidant, Asadollah Alam. This marked the beginning of the shah's direct personal rule.

Land reform and the revolt of June 1963

In January 1963, the shah took many, including his democratic and leftist opposition, by surprise when he put a six-point reform programme, described as the White Revolution, to referendum, which by official manipulation returned a staggering ninety-nine per cent 'yes' vote. In different ways, the most important and controversial of these points were land reform (which had already begun under Amini a year before) and women's suffrage. Mosaddeq's hope to enfranchise women had been frustrated by the religious

Mohammad Reza Shah with President Kennedy and Secretary of Defense Robert McNamara. White House, Cabinet Room, 1962. (Source: US National Archives and Records Administration via Wikimedia)

establishment's hostility towards it, and this time there was similar opposition by many if not most leading religious leaders. In practice, all elections were controlled by the state, but even so the act itself followed by sending a few women to parliament, had an important symbolic social value and would encourage greater emancipation and participation of women – limited, of course, to upper- and modern middle-class women – in society.

Land reform was still the most controversial point of the White Revolution. It was well known that the shah was opposed to Amini; therefore, the landlords and religious establishment who had provided the strongest social base of the regime after the 1953 coup expected a disruption of the land reform policy.

Many ulama were opposed, regarding it as a violation of private property, both in response to the landlords' appeal to them for support and because they were anxious over its consequence for the *owqaf*, or religious endowments, which were an important source of revenue for religious institutions. In reality, the land distribution programme was diluted when it moved to its 'second stage', but this was not apparent from the general policy principle in the shah's referendum.

At least as worrying for the landlords and the religious establishment was the fact that, in the long parliamentary recess, the shah had assumed personal rule and had in effect abandoned his old allies. He brushed aside personal representation by pillars of the establishment and banished them from court.

It is highly instructive that at this time Taqizadeh, who was greatly in favour of both land reform and the women's vote, and who had not made any notable political pronouncement for more than a decade, drafted a letter addressed to the shah, complaining about the parliamentary recess and violations of constitutional law. It was intended to be signed by a number of elder statesmen, but was never actually sent. There is no reference in the letter to land reform or the women's vote. It shows the deep concern of the political establishment for the shah's assumption of arbitrary power, as opposed to the mere dictatorship in which they had acquiesced since 1953.

Likewise, the modern middle classes were not opposed to the principles of land reform and the women's vote. But they were opposed to dictatorship, and were nostalgic about the freedoms enjoyed under Mosaddeq, who by this time had assumed an almost mythological status among the politically minded, particularly students, intellectuals and the bazaar. The strongest response came from the ulama and the religious community in general and Ayatollah Khomeini in particular, who – though well known in the Qom seminary and in specialist circles – came to wide public notice as a result of this personal challenge, quickly becoming a national figure. This led to the revolt of June 1963.

On 3 June or *Ashura*, the day of martyrdom in Karbela, demonstrators carried portraits of Khomeini and chanted pro-Khomeini and anti-shah slogans. Defying government orders, Khomeini delivered a powerful sermon at a theological college in Qom, strongly attacking the shah himself. His arrest early next morning led to a public revolt, which reached its peak the following day, 5 June, known in Persian as The Fifteenth of Khordad. The riots were violently suppressed, with heavy loss of life. There followed a clampdown on the religious community, especially in Qom and Tehran.

Khomeini was later put under house arrest and only released after eight months. Still later, he was arrested and exiled to Turkey, whence he was allowed to live in the holy city of Najaf in Iraq. This happened when he broke his silence and delivered a long and stinging sermon against a new law which granted immunity from prosecution in Iranian courts to American technical and military advisors and personnel and their dependants in Iran, a highly unpopular law which was reminiscent of the hated capitulation agreements under the Qajars. Khomeini said in the sermon:

> If some American's servant, some American's cook, assassinated your *maraje'* [grand ayatollahs] in the middle of the bazaar, or ran him over, the Iranian police would not have the right to apprehend him . . . Even if the shah himself were to run over a dog belonging to an American he would be prosecuted. But if an American cook runs over the shah, the head of state, no one will have the right to interfere with him.

The revolt of June 1963 marked a watershed in the relationship between state and society and between dictatorship and arbitrary rule, and inaugurated a new era which ended with the revolution of February 1979.

The return to arbitrary government

The shah personally ruled Iran between 1963 and 1978. He tried to combine the role of a traditional arbitrary ruler with that of modern revolutionary leader. In a brilliant observation made to close friends, Senator Hasan Akbar said as early as 1964: 'His Majesty is trying to become both Xerxes and Fidel Castro; but this is impossible.'

From the mid-1960s on, Iran began a process of rapid economic and social change. The most important single factor in determining both the pattern and speed of economic change and industrialization was oil revenue. Oil revenues are in the nature of economic rent: the cost of producing crude oil is little compared to the revenues that proceed from it. The revenues accrued to the state, and it was their disbursement by the state that determined the whole direction and character of industrialization and social change. Therefore, the combination of oil and state played the chief role in deciding the course of events. That need not have resulted in the same *pattern* of events, and the same or a similar *outcome*, had there not been an arbitrary government, which would neither be subject to legal restraints, nor would allow any independent advice or mediation.

The failure of long-term development in the period concerned was neither for want of economic resources, nor even because of political dictatorship. Dictatorships do allow for politics. They are based in law, even if the law may be unfair and discriminating. They have a social base either among the privileged social classes or some sections of 'the masses', or among both, as in some fascist and populist regimes. The government is not democratic, but nor is it moved by the personal whim and will of one individual. As we have seen, Iran had already been a dictatorship since 1953. From 1964 onwards there was not just a lack of political development; rather, politics itself began to disappear from the public sphere.

The regime lost its social base among the landlords, provincial grandees and religious establishment, without wishing to replace it with other, existing or emerging social classes. Even as early as 1964, when the state had beaten all opposition, substantially improved its foreign relations and was looking forward to economic growth and prosperity, its fundamental failure was not lost on some, such as Martin Herz, the political secretary at the American embassy, who wrote in an unusually long dispatch that not even the regime's clients and beneficiaries supported it:

> Here, and not in particular activities of the exponents of the opposition, lies the real weakness of the regime . . . the Shah's regime is a highly unpopular dictatorship, not only by its opponents, but far more significantly, by its proponents as well.

Herz's reference to 'a highly unpopular dictatorship' meant arbitrary government or *estebdad*, for which he had neither the concept nor the terminology. What was true in 1964 was scarcely less true in 1977, when a limited opening of the political sphere by the regime quickly led to mass protests and revolution.

Asadollah Alam, the shah's most loyal servant and confidant, who was minister of the royal court, had dreaded this state of affairs. Alam's extensive confidential diaries, covering the period 1969–77, provide a first-hand account of the nature of the regime, its real weaknesses in the face of apparent success and, indirectly, of the psychology of the man who was in complete command of all the key policies, domestic and foreign.

The diaries, which were published in 1991 (long after both Alam and the shah had passed away), contain ample evidence to refute the almost universal belief of the Iranian people that the shah was in the pocket of America. On the contrary, they clearly show that, rather than subservience to America, arbitrary government combined with superficial modernism as well as the shah's own persona were the real determinants of the shah's policies, which culminated in the revolution of 1979.

The shah was certainly pro-American. Yet Alam's diaries amply demonstrate that – at least from the late 1960s onwards – he saw America as his chosen grand and admired partner, rather than the master to whom he was slavishly bound by money or power. It is ironic that the diaries also contain much direct evidence, not just of the shah's own acute Anglophobia, but his firm belief in the conspiracy theory of international politics, a belief that extended to include the United States.

Having given himself the title Aryamehr ('Aryan Sun') in the mid-1960s, the clearest manifestation of the shah's pan-Persian Aryanism was the fabulous international celebrations, in October 1971, of the 2,500th anniversary of the Persian empire, at a cost of \$22 million when the country's annual income per head was around \$350. The festivities were deeply resented by almost the entire society. Alam says in his diaries that even the queen, now entitled Shahbanu, had been opposed to them.

Shortly after the quadrupling of oil prices in 1973 and 1974, in which the shah had played a significant role, he told Alam that his ambition was to turn Iran into a world power. A year later he wrote in his book *Towards the Great Civilization* that 'To take the Iranian nation to the age of the great civilization is my greatest wish', and he went on to add that 'the great civilization towards which we are now moving is not just a chapter in the history of this land. It is its greatest chapter.' A few months before, Alam had been horrified to learn that 'only one per cent of our villages has been supplied with clean, piped drinking water . . . far more shameful is the fact that only one in twenty-five villages has electricity'.

The military, the parliament, the long-standing administration of the cultured but subservient Amir Abbas Hoveyda had no will of their own, and when the loyal Alam told the shah that he could at least allow free municipal elections, the shah replied that even that would be harmful 'because the people would then want to talk about such matters as inflation'.

One-party state

In March 1974, shortly after the fourfold increase in oil prices, official party politics took a dramatic turn. At a hastily convened press conference, the shah disbanded the two official Mardom and Iran-e Novin parties and replaced them with the single National Resurgence party. Membership of the new party was made compulsory for all Iranians. In a famous speech, the shah classified his subjects into three groups: the great majority who, he said, were behind the regime; those who were passive and neutral and should therefore 'expect nothing from us'; and dissidents and critics, for whom there was no room in the country and who were free to apply for passports and leave Iran. The people, great as well as small, felt insulted and humiliated. Abolhasan Ebtehaj, former head of the Plan Organization, later remembered that 'I telephoned Hoveyda, who was the party's general secretary. I said, "This means that I have to join the party, because I can't leave Iran." "Yes," he said. I said, "What should I do?" He said he would send me a piece of paper to sign . . . meaning that I had become a party member. That's all, just a signature.'

The shah's grip on the military was tight. The power and privileges of military officers went considerably beyond their good pay and conditions. Their military uniform, which they regularly wore, conferred extraordinary authority, and they could intimidate ordinary people in public. Military organizations could also violate private property (especially urban land) whenever it suited their purpose. All this served to cause a great deal of general resentment towards military officers and networks.

But as powerful as the military organizations were in relation to the ordinary public, they were completely powerless regarding their own professional tasks and activities. The shah was personally in charge of all arms purchases; he made all the appointments and promotions of senior and general staff, and heads of services, departments and operations had to report directly to him.

The highly regarded General Fereydun Jam, chief of staff from 1969–71, resented the fact that 'officers were all responsible without having power . . . Not even the army commander had the right to use more than a company in his area . . . It is clear that such an army which in normal times would have to seek permission to breathe, will have no one to lead in a crisis, and will disintegrate . . . exactly as it in fact did.' General Jam, General Hasan Toufanian and Admiral Amir Abbas Ramzi Atai are at one in emphasizing the lack of coordination between various military establishments, and the requirement that all service chiefs both report directly to the shah and obtain permission from him for the least decision.

SAVAK, founded in 1957, was the shah's secret police, though there were other security and intelligence-gathering networks, each watching the others and all of them under the shah's direct control. SAVAK was a large and ruthless security organization whose power, influence and sphere of operations grew from the mid-1960s as a consequence of the growth of the shah's arbitrary power alongside the steady, and later explosive, increase in oil revenues. It not only suppressed political dissidence and the urban guerrilla movements, but also struck widespread fear into the hearts of high and low alike in an attempt to obliterate any word of criticism, however harmless, even in private. This played a significant role in spreading anger and frustration against the regime.

Foreign policy

From 1963 onwards, the shah himself conducted his own, largely successful foreign policy. American ambassador Armin Meyer recalled that after his audiences with the shah, the foreign minister would 'pick my brains to educate himself as to what was on the shah's mind'. Most important in the field of Iranian foreign relations were the United States (and Britain), the Soviet Union (and the Eastern European countries) and the Arab (and Islamic) world. In the period of his absolute rule, the shah managed to maintain and enhance the support of America and Britain, establish friendly relations with the Soviet Union and Eastern European countries, be on good terms with Arab kingdoms, maintain friendly relations with Israel and even reach an accord with Mao's China. At the same time, the defeat of the Egyptian leader Gamal Abd al-Nasser in the 1967 Arab–Israeli war and his death a few years later largely removed the threat of Nasserism, the symbol at the time of Arab nationalism. The shah even managed to bring Saddam Hussein to heel in 1975.

The shah's American card became much stronger on Richard Nixon's assumption of the presidency (1969–74). Nixon almost gave the shah carte blanche for ordering arms from the US, and openly asked him to keep the peace in the Persian Gulf on behalf of America. Relations remained unchanged under Gerald Ford (1974–6), but they took a new turn on the election of President Carter with his more liberal international policy and public espousal of human rights.

Relations with the Soviet Union improved and normalized in the 1960s and 1970s, although not to the extent of disturbing Iran's alliance with the West. This included better trade relations, the most important results being the Soviet construction of Iran's first modern steel plant in Isfahan, a machine-tools factory in Arak and the export of Iranian natural gas to the Soviet Union as well as purchases of arms and military equipment from Russia and some Eastern European countries.

The shah's most engaging foreign conflict in the late 1960s and early 1970s was with neighbouring Iraq. The Iraqi regime was fiercely nationalist as well as pro-Soviet, and saw itself as Iran's rival power in the Persian Gulf. But the specific cause of conflict with Iraq was the age-old dispute over Iran's rights in the Shatt al-Arab waterway. Iraq welcomed General Teymur Bakhtiar, the founding SAVAK chief who, having been sacked, was now plotting against the shah but who was killed by an Iranian undercover agent in 1970. In 1971 and 1972, Iraq resorted to the persecution and mass expulsion of Iraqi Shi'ites of Iranian origin. And so, when the Kurdish revolt in Iraq ignited, the shah used it as an opportunity to retaliate and to stem Iraqi hostility by providing effective support for the Kurdish insurgents. The tactic worked, and in 1975, at a summit of the Islamic countries in Algiers, Saddam Hussein capitulated and made peace with the shah. All the while, the highly dictatorial Iraqi Ba'thist regime was becoming very popular with the Iranian people, not least with intellectuals. Admiration of the Iraqi confrontation of the shah's regime was further proof of the fundamental conflict between state and society in Iran, especially now that the state was so strong and repressive.

The most sensitive issue facing the shah in his relations with both Britain and his Arab neighbours in the Persian Gulf was the question of Bahrain's independence after the British withdrawal from the Gulf. Iran had a historical claim to Bahrain, as well as to the islands of Abu Musa and the Greater and Lesser Tunbs, which are virtually uninhabited but which are strategically located in the Strait of Hormoz, and to which the then Trucial States (now the United Arab Emirates) also lay claim. The shah did not want to go to war with Britain or the Arabs over Bahrain, whose population was overwhelmingly Arab. In the end, long and protracted negotiations with Britain led to Iran's recognition of Bahrain in 1971 as a sovereign country, following the report of a UN mission that the people of Bahrain wished their country to become fully independent after British withdrawal. But Iran would not leave empty-handed. The day after the British withdrew from the Persian Gulf, the Iranian navy occupied all the three islands mentioned above. The departure of Britain, combined with the support from President Nixon and the end of Iraq's confrontation with Iran, meant that by the mid-1970s Iran had become the foremost player in the Persian Gulf.

Thus, by the time the anti-regime protest movement began in 1977, the shah's regional and international policy had been so successful that his only enemy was Colonel Gaddafi of Libya. Nevertheless, he came to believe that the revolution against him had been engineered by America and Britain.

The impact of the White Revolution

In 1979, Iran was incomparably richer than it had been fifteen years earlier, and – though unevenly – all sectors of the economy had expanded considerably.

None of this would have been possible without the steady growth, and later explosion, of the oil revenues. In 1963 they were $300 million; in 1977, they had risen to $24 *billion*. Oil therefore was the engine of growth, and the cause of a substantial rise in general living standards, but given that it was almost a free gift and the state received its revenues directly, it also led to negative impacts on political, economic and social development.

In the crucial years following the restoration of arbitrary rule, growing oil revenues enhanced the power of the state, making it free from the need for foreign aid and credit, and much more independent from world powers in choosing its foreign as well as domestic policies. Likewise, the oil revenues made the state largely independent from the domestic economy such that, by 1977, oil contributed almost eighty per cent of state revenue, which was received in foreign exchange. It was state expenditure that determined the course and strategy of social and economic change, and the state sector grew much more rapidly than the private sector, although the latter's growth itself was mainly due to state outflow.

The first six principles of the White Revolution of 1963 were later extended to include other measures without further referendums, leading to a sense of social insecurity, so that by 1977 many believed that the next principle of the White Revolution would nationalize all urban property except for personal dwellings.

The second stage of the land reform that followed Amini's first stage was similar to the first, but it was more favourable towards landlords. In both cases peasants without traditional rights of cultivation – about one-third of villagers – were excluded, and this encouraged many of them to migrate to towns. Hasan Arsanjani, the architect of the original first stage, wanted a relatively autonomous cooperative movement run by the peasantry, but the shah later opted for a system that was bureaucratically controlled.

The third and fourth stages could not realistically be described as land reform. The shah's vision was to turn Iran into a modern industrial society within a short time frame. But, on the one hand, the reliance on petrodollars apparently removed the need for agricultural exports to provide the necessary foreign exchange; and, on the other, the shah believed that in the eyes of the world, a fairly large rural society was a sign of underdevelopment. This attitude was behind his agricultural policy from the late 1960s onwards.

The third stage was the creation of agricultural corporations for each of several villages taken together, in which the peasants would receive paper shares on the basis of the size of their plots. In practice, this forced the small shareholders to sell their shares and become rural or urban labourers. The fourth stage of the agricultural policy was even more destructive and less relevant than the third stage. It involved creating giant agribusiness companies in some of the most fertile areas of arable production.

The peasants were forced to sell their lands as well as their homes at administrative prices and become landless farm labourers on a daily wage, living in substandard housing estates that lacked the communal environment of the village. In one case, in the Khuzistan province fifty-eight villages were demolished to make way for one agribusiness company. But as with the farm corporations, the agribusinesses performed less efficiently than the existing agricultural systems.

Educational policy was much more successful. Now that oil revenues were flowing in, the economy was expanding rapidly, incomes were rising and there were greater job opportunities for educated men and women. As a result, the demand for more education grew fast, with more social classes expecting their children to be educated at the highest levels. New schools came into being all over the country, though much more so in towns than in villages. The number of primary-school students, girls as well as boys, increased more than threefold between 1962 and 1977. The growth of secondary education was even more impressive: there was a higher than eightfold increase between 1962 and 1978. However the philosophy, style, quality and results of secondary education were criticized by some educationalists for their insufficient focus on science and technology, and the emphasis on memorizing rather than on acquiring a critical faculty.

Higher education also expanded rapidly both at home and abroad. Following 'the educational revolution' in the late 1960s (one of the principles of the White Revolution) the state decided to raise intake at universities and colleges. In 1962 the number of university students stood at 27,000, but by 1977 it had risen to almost 70,000, although once again there were complaints about standards regarding both teaching and research. True to the sharp conflict between society and state, not only university and secondary-school students, but eventually even primary-school children joined the anti-shah demonstrations in 1978 and 1979.

The growth of oil revenues and, therefore, middle-class incomes, and the demand for higher education still being greater than its supply, along with the obvious prestige and income prospects attached to a Western education combined to lead to the rapid growth in numbers of students departing for Western Europe and the United States. Numbers rose from about 15,000 in 1962 to 40,000 by 1977 – a huge leap – which occurred mostly in the 1970s, especially after the quadrupling of oil prices in 1973 and 1974.

There was a continuing rise in the number of girls at schools; there was also a corresponding increase in the number of women attending college and university, and even going abroad. This, together with a more open attitude on the part of state and society, and the introduction of modern means of birth control, led to the growth of female employment in the modern economic sectors and the professions. By 1977, there had been a number of women Majlis deputies, senators, ministers and higher civil servants. The law still discriminated against women regarding divorce, inheritance and custody of children. But there was a growing tendency for modern women to obtain the right of divorce in their marriage contracts. Furthermore, the Family Protection Law of 1967 made it possible for other women to apply to an appropriate court for divorce on certain grounds; and while it did not abolish polygamy, it applied certain restrictions to it. In general, the 1960s and 1970s saw significant advances in the position and status of women, albeit mainly among the upper and middle classes.

The economy expanded fast, thanks to the oil revenues received and disbursed by the state: in 1975, oil contributed eighty-four per cent of government revenue, sixteen per cent being provided by other sources. The population also grew rapidly, at an average annual rate of about 2.7 per cent, as a consequence of falling death rates and rising birth rates, both of which were directly or indirectly influenced by rising living standards.

Oil revenues made possible the importing of modern technology and machinery, enabling high levels of investment in modern manufacturing, services and construction. Though while modern economic sectors expanded, economic development did not progress in any long-term, self-sustaining sense because the strategies pursued by the state were unhelpful to the objectives of enduring, irreversible economic development.

In particular, the import substitution – as opposed to export promotion – strategy of industrial development did not allow for the emergence of a modern export sector. In other words, the economy was permanently dependent on oil revenues. The decline of agriculture made matters worse. It ceased to be a net export-earning sector, for, among other problems noted above, Iran's currency was overvalued, and this made her agricultural products expensive in the international market. Throughout the period, the rate of exchange was maintained at between 70 and 75 rials to the American dollar because the shah attached prestige value to a high rate of exchange.

Foreign exchange receipts being due to an unpredictable gift of nature, and saving rates being low or negative, by the time of the revolution of February 1979 Iran had not achieved self-sustaining development, and nor had she in 2012, in spite of the considerable expansion of the economy.

Economic growth, although high, was uneven. Apart from oil, it was services rather than manufacturing that had the highest share in national output. In 1977 the share of modern as well as traditional manufacturing, and construction in non-oil output, was 29.7 per cent, whereas the share of services was 55.6 per cent. Agriculture – on which about half the population depended – claimed the remaining 14.7 per cent. The share of oil and services put together was almost seventy per cent of total national output.

While national income grew in all sectors of the economy, its distribution was highly unequal. This was partly due to the different rates at which the economic sectors grew, and partly as a consequence of state expenditure policies. In particular, the continuing relative decline of agriculture and the urbanization policies of the state meant that rural society was constantly losing in incomes and welfare relative to the towns. In 1977, while the rural population was about fifty-five per cent of the total, its share of total consumption was almost one-third of urban consumption. This led to an increasing rate of rural-to-urban migration, creating problems for urban employment, housing and so on.

The shah's strategy of economic development led to constraints, bottlenecks and inflationary pressures and, above all, the frustration of expectations, despite the fact that almost all sections of the population had gained in welfare over the period 1963–77. Such an economic landscape contributed to social discontent and revolutionary trends. But it was by no means economic factors alone, or even primarily, that determined the fundamental causes of the revolution of February 1979, when the whole of Iranian society, rich as well as poor, high as well as low, burst out in a historic revolt against the state.

5

The 1979 revolution and the Islamic Republic

The main principles of the shah's White Revolution of January 1963 were land reform and women's suffrage. Neither of these would quite have required a revolution as such; comparable Third World countries had achieved similar reforms without the need for revolution. The real revolution in 1963, following the suppression of the revolt in June and the successful implementation of the politics of elimination, was the reimposition of absolute and arbitrary rule following a period of dictatorship in which individuals and groups other than the shah also had a role to play.

The conservative establishment as well as the religious establishment were thus eliminated as political forces, much as Amini and the liberal democrats and communists had been before it. In other words, politics was abolished and the state lost its base among landlords and the ulama. At the same time, leaders of peaceful, liberal political groups were silenced or sent to jail. The shah described his new regime as classless for that very reason, and reinterpreted the democratic Iranian constitution as *nezam-e shahanshahi* (the imperial system), essentially an absolute and arbitrary regime. However, this had a dialectical effect, since while it led to the elimination of conservatives, liberals and democrats from politics, it encouraged the development of their opposites, namely beliefs, ideologies and movements which, one way or another, sought to overthrow the regime and eliminate the shah himself.

The familiar Iranian state–society conflict thus began to reach its highest point from the late 1960s onwards. Society regarded as harmful any and all views or decisions taken by the state, and believed that, by its very nature, the state was incapable of doing any good for society: whatever the state did was either 'on the order of their foreign [mainly US] masters', or 'so that they can loot the country's riches'.

Iranian intellectuals and the wider intelligentsia had for decades blamed the state for social and economic underdevelopment, and had been highly critical of the regime's association with the religious establishment, demanding a greater degree of secularism. It was a common jibe at the state that 'this country has even got to import needles', pointing to the absence of a modern steel industry in the country. Before the White Revolution they had been demanding modernization, industrialization, social and economic development and Western-style standards of material and cultural consumption. But no sooner had the state begun to break its ties with religious and traditional forces, invest in modern industry and encourage Western culture in the 1960s, than the intelligentsia began to make what almost looked like a U-turn. This was not development, they argued, but dependency on Western imperialism, promoting as well as promoted by the 'comprador bourgeoisie', or capitalists dependent on the West and serving Western interests. Land reform had been carried out on the orders of American imperialism, partly to forestall the danger of a socialist revolution and partly to provide a better market for Western consumer goods. And so it went.

In tandem, many of the most secular intellectuals – virtually all leftists, and most of them Marxist-Leninists – hitherto highly critical of religion and the state's peaceful relationship with its leaders, began to hark back to the country's religious culture and traditions, decry *gharbzaedgi*, or Weststruckness, and advocate cultural authenticity and 'nativism'.

MARXISM-LENINISM

Marxism-Leninism was a familiar ideology which, at the time, was popular in many so-called Third World countries. Even in advanced countries young people were influenced by it. In the 1960s and 1970s, Iranian Marxist-Leninists were either Maoists of various colours, or pro-Soviet or Trotskyists of different tendencies. They had virtually unresolvable conflicts among and within themselves, although theoretically they all advocated a proletarian revolution followed by the dictatorship of the proletariat. But what united them all was an intense hatred of the shah and the West, and especially America, in which most other opposition trends, notably the Islamist movement, also concurred.

The rise of anti-Westernism

Serious criticism of modernization and Westernization had begun at the beginning of the twentieth century, perhaps the most important figures in which were Sheykh Fazlollah, who was executed in 1909 by the constitutionalists (see Chapter 3), and the deeply religious but anti-Shi'ite scholar Ahmad Kasravi, who was assassinated by the fundamentalist Fada'iyan-e Islam group in 1945. Yet in his book, *Weststruckness* (*Gharbzaedgi*, 1962), Jalal Al-e Ahmad put forward a new line of argument which was an amalgam of familiar anti-colonialist theories and a critique of pseudo-Westernism. However, now that the regime had 'gone modern', so to speak, the time was ripe for the term to be turned into a slogan, indeed a potent weapon, which almost every social class used to condemn the regime, the West and everything and anything they did not like.

The term 'Weststruckness' which, in 1962, Al-e Ahmad had used to attack superficial Westernism, in a short time became all things to all men in attacking anything that vaguely related to the West, or indeed a powerful instrument for denouncing any undesirable idea or object. Al-e Ahmad's critique, though not faultless, had intended mainly to denounce an uncritical, superficial and comprehensive aping of the West. Out of his hands, his concept became a key tool in all anti-Western propaganda.

Ultimately this meant that, in matters regarding Europeanism, modernization, tradition and authenticity, there was a changing of places between the state on the one hand and society and its intellectuals on the other. For the opposition to the state to remain – even to intensify in the face of absolute and arbitrary rule – the intellectuals had to switch sides from the advocacy of modernization and development to authenticity, religion and return to self. Most of them espoused or sympathized with Marxist-Leninist ideology, but few saw this as conflicting with their swing back to tradition.

The search for authenticity and the critique of rapid and uncritical conversion to Europeanism went back at least to the 1920s and the dawn of Reza Shah's purportedly modernist reforms, though, as noted above, it had its origins among the opponents of the Constitutional Revolution. In the 1960s, however, it began to make a serious impact on intellectuals and the modern middle classes, chiefly because of the shah's intensive arbitrary rule and the Americanism and Aryanist nationalism of his last phase. But it was helped by regional and international factors as well, the emergence of peaceful coexistence between the US and the USSR, the challenge of Maoism, the revolutions in Cuba and Algeria, the Arab–Israeli conflict and the Vietnam war, all of which fuelled anti-imperialist sentiments in Iran.

It was also in the early 1960s that Ali Shariati obtained his doctorate in Persian literature from the University of Paris and returned to Iran. From his youth he had been both religious and Mosaddeqite, and later had been close to Bazargan's Freedom Movement party. Shariati had been impressed with Jean-Paul Sartre's existentialism, leftist French sociology as well as such Third Worldist figures as Frantz Fanon, ready to put forward a utopian Islamic ideology – which was at once anticlerical and a harbinger of return to early Shi'ite purity – and advocate an Islamic revolution which combined pure faith with modern radical ideologies. This was 'a return to self' fundamentally different from Al-e Ahmad's critique, but it was easily identified with it, not least in the minds of the emerging new social classes, whose younger generations demanded social and political change – even some vague socialist ideals – which were not in conflict with their religious faith. Shariati made a significant impact on this generation of an emerging modern religious class, many of whom sympathized with the People's Mojahedin, the leftist Islamic guerrilla movement.

Opposition at home and abroad

Meanwhile, Ayatollah Khomeini, the hero of the revolt of June 1963, continued his opposition to the shah's regime from his place of exile in Najaf, Iraq. He kept in close contact not only with his former students and a large number of devotees in Iran, but even with such opposition organizations as the Confederation of Iranian Students and the Islamic Students' Association, which were based in the West. Both in private communication and in public statements, he advocated the complete overthrow of the regime, and so became a symbol of resistance even for most non-religious Iranians. In a highly original book *The Guardianship of the (Shi'ite) Jurist*, he argued that, contrary to the traditional consensus of Shi'ite ulama, they should not only participate in government but that they alone had the right and duty to rule a Shi'ite country. This was a generally technical book addressed to the ulama and remained largely closed to the eyes of lay people, religious as well as secular, but immediately after the revolution it became – and still is – a great bone of contention even among the ulama themselves. While it is supported by many of the ulama – especially those involved with the Islamic state – there are others who stick to the traditional view that they should not be involved in governing society.

The Tudeh party, while exiled in Eastern Europe, was engaged in some activities, mainly journalistic, but it was obliged to keep within limits that would not jeopardize the shah's friendly relations with its hosts, the Soviet Union and East European countries which wanted to maintain good relations with the shah. This alienated many of its student members in Western countries, which happened to coincide with the rise of international Maoist Third Worldism, a movement that encouraged them to break with the Tudeh and convert to Maoism. Not only did Maoism as a fresh anti-Soviet communist ideology manage to convert large numbers of Tudeh dissidents, but it even persuaded most of the old National Front supporters abroad to set up their own Maoist organizations.

These and other dissident students and ex-students in Western countries were mostly gathered together under the umbrella of the Confederation of Iranian Students, which in the late 1950s began as a students' union, but which after a few years turned into an opposition movement. By 1970 it was hard to find a few among its members who were not Marxist-Leninist of one denomination or another. The confederation played an important role in bringing constitutional and human rights abuses in Iran to the notice of European human-rights groups, liberal and socialist political parties and, eventually, the general public. This cost the shah dearly when the chips were down, a situation his own open hostility towards democracy in Western countries had done nothing to mitigate.

The most active Marxist-Leninists in Iran, mostly students and ex-students, were either members or well-wishers of the guerrilla organization People's Fada'is, who began their operations – in many cases, the assassination of army and security personnel – in the early 1970s and continued until the revolution. The leftist Islamic guerrilla group Mojahadein's network was infiltrated and largely broken up by SAVAK (the secret police) in the mid-1970s, and were further weakened by a splinter group, later renamed Peykar, which had turned Marxist-Leninist.

Origins of the revolution of 1979

The revolution had many causes, both deep-rooted and more superficial, though it would not have turned into a revolt of the whole society against the state had the state enjoyed a reasonable amount of legitimacy and a base among some – at least the propertied and the modern – social classes.

A major consequence of the high economic growth rates generated by increasing oil revenues was the rise of new classes in society amid a high population growth rate. Far from having a sense of gratitude towards the state, they were discontented and rebellious on many grounds. They, like the rest of society including the clientele of the state (those who drew significant benefits from it), believed that the rise in their standard of living was simply due to the huge oil revenues, for which they did not give any credit to the state. On the contrary, they pointed to the much greater rise in the fortunes of the privileged groups, the widening gap between the wealth and luxury consumption of the state and the small minority as compared with the large majority, and the existence of absolute poverty as evidence of injustice and corruption.

Large numbers of people were also alienated from the state and from modern Iranian society on cultural and religious grounds. Unlike the latter part of Reza Shah's rule, the state did not ban religious activities and rituals. On the other hand, the opening of bars, nightclubs and cabarets, and the growing number of modern women wearing miniskirts and the like was an affront to the sensibilities of the religious and traditional classes, both male and female. The television, which now many if not most people could afford, represented mostly Western values, standards and habits in its programmes and shows. This led to an increasing number of clerics advising their followers that it was sinful to watch television.

Accordingly there developed a large community of traditional classes with good or reasonable standards of living and a modern education who regarded the state as alien and oppressive towards their cherished values. Large numbers of their young people adopted revolutionary attitudes towards the regime. They, like all other dissidents, believed that the regime was in the pocket of the West, and therefore extended their anger against it to Western countries, especially America, which was its strongest ally and had a considerable presence in the country.

However, the state's biggest failure from the point of view of its own interests was that it alienated the modern and secular social classes as well, at least some of which should have formed a natural social base. That would have been the case if the regime had been a dictatorship instead of one-person rule or *estebdad*, since it would have involved the participation of a political establishment in the running of the country, benefiting from some critical discussion and advice without the opposition not being blanket and comprehensive.

Not only were traditional propertied classes such as merchants and traders being alienated from the regime, not just the growing modern middle-class professionals and middle-income groups such as civil servants and university teachers, but also the modern business class, who owed much of the rise in their fortune to oil revenues. They had no independent economic or political power, and there was no forum or channel for airing their views, where they were critical of some of the economic policies of the state. In any case, no criticism of the regime, however mild and well intentioned, would be tolerated, even if expressed in private. This was the greatest single grievance of intellectuals, writers, poets and journalists against the regime. Censorship was heavy, but, as we have seen, any verbal criticism, if reported, would be duly punished.

The impact of the oil price rise

For most of the twentieth century until the early 1970s crude oil prices hovered around $1.80 per barrel, which alone since World War II had lost thirty per cent of its purchasing power. The Organization of Petroleum Producing Countries (OPEC), founded in 1962, had been ever more critical of low oil prices, and by 1972 had managed to push up the price of crude to around $3.45 per barrel. When the Yom Kippur War between and Egypt, Syria and Israel broke out on 5 October 1973, the United States and other countries in the Western world showed support for Israel. In reaction to this, several exporting Arab nations imposed an embargo on the pro-Israel countries. Iran did not join the embargo, but in the panic that ensued among oil-consuming countries, managed temporarily to bid the price up to around $17 per barrel. Thus the settlement that ensued between OPEC and the international oil companies raised the agreed price up to around $12 per barrel.

Ironically, the oil revenue explosion of 1973 and 1974 had negative consequences for the regime. It greatly enhanced its sense of self-confidence and its policies of repression. As noted in chapter 4, in March 1974, shortly after the fourfold increase in the oil prices, official party politics took a dramatic turn. At an emergency press conference, the shah disbanded the official Mardom and Iran-e Novin parties and replaced them with the single National Resurgence party, membership of which was mandatory for all Iranians. Then he followed his mandate with the famous speech that divided the nation into three groups: supporters of the regime, neutrals who could expect nothing from the regime and critics of the regime, who, he declared, were free to leave the country.

But more was to come. The oil price revolution almost immediately led to a massive increase in public expenditure. As both state and private incomes rose sharply, so did consumption and investment expenditure, rapidly increasing aggregate demand and fuelling demand-pull inflation. At the same time, since the supply of many products ranging from fresh meat to cement could not quickly be raised from domestic sources, supply shortages developed in the midst of financial plenty. Imports could not relieve the situation adequately partly because they would take time to deliver, but chiefly because of limits to the existing means of delivery, such as port facilities, warehouses, roads, lorries and drivers.

The state blamed rising inflation on producers and traders. Prices of a number of commodities were reduced by fiat. A public campaign was launched against 'profiteering' (*geranforushi*), whereby thousands of young men were sent to find the suspected culprits and take swift arbitrary measures against them. Hundreds of merchants and traders, including a few leading businessmen, were arrested and expropriated. Others were fined. Shops were closed down and trading licences were cancelled. While this was seen as an outrage by the business community, the public saw the traders as scapegoats for the state's arbitrary policies.

The protest movement of 1977

By the end of 1976 when Jimmy Carter was elected US president, Iran was ready for revolt. This was greatly encouraged by the new president's special emphasis on universal human rights. The shah interpreted this as a message to himself, and slowly began to allow limited freedom of speech and to release 'repentant' political prisoners. Yet, at the same time, the official press led a bizarre campaign implying that American imperialism was planning to bring its agents such as Ali Amini (whom the shah disliked and had dismissed as prime minster in 1962) to power to serve its interests. The shah himself felt that America's real intention was to make him stop pushing for higher oil prices and so, later in 1977, he said that he would not do that.

Iranian society was greatly emboldened in the erroneous belief that Carter had literally ordered 'the American agent' shah to open things up and to some extent allow views and criticisms to be aired. Campus demonstrations became frequent, and various legal, intellectual and political groupings began to demand liberty and the rule of law, which had disappeared with the politics of elimination. Trying to weather the storm by using the tactic he had applied in the early 1960s in response to President Kennedy's election, the shah dismissed Hoveyda's thirteen-year premiership and put Jamshid Amuzegar, a senior minister, in his place. The new cabinet was younger and more efficient than previous ones and began certain technical, bureaucratic and economic reforms, but those in Iran who were looking for fundamental change saw this as more of the same, and the protest movement became bigger and more active. SAVAK and other instruments of coercion retaliated by bombing the offices of liberal lawyers and attacking a large National Front meeting held outside Tehran, but, if anything, this simply amplified public indignation.

The campaign for freedom and human rights, still short of a general call for the overthrow of the regime, peaked during ten nights of poetry-reading sessions, held in November at Tehran's German cultural centre, the Goethe Institute. Attended by thousands of people, they were organized by the Writers' Association and became known as the Poetry Nights.

Also in November, the shah paid a state visit to the United States, and while he was being welcomed by President Carter on the lawns of the White House, Iranian students demonstrating against him clashed with a small number of well-wishers. The police used tear gas, which resulted in the shah, Carter and their suite appearing to weep live on television. The shah returned to a warm but officially organized welcome, and a few weeks later Carter celebrated the New Year as the shah's guest in Tehran. Both in Washington and in Tehran, the president was fully supportive of the shah, emphasizing Iranian–American friendship and cooperation.

Protest turning into revolution

Up until that time, the campaign for change had looked like a reform movement, but revolutionary forces were ready to come forward at the right moment. The first such opportunity was offered in the form of an article against Ayatollah Khomeini, ordered by the shah and organized by Hoveyda, now minister of the royal court. Signed under a pseudonym, it was published on 7 January 1978 in the leading semi-official daily *Ettela'at* despite its editor's fears of a strong public backlash. It described Khomeini as an agent of both Black (British) and Red (Soviet) imperialism, 'an adventurous cleric, subservient to centres of colonialism'.

There was a public outcry in Qom. The religious colleges and bazaar were shut down. There were clashes with the security forces leading to civilian casualties, the official figures being two dead; the opposition figures, seventy dead and five hundred injured.

Khomeini's direct and open attack on the shah had made him popular, not just with his religious followers but with a wide spectrum of people, simply because this was what they wished to hear, and he was the only person who could and would do it from his place of exile in Iraq. The incident opened a new chapter, undermining moderate and reformist views and encouraging riots and confrontations with the police and, later, the army.

Qom, then, was the first major turning point of the revolution. The second turning point occurred on 19 August 1978. The Cinema Rex at Abadan – Iran's oil capital – was set ablaze by unknown arsonists, resulting in the death of more than four hundred people inside. The crime was never convincingly investigated either before or after the revolution, but the public blamed it on the state. Within a few days the shah dismissed Amuzegar's cabinet and appointed an old hand, Ja'far Sharif-Emami, chairman of the senate and head of the shah's business concern, the Pahlavi Foundation. This was not a good choice in the circumstances because, rightly or wrongly tainted by major financial corruption, Sharif-Emami had virtually no credit left with any part of the public.

The third key turning point came on 8 September, subsequently dubbed Black Friday. A rally was called for Friday 8 September (Friday being the weekend in Iran), but the night before martial law was declared in Tehran and twelve other cities and all public meetings were banned. An anticipated huge crowd gathered in Zhaleh Square at the appointed time and, after a round of warning shots let off into the air, the soldiers fired on the crowd. The official figure for the dead was below one hundred; the opposition's, more than four thousand.

Meanwhile, Ayatollah Khomeini had been issuing written and spoken statements and, in accordance with the deep desire of most people, insisting on the overthrow of the regime. The Iranian government pressed the Iraqi government to restrict his activities, and on 6 October Khomeini flew to Paris. Once in France, he became the focus of attention for the Western press and media, and the object of pilgrimage for thousands of

Iranians everywhere. He was given the highly honorific title of Imam and, not long afterwards, the rumour spread that Khomeini's image could be seen on the moon. The rumour was believed by a significant number of Iranians, educated as well as secular, many of whom would testify to have seen it themselves.

Total revolt

By now the oil company, civil servants, the judiciary, the business community – the entire nation except the military, the police and security services – were on a general strike. On 5 November the people of Tehran ran riot. A BBC television reporter was puzzled when he saw a man in smart suit and tie dancing around a burning tyre and shouting anti-shah slogans. At the same time, following a meeting in Paris, Karim Sanjabi's virtual submission to Khomeini as the supreme leader of the revolution boosted Khomeini's standing both at home and in the West, Sanjabi being the leader of the secular liberal democrats, the fourth National Front.

The shah, who had only just realized the gravity of the situation, was hoping for a Sanjabi premiership, but Sanjabi's Paris statement spoilt this. The shah then appointed the moderate general Azhari prime minister, though many members of his cabinet were civilian. Regardless, large numbers of both secular and religious people began to shout the religious slogan *Allah-o Akbar* (God is the Greatest) from their rooftops every night. Talking the incidents down, Azhari said in the parliament that the slogans had come out of cassette tapes. The next day the people were shouting in a massive demonstration, 'Miserable Azhari! / Four-star donkey! / Keep saying it's tapes / But tapes have no legs.'

On 6 November, the day Azhari took office, there took place one of the most remarkable events in the Iranian revolution: the shah's television broadcast to the 'dear people of Iran'. It was delivered in a most humble manner, acknowledging their revolution and promising the abandonment of arbitrary rule, the removal of injustice and corruption and free elections and democratic government, and begging them to restore peace and order to make it possible to proceed with these reforms.

Ten per cent of such a move six months before – and not even so blatantly spelt out – followed by action, would have gone a long way to defuse the situation. But now it was too little, too late. Political leaders (other than the Islamist and Marxist-Leninist forces) who had hoped for dialogue and compromise, or at least an orderly transfer of power, were sidelined by the might of acute public anger: the most popular slogan was 'Let him [the shah] go, and let there be flood afterwards.'

All this took place while the shah's greatest Western allies, Britain and America, were watching events with bewilderment, not sufficiently able to understand or assess the situation. The shah regularly saw their ambassadors and sought their advice. He was certainly suspicious of Britain, especially as the BBC Persian Service was faithfully reporting the news of the revolution. Both powers publicly, repeatedly and almost continuously declared their support for the shah. However, given the gradual build-up of Western public opinion in its antipathy for the shah, and the scale and intensity of the Iranian people's revolt against him, the two world powers would not advise him to adopt an 'iron fist' policy, a euphemism for heavy and sustained military repression. Yet that is exactly what the shah wanted to hear from them, now that he had no social class or political party to turn to in the country. And that was the real reason why he later blamed the revolution on Britain and America, saying more or less openly that either or both of them had instigated and inflamed the revolution.

Alone, on 16 January 1979, the shah eventually offered the premiership to Shapour Bakhtiar, the deputy leader of the National Front and one time deputy minister under Mosaddeq, while he and the queen left the country for 'rest' in Egypt, then Morocco. The people rejected Bakhtiar out of hand, calling him 'a powerless lackey' in their street slogans, and he was expelled from the National Front. Bakhtiar did try to obtain Khomeini's consent, but was told that he had to resign first.

On 1 February, Ayatollah Khomeini returned to Iran to a tumultuous welcome. Shortly afterwards, and as his alternative government, he asked Mehdi Bazargan to form a provisional government. Bazargan was a Muslim democrat and leader of the Freedom Movement who regularly wore a tie, and had been Bakhtiar's colleague for a while in the second National Front. He resisted the idea at first, but agreed under pressure on the condition that he would have a free hand, which was granted but later not honoured. However, he himself did not adopt a belligerent attitude towards Bakhtiar, hoping that some kind of peaceful settlement could be worked out.

The final act of the great drama was the result of an accident. Early in February a troop of the elite Imperial and Immortal Guards still zealously loyal to the shah decided to teach a lesson to some air force personnel who were watching the taped broadcast of Ayatollah Khomeini's return to Iran, and attacked their barracks in Tehran. The airmen took up position and began to fight, and appealed to the people for help. Large numbers of people, including young guerrillas, went to their aid and attacked the guards from the rear. Quickly, the situation got out of control for both the revolutionary leaders and the government. Fearing civil war, on 11 February the army declared neutrality and withdrew to their barracks. The government, whose only power base the army was, thus collapsed and Bakhtiar went into hiding, only to appear in Paris some time later. But, despite appeals by Bazargan's provisional government for calm, the people went on to attack the main prisons and the military barracks, almost all of which surrendered without a fight.

Now it was time for the revolutionaries to turn on each other, which eventually resulted in the complete triumph of the Islamic takeover.

The nature of the revolution

The revolution in Iran did not conform to any European revolutionary pattern because of the arbitrary nature of the state and society. The most obvious difference was the fact that it was a revolt of the entire society rather than, as in Europe, a rebellion of the lower against the upper classes: no social group or political party stepped forward to defend the state. Later, the emergence of the Islamist state puzzled many, including Western and Western-inspired analysts and commentators who had expected a 'progressive' outcome *à l'Europe*.

The reason why the later analysts found the revolution 'enigmatic' or even 'unthinkable' after the event was that they had based their expectations on their knowledge of Western history and society. Whereas, as we know, Iran was a 'short-term' society, normally subject to absolute and arbitrary rule and therefore inclined towards disobedience and rebellion. Not even the upper classes could be described as the state's social base; in that case, they would have had some share in power, and rallied to the state in times of adversity.

Although there were great differences between the various agendas of the Constitutional Revolution and the revolution of 1979, they each answered to the characteristics of traditional Iranian revolts as described above. In the Constitutional Revolution the fight was against an archaic and traditional state, and therefore the secular, modern agendas gained the upper hand and they were the winners, in the main. In 1979, the struggle was against a modernist, Westernist absolute and arbitrary regime, and so the Islamist and anti-imperialists gained the upper hand, with the ultimate victory going to the Islamists.

This outcome resulted from a short-term consensus of society at large that the shah must go – a negative agenda without any common vision at all about what should follow the shah's fall. Putting aside the Muslim and secular democrats who had a small following, the Islamist, Islamic-Marxists and Marxist-Leninists of various hues had agendas which, by their very nature, would result in the elimination of the others from politics. Out of these three broad groups, the Islamists won because they had the great majority of the people, led by Ayatollah Khomeini, behind them, using the highly potent instrument of religion which most of the people understood and obeyed.

Like all other revolutions, the Iranian revolution did not stop after February 1979. The single unifying aim of overthrowing the shah and the state having been achieved, it was now time for each party – except for 'the liberals' – to try and grab as many of the spoils of the revolution as possible. None of them was interested in *sazesh*, or compromise, which in Iranian politics was tantamount to betrayal.

The Islamic revolution (1979–81)

There were two stages in the completion of the specifically Islamic revolution. The first was the taking hostage of American diplomats in November 1979. The second stage was the impeachment and dismissal in June 1981 of Abolhasan Banisadr, the Islamic Republic's first president. But first and foremost in the minds of Ayatollah Khomeini and his lieutenants was the formal declaration of an Islamic republic.

In a referendum held on 30 and 31 March 1979 the overwhelming majority of Iranians – men and women, secular and religious, rich and poor – voted for the creation of an Islamic republic; the official figure of 98.2 per cent was probably close to reality. However, many of those who voted for an Islamic republic saw it as the alternative to the monarchy, which was the only other choice they had in the referendum. Thus for them it was a political, not a religious act, the consequences of which they had not contemplated. There were a few dissenting voices, since the nature of the republic had not yet been defined, and they had only one alternative offered to voters – the monarchy, which they had actively rejected. Bazargan was much criticized by the Islamists when, at the polls, he emphasized that he was voting for a *democratic* Islamic republic.

One thing on which all the revolutionaries and their supporters other than the liberals were at first united was a systematic attempt to punish those associated with the former regime and to dismantle, as far as possible, the state's military and civilian apparatus. The person and property of a very rich person who had had no connection with the state were respected and protected. But any middle-ranking or senior civil servant, however conscientious and living on a relatively moderate income, would be in danger of expulsion and expropriation, as most of them were in the end. In general, and putting aside the cases of a few top generals and high officials, guilt or innocence, wealth and income had little to do with determining the fate of such people; it was their connection to the state and, through it, to the West that was the deciding factor. The only 'crimes' cited for executing General Nader Djahanbani were that he was blue-eyed (since his mother was Russian) and had four horses which he kept in stables on fitted carpets. The revolutionary judge Sadeq Khalkhali added in an interview that Djahanbani was related to the shah, and so did not criticize his regime 'for the sake of maintaining his parasitic existence'.

Four generals, including the SAVAK chief Nasiri, were executed first with minimal judicial formalities. There then followed the trial and execution of many military and civilian officials, including Prime Minister Hoveyda, chairman of the senate and speaker of the Majlis. The charges often included 'waging war against God' and 'waging war against the Hidden Imam'. The standard of the judicial procedures used may be gauged from Judge Khalkhali's public statement that no defence lawyers would be allowed in court 'unless the defendant is dumb', that is, unable to speak.

This revolutionary judicial procedure and anti-Americanism was as much as the radicals of all sides and their supporters agreed on, unsuspecting that their own turn would soon arrive. There were attacks on the press for not being sufficiently loyal to Islam or to the revolution, and almost daily clashes in the streets by secular leftist militants and Islamist gangs described as Hezbollah (Party of God). Such street clashes later became common also between Hezbollah and the Hojjatieh Society's supporters, an anti-Baha'i movement generally believed to have been encouraged by SAVAK which prayed for the imminent advent of the Hidden Imam, and which by implication regarded clerical rule as a usurpation of His government. The Baha'is were subjected to both official and unofficial harassment and persecution, their property being destroyed or confiscated, while several of them were hanged or faced the firing squad. They were excluded from schools and universities, and later their own informal institutions of higher education were also banned. The government's maximum charge against them was that the entire Baha'i community was a Russian-British-American-Israeli spy network; the minimum, that it was an illegal political party. Only during Mohammad Khatami's presidency (1997–2005) did they experience some relief, but Hojjatiyeh ideas became particularly powerful and influential in Mahmoud Ahmadinejad's presidency (2005 to the present).

Back in 1979, the masses were still loyal to Khomeini. Yet the collapse of the former regime led to the assertion of old provincial grievances, at first in Gonbad and the Turkaman area east of the Caspian, and in the Kurdish areas and later in Azerbaijan and among the Qashqa'i chiefs, all of which were, in time, put down. The Kurdish Democratic Party leaders went into exile in Europe; their leader, Abdorrahman Qasemlu, to be assassinated in Vienna in the late 1980s, for which the Islamists largely took the blame. In 1992, four Kurdish leaders were assassinated in the Mykonos restaurant in Berlin, the German court later finding agents of the Islamic Republic responsible.

The Marxist-Leninist Fada'iyan and the Islamic leftist Mojahedin were in opposition. The Tudeh leaders unreservedly supported Khomeini and the Islamists, but were generally unpopular because of their record under Mosaddeq and after the 1953 coup as well as their dependence on the Soviet Union. On the other hand, they were very well organized, had an effective propaganda machine and used their Soviet connection to their advantage. They penetrated and organized a secret military network in the regular army, the exposure of which by a Soviet defector played a major role in their downfall together with the Majority Fada'iyan, who had later dropped their opposition and were collaborating with the Tudeh. Meanwhile two religious parties had come into being: The Islamic Republican Party, patronized by Ayatollah Khomeini, and the Muslim People's Republican Party, which was close to the liberal Ayatollah Shariatmadari, a senior *marja'* in Qom, most of whose following was in his native Azerbaijan.

At the fall of the former regime, the Islamists, Marxist-Leninists and Mojahedin began to arm themselves. They felt highly insecure vis-à-vis each other and, no less, the regular army, which, though demoralized, was still largely intact but was quickly decapitated. Within a short period, an official paramilitary organization was created to defend the new regime against all comers: The Islamic Revolutionary Guards Corps, generally known as Pasdaran. Beginning with 5,000 young men, this force was to grow rapidly in size and sophistication to become the most powerful and influential military force in the service of the Islamic Republic, with considerable involvement in the production of goods and services.

At first the main Islamic campaigners were the Islamic Republican Party (IRP) and the Muslim People's Republican Party (MPRP). The IRP was the Islamist party par excellence, and was led by clerics close to Ayatollah Khomeini, notably Ayatollah Seyyed Mohammad Beheshti and Hojjatoleslams Ali

Akbar Rafsanjani, Mohammad Javad Bahonar and Seyyed Ali Khamenei. In the few years that the party remained active it played a pivotal role in the politics of the Islamic Republic, but dissolved itself in 1987 when, in effect, it had become one with the government. Another influential Islamist grouping was the pro-regime Coalition of Islamic Societies, a conservative organization with its main base in the upper layers of the bazaar community. There was also a radical, small but very active 'Mojahedin of the Islamic Revolution' (not to be confused with the old Mojahedin), which, later in the 1990s, was to change its attitude and back liberalizing reforms.

The MPRP was in its broader political outlook not far from the Freedom Movement, a Muslim organization with democratic tendencies. It had its strongest following in Shariatmadari's ethnic Azerbaijan, and its fortunes were largely bound up with his position. Shariatmadari fell when, in 1982, Sadeq Qotbzadeh confessed to planning a military coup which would have involved killing Khomeini. Rightly or wrongly, Shariatmadari was implicated in the plot.

Qotbzadeh, Abolhasan Banisadr and Ebrahim Yazdi were former members of Bazagan's Freedom Movement who, in the late 1970s, had become Khomeiniites and had served the Ayatollah himself while he was in Paris. Yazdi was to fall out with Khomeini and become leader of the Freedom Movement after Bazargan's death in 1995, and is currently serving an eight-year jail sentence, though as of 2012 he is under surveillance pending his appeal. Banisadr, as noted above and further below, was to become the Islamic Republic's first president and to end up in exile in July 1981. Qotbzadeh was to face the firing squad following his confession to have tried to organize a coup in September 1982.

The dichotomy of a republic based on religious principles is most evident from the constitution of the Islamic Republic, which was finally approved in mid-November 1979 and put to popular vote shortly afterwards. It included features and principles that closely resembled the former constitution, which had been a product of the Constitutional Revolution, as well as precepts and provisions which were entirely Islamist: separation of executive (then including a president and a prime minister), legislative and judicial powers, but headed by a virtually unelected supreme arbiter.

From the outset, Bazargan's government had begun to try and return the country's economy and administration back to a normal state, a 'step by step' policy. It soon became clear that theirs was a government with much responsibility and little power and authority, and it did not have Khomeini's confidence. To hard-line Islamists Bazargan represented 'American Islam'; to most of the leftists he was a 'liberal' (for them as well as for the Islamists, a highly pejorative term), a 'friend of America' and 'representative of the well-to-do bourgeoisie'. Seldom in history has a near-powerless man been given a task as hopeless and thankless as Bazargan's.

Hostage-taking

On 4 November 1979, a group of students describing themselves as 'Muslim student followers of the Line of Imam [Khomeini]' attacked and occupied the American embassy and took its diplomats hostage. Bazargan had recently met America's national security advisor Zbigniew Brzezinski in Algiers, raising further typically Iranian suspicions (arising from disenchantment) among large numbers of all colours and creeds that the revolution had been sold to America from the start, perhaps by Ayatollah Khomeini himself in Paris. On 22 October, the shah had been admitted into the United States to follow the treatment of his cancer, and Khomeini had denounced America as the Great Satan.

The Line-of-Imam students eventually kept fifty-two of the diplomats hostage. Along with other demands, they required that

America return the shah to Iran 'to be tried and executed'. Within a few days Khomeini endorsed their action and Bazargan's government resigned. The efforts of many, in the meantime, including Yazdi and Qotbzadeh, to have the hostages released were frustrated, and secret military action by America for their release met with bad luck and the loss of eight American soldiers in a desert storm in north-eastern Iran.

Khomeini's endorsement led to renewed public frenzy comparable to the early days of the victory of the revolution. Everyone, modern and traditional, Marxist-Leninist and Islamist, rich and poor (except the few 'liberals') rallied to the anti-American battle cry. Many who had begun to be disillusioned by the decline of mass fervour and spread of political conflict found a new channel through which to steam off their revolutionary zeal anew. Once again the country was united over what it did *not* like, in this case America.

It was in this atmosphere of fury and frenzy on the one hand, and fear of persecution on the other, that the draft constitution (drawn up by a constituent assembly known as the Assembly of Experts) was put to vote, making it impossible for its opponents and critics such as Bazargan to present their views. Not even the Marxist-Leninists raised any objection to the rule or guardianship of the (Shi'ite) jurist, (Velayat-e Faqih), now that the struggle against American imperialism was in full sway. The Tudeh, the Fadai'iyan, the Mojahedin and others came out in full support of the hostage-taking, while writers and intellectuals were busy collecting signatures in its support.

The hostages were eventually released on 20 January 1981 after 444 days of captivity, the day Ronald Reagan formally became president, after the Iranian-American Algiers Accord of 19 January. It took so long partly because of its usefulness for manipulating the domestic situation, and partly as a result of differences among rival factions on the terms and conditions of the release. This concluded the first phase of the Islamic revolution, the second phase being completed with the fall of president Banisadr in June 1981. In the meantime, the shah had been invited by President Sadat of Egypt to Cairo for hospital treatment and died there in July 1980.

The fall of Banisadr

The successful referendum for the Islamic constitution was followed by presidential and parliamentary elections. The IRP won the parliamentary majority, but Abolhasan Banisadr forty-four was elected president with Khomeini's implicit support. In his political views Banisadr was closer to Bazargan than the Islamists, although he had shown himself to be committed to Khomeini to remain in the mainstream of revolutionary politics. Hence from the word go the IRP parliamentary majority began to restrict his choices and decisions.

While Khomeini was naturally inclined towards the IRP, the overtures of Banisadr towards Mojahedin made him both suspicious and angry, and he eventually decided to abandon him, since the Mojahedin, though not yet confronting him, were opposed to the IRP and refused to lay down their arms. It may look confusing that the Islamists and Mojahedin should be at loggerheads, but this was due to their different political backgrounds and ideology as well as the requirements of power struggles, the wish of every party to come on top.

In June 1981 the chips were finally down, and in a highly charged atmosphere, the Majlis, prompted by Khomeini, impeached and dismissed Banisadr in his absence. On 20 June 1981, the Mojahedin led a public revolt which resulted in armed conflict and many casualties. They were joined by all leftist groups except the Tudeh and 'Majority' Fadai'iyan who, following a split in their organization, held to the general Tudeh line of supporting the regime, while the 'Minority' Fada'iyan opposed it. Eight days later a powerful bomb exploded in the

IRP headquarters, killing more than seventy of its leading figures including Ayatollah Beheshti. Two months later another bomb exploded in the presidential office, killing Banisadr's replacement, President Raja'i, and Prime Minister Bahonar. It was strongly suspected that both explosions were the work of the Mojahedin, though they did not confirm it themselves. The Islamists reacted by unleashing a reign of terror, which was countered by Mojahedin assassinating Islamist politicians and religious figures. For a while the situation began to resemble an urban civil war, while the war with Iraq was still raging at the front. Meanwhile, in July 1981, Banisadr and Mas'ud Rajavi (the Mojahedin leader) managed to escape to Paris, where they formed a coalition which later fell apart when the Mojahedin entered an agreement with Iraq.

The Islamic Republic

As soon as Banisadr fell, the Islamic revolution, that is, the process of Islamization of social and political life, rapidly reached its completion. From then on all women (and not just public employees) had to observe the Islamic dress code. A massive purge of government offices began, making redundant many non-Islamist employees and expelling the higher civil servants, in some cases confiscating their property as well. This was conducted largely by Islamist teenage boys sitting in government offices who, typically, would just enter in a printed expulsion form the name of the civil servant, describe his position in the department as 'agent of the hated Pahlavi regime' and his offence as 'looting the public treasury'. There was no charge, no hearing and no defence. This was followed by a thorough purge of the universities by the Council of Cultural Revolution, since most of the students and professors, whether leftist, liberal or non-political, did not conform to the political and educational requirements of Islamist ideology.

That is how the *Islamic* revolution, which had been in process since the hostage-taking of November 1979, was accomplished. Thus began the first major wave of emigration of many disillusioned, frightened and dispossessed Iranians from their country, mainly to the West, and the modern Iranian diaspora came into being.

The Iran–Iraq war (1980–8)

Meanwhile the war that had been started by Iraq in September 1980 and had further boosted the position of radical Islamists, was to rage for almost eight years before Iran accepted the UN ceasefire resolution in July 1988. The Iranian revolution had made a profound impression on Muslim peoples almost everywhere and notably among the Shi'a majority in Iraq, who had long been treated as second-class citizens by their rulers, and there was talk of exporting Iran's revolution to neighbouring countries. Saddam Hussein, who had been deeply wounded by his 1975 surrender to the shah, now believed to have both the pretext and the power to renounce the Algiers accord, overrun the Shatt al-Arab waterway, annex the Khuzistan province and hopefully bring down the Islamist regime. He was a ferocious secular dictator, despised by most Iraqis, including the Shi'a majority, bent on rapid industrialization and militarization of his country and hoping to become master of the Persian Gulf region.

Saddam's undeclared invasion at first caught the Iranians by surprise, resulting in the ruin and loss of the border town of Khorramshahr. In May 1982 the town was to be liberated by Iranians, compelling Saddam to begin to sue for peace. Many young and old volunteers joined the Revolutionary Guards, a new and virtually selfless paramilitary force called Basij ('Mobilization') was launched and the regular army managed to demonstrate its loyalty to the revolutionary regime by effective participation in the war. The heroism and quest for martyrdom of the Basiji boys became a daily event.

The Islamic Republic turned down Saddam's peace moves, and the Saudi-led plan of offering substantial reparations and indemnity to Iran in June 1982 was rebuffed. 'War, War until Victory' became a regular official slogan as long as the war lasted. Realizing that he was in a no-win situation, Saddam began sending rockets to Iranian cities and using chemical weapons in battlefields, even among civilians, the most notorious example of which was the massacre in Halabja of Iraqi Kurds who were suspected of sympathizing with Iran. In March 1984 Iranians captured parts of the Majnun Islands, whose oilfields had economic as well as strategic value.

The war of attrition which began in 1984 was to go on for another four years, Iraq depending mainly on weapons and credit from its Arab and Western backers, while Iran pushed nationalist sentiments, revolutionary zeal and the Shi'ite cult of martyrdom to their utmost limits to compensate for its complete isolation.

The economy being largely geared to the war machine, shortages of consumer goods were inevitable and a system of rationing was introduced, which, although far from ideal from the public's point of view, was on the whole managed well. There was a sustained decline in the average standard of living, and in general, overall economic performance deteriorated.

In 1986, Iran's secret contacts and deals with the United States were exposed, and later became known as the Iran-Contra affair or Irangate. The main deal was the secret sale of limited US military equipment via Israel to Iran, in exchange for Iran's help in getting American hostages released in Lebanon. The extreme Islamists who exposed the deal were tried and executed.

If political critics of the regime were weak and suppressed, it was different for those in the business community, who increasingly disliked the government's pushing statist and egalitarian legislation through the parliament in which it had a majority.

This was increasingly met with resistance from the conservative Guardians Council, the constitutional body which vetted parliamentary legislation to ensure that it was consistent with Islamic and constitutional laws. Thus a confrontation ensued between the two most powerful faces of modern Islamism: the radical, statist and egalitarian, and the conservative, capitalistic and market-oriented. This had already taken an institutional form in the split, in 1987, of the radical Association of Militant Clerics from the conservative and influential Society of Militant Clergy.

Khomeini sided with the radicals over the case of a bill which the Guardians Council had rejected, saying that the absolute guardianship of the supreme leader gives him the power temporarily to suspend *shari'a* laws in the interest of Islam. There followed a few days of legal and political argument until it was decided to give this power to a permanent Expediency Council which would take the final decision in such cases.

Meanwhile the war was still raging, and in February 1986 Iranians took the Al-Faw Peninsula in a notable victory. This was another moment the Iranians missed for making triumphal peace. However, with virtually every power supporting Saddam Hussein in any way they could, by mid-1988 the Iranians began to realize that they had practically taken on the whole world, and that if there was to be any victory in that war, it would not be theirs.

On 3 July 1988, the US navy cruiser USS *Vincennes*, whose captain later admitted that it had been in Iranian territorial waters at the time, shot down an Iranian passenger airliner with the loss of 290 passengers and crew. Nevertheless, the Iranians accepted UN Resolution 598 late in July 1988, and by 20 August the ceasefire came into effect. It was not a defeat, but it negated eight years of optimism and the promise of definite victory to the Iranian people.

The war did not quite end at that point. After the Iranian government had accepted the ceasefire resolution, the Mojahedin who, backed by Saddam Hussein, had been camping over the border in Iraq for a couple of years, launched an attack on Iran. At first they benefited from Iraqi air cover, but the US apparently advised Saddam Hussein to stop this. Subsequently the Mojahedin forces were routed, leaving many casualties and prisoners.

Montazeri resigns

At first it looked as if revolutionary fervour had died down, but not for long. The British author Salman Rushdie's book *Satanic Verses*, published in September 1988, was seen by Muslims everywhere as a great insult to Islam and the Prophet Mohammad. Ayatollah Khomeini issued a *fatva* (or *fatwa*) – an edict the observation of whose content is incumbent on all believers – sentencing Rushdie to death, which led to the deterioration of Anglo-Iranian relations just as they were about to improve. (An exchange of ambassadors took place about ten years later, when President Khatami's reformist government declared that it would not implement or encourage the sentence.)

On 29 March 1989, Ayatollah Montazeri, Khomeini's deputy and heir-designate, resigned his position. It came in the wake of Khomeini's direct attack on him, following the leaking of three letters – two of them to Khomeini himself and the third to some judicial and security authorities – protesting against the killing in jails, the figures estimated at between 2,000 and 5,000, of the regime's opponents. In fact it was the climax of a long-running conflict of opinion between the two leaders.

But it was the leaking of these letters outside Iran that led to Khomeini's direct attack on Montazeri and which provoked his resignation, for otherwise Montazeri had seldom made a secret of his unhappiness with some of the regime's arbitrary and illiberal decisions. From this point on, Montazeri was to continue his criticism of the regime and essentially advocate democratic government, a position that often resulted in his censure and house arrest, until his death in 2009, surviving Ayatollah Khomeini by twenty years.

Ayatollah Khomeini passed away on 3 June 1989, little more than two months after Montazeri's political disgrace. He had been suffering from chronic heart disease, and his death occurred as a consequence of a series of heart attacks. He was eighty-nine. Khomeini's funeral drew millions of mourners to the streets, and there was such a frenzy that some of them died or were injured in the process. Iran, a country of martyrs and mourners, had not seen such a vast, passionate and emotional funeral procession in living memory.

6

Post-Khomeini Iran

The Islamic Republic in Iran has undergone significant changes in all spheres of life since 1989, but the major domestic and foreign problems have remained, and some have even intensified. Four distinct political factions emerged within the Islamist fold: fundamentalist, conservative, pragmatist and reformist. The regime went from a relatively moderate pragmatist-conservative presidency under Hashemi Rafsanjani (1989–97) to a reformist-pragmatist one led by Mohammad Khatami (1997–2005), for a time raising hopes of steady and peaceful reform and development. These hopes ended as the fundamentalist-conservative presidency began, led by Mahmoud Ahmadinejad (2005–present), and the eventual opening of a seemingly unbridgeable rift within the Islamist movement itself. Once the reformers were politically eliminated, however, the ruling powers broke up into a number of new factions, each once again struggling for power.

Back in 1988, the ceasefire, followed by Khomeini's demise the following year, apparently initiated a new era of peace and reconstruction, but the short-termist nature of the Iranian state and society did not allow for long-term, irreversible progress. In April 1989 a constitutional review conducted by the Assembly of Experts laid it down that the supreme leader did not also have to be a *marja'*, or source of religious emulation. While providing further proof that Iran was not a theocracy in any precise sense of the term, at the same time it brought a landmark change in the Shi'a hierarchy, now that a less prominent cleric's pronouncements could be regarded as law, although in later years Khamenei was elevated to the position of a *marja'*. This emphasized the political aspect of the system over the religious.

The constitutional review also removed the office of prime minister and thus created an executive presidency, where the president combines the functions of prime minister as well as president. This enabled Rafsanjani to be the first man to stand for, and win, the presidential election in August 1989.

SEYYED ALI KHAMENEI

Born in Mashhad in 1939, Seyyed Ali Khamenei studied in the seminaries of Mashhad and Najaf, in Iraq, before settling in Qom in 1958 where he studied under Ayatollah Khomeini, among others. He was involved in the revolt of June 1963 and was imprisoned. For the rest of the 1960s and the 1970s leading up to the revolution, he spent time teaching and preaching, interspersed by terms of imprisonment and banishment due to his Islamist revolutionary activities. He was Khomeini's close confidant and became Tehran's Friday Prayer leader, and in October 1981 was elected president of Iran. Shortly before that, Khamenei narrowly escaped an assassination attempt, which led to serious injury, and he lost the use of his right arm. Khamenei helped guide the country during the Iran–Iraq War in the 1980s, and developed close ties with the now powerful Revolutionary Guards. As president, he had a reputation for being deeply interested in the military, the budget and administrative details. After the Iraqi army was pushed back from Iran in 1982, Khamenei became one of the main opponents of Khomeini's decision to counter-invade into Iraq, an opinion Khamenei shared with the then prime minister Mir-Hossein Mousavi – with whom he would later conflict over the result of the 2009 presidential election protests – but their counsel did not prevail. After the demise of Ayatollah Khomeini, the Assembly of Experts elected Khamenei his successor as supreme leader in June 1989.

From pragmatism to reformism

Rafsanjani was an old devotee of Khomeini, a Majlis speaker as well as war leader in the 1980s. He was nevertheless a pragmatist or realist as far as both domestic and international politics were concerned. For example, after the acceptance of the UN cease-fire resolution in July 1988, he said: 'The main thing is that we can stop making enemies without reason because of this new move.' This was reflected in the helping hand he gave in the release of Western hostages held in Lebanon.

Rafsanjani took over the executive running of a country that was ravaged by war and revolutionary struggle, had lost much of the inflated optimism of the late 1970s and early 1980s and was isolated in the region and in the eyes of the world. The revolution had not delivered the moon, and the war had ended without conquest or compensation. Instead, the economy was in very poor shape and public morale was at its lowest since the late 1970s. Between the late 1970s and 1990, the standard of living had declined by one half, as a result of the steady fall in oil prices and the considerable rise in the population growth rate of up to 3.6 per cent.

Meanwhile, the high cost of the war had left little room for investment, while both war and revolution had led to a flight of financial as well as human capital. Inflation and unemployment rates were high, money was scarce and foreign borrowing was extremely difficult due to the country's isolated position internationally.

These were the circumstances in which Rafsanjani and his team launched their first Five-Year Plan, trying to moderate government economic supremacy and relax some of the heavy restrictions on the market. Yet the sudden opening up of the economy to the outside world led, among other things, to short-term debts of between $20 and $30 billion, which, as indicated, could not be repaid by international borrowing. Notwithstanding his 'dual containment policy' vis-à-vis Iran and Iraq, President Clinton might have adopted a less punitive approach towards Iran had it been allowed by pro-Israeli lobbies and the Congress.

Meanwhile, as oil prices were still as low as around $15 to $20 per barrel, and so not generating sufficient revenues, the government and its licensees began to sell crude oil over and above the OPEC quota, sometimes for as little as $8 per barrel. Thus high foreign debts, shortage of foreign credit, erratic changes in the foreign exchange regime and the rate of exchange, among other factors, impelled the government to discontinue some of its trade liberalization policies from the mid-1990s. The activities of giant and virtually autonomous foundations or *bonyad*s were also unhelpful to the process of economic policy. According to an extensive study, these foundations used their power to redirect the privatization of state enterprises from the private sector to themselves. This was a foretaste of the Revolutionary Guards' military industrial complex which in recent years has been the strongest sector of the economy.

Rafsanjani also had to face the growing opposition of the fundamentalists, who opposed his softer approach to foreign relations as well as towards the private sector. 'Death to the capitalist' was a regular slogan in their street demonstrations, leaving little doubt as to who 'the capitalist' was, considering Rafsanjani's large personal business concern. Almost at the opposite end of the spectrum were the complaints of the growing reformist faction who, through their influential journals, began to look like an Islamist social democratic movement. By 1995, two years before the end of Rafsanjani's second term, a considerable amount of economic reconstruction had been achieved. But in the remaining two years, he abandoned his original strategic initiatives and lacked a clear line for moving forward.

While there had been relatively less political turmoil since Rafsanjani's election to the presidency, there had been little political development. He later showed that he favoured gradual political development, but his pragmatic style would not allow him to risk it too far beyond mentioning 'the rehearsal of democracy' from time to time. Regarding the position of women and young people, he made two celebrated gaffes, perhaps deliberately just to see how far he could go. He once said that if 'ladies' did not like the Islamic dress code, they could wear two-piece suits instead. Facing the immediate outcry of conservatives and fundamentalists, he explained that he had meant they should wear a chador over the suit as well. On the other occasion, he said that young men and women could enter a loving relationship through the Shi'a institution of temporary marriage, upon verbal agreement. This time even some modern middle-class women objected. The president then backtracked, explaining that he meant they should go through a legal marriage ceremony.

Thus Rafsanjani's economic policy was in retreat; his foreign policy had reached a stalemate, despite improved relations with the main regional players and the beginnings of a dialogue with EU countries (especially Germany and France), largely because of the continuing US–Iranian stand-off and the opposition of the other three factions – reformist, fundamentalist and now also conservative – to his government. In particular, the conservatives, who had supported Rafsanjani for a few years, were now looking towards his replacement by one whom they could truly call their own. All the signs strongly indicated that the conservative candidate would win the 1997 presidential election, hardly anyone suspecting a highly unpredictable, though historically familiar, Iranian overturn of fortunes and refutation of normal predictions.

The rise and decline of Islamic reformism

On 23 May 1997 in the Islamic Republic's seventh presidential election Seyyed Mohammad Khatami won a landslide victory.

Even more encouraging than the sixty-nine per cent of the votes perhaps was the great enthusiasm with which most of the public, especially young people and women, both participated in and celebrated the victory.

SEYYED MOHAMMAD KHATAMI

Khatami, then fifty-four, had read Western philosophy and education at two universities before attending the seminary in Qom and qualifying as a cleric. He already had two books and several articles to his name, but was little known among the general public. He had been a minister under Mousavi as well as Rafsanjani, and was admired by the elite for his virtual ending of book censorship as minister of Guidance and Islamic Culture, especially as, when the pressure had got too much, he had resigned his office rather than change his policy. His pleasant looks, charming smile, sartorial neatness and, above all, fluent speech were important vote-winners. His talk of the rule of law, tolerance, the development of civil society and the rights and welfare of women and young people struck a chord with educated people both modern and traditional, especially the young and women: before the election, a woman fully clad in ski gear, at a ski resort north of Tehran, said in English to a British TV reporter: 'All women love Khatami!'

Having already taken important political, social, educational and cultural strides, women were now ready to take their efforts to higher levels for more rights and greater equality, especially before the law. Many if not most of the young were first-time voters, had no memory of the revolution and were looking for jobs and social and cultural opportunities. At the level of the political and intellectual elite, both the old radicals, who now made up the bulk of the reformists, and 'the religious intellectuals' had been advocating reform through their press, books and meetings, which mainly influenced the young people.

Mohammad Khatami. (Source: Copyright World Economic Forum, Remy Steinegger, via Wikimedia Commons)

Of special significance was Khatami's and his supporters' great emphasis on the rule of law. In this, they were explicitly mindful of the legacy of the Constitutional Revolution a century before, and its long-forgotten but most fundamental programme of abolishing arbitrary rule and establishing a government based in law. A certain amount of lawless behaviour still prevailed, not least in the treatment of peaceful political dissidents, who would sometimes be dragged from their homes, physically and mentally abused and brought to television to confess and recant, and who sometimes died in custody. Such practices did not entirely cease under Khatami, but the scale of them was considerably reduced: most of the arrests were now made following a legal procedure, and Khatami always condemned official lawless behaviour whenever it was suspected. Still, given Khatami and the reform movement's acute and frank awareness of the country's long tradition of arbitrary rule – Khatami often saying that 'arbitrary rule and chaos are two sides of the same coin' – the question of the rule of law went far beyond that, the pitch going so high that Khamenei himself emphasized it in his public speeches, saying more than once that no one, including himself, was above the law.

Khatami's liberalization policies restricting censorship and allowing greater cultural freedoms met with increasing resistance by his opponents, and by the time he had reached the fourth year of his first term, he and the reformist movement had already lost significant ground. However, the growing conflict and disillusionment within the reformist camp began to emerge through his second term (2001–5).

On Khatami's first election in 1997, the reformists and their supporters were highly optimistic about the prospects for reform, but events proved them to have been too hopeful. They had won a landslide victory, in which Rafsanjani had played an effective role by preventing vote-rigging. They enjoyed the support of women, students and the young in particular. Apart from their own organizations, a considerable number of prominent modern Islamic political theorists and 'religious intellectuals' were campaigning for political and religious reform. Rafsanjani and his Servants of Reconstruction party also gave them support, although, as the movement began to turn more to the left, they attacked and alienated Rafsanjani at a time when they most needed his support.

The reformists also enjoyed critical support from the fellowship of various groups and individuals who were now dubbed as the Melli-Mazhabis. Best described as religious democrats or religious Mosaddeqites, their strongest organization was Bazargan's old Freedom Movement, which now, after his death, was being led by Ebrahim Yazdi, who had been an old hand in the party and Bazargan's foreign minister after the revolution and, despite his advanced age, has since been in and out of prison. Because of their relatively long history, their religious commitment along with a commitment to parliamentary democracy, and their association with Mosaddeq's legacy, the Freedom Movement and other Melli-Mazhabis were qualitatively important. At the same time, these groups began to attract the attention of a sizeable number of the young who were warming up to Mosaddeq's memory. This new-found popularity of the Melli-Mazhabis upset not just the radical fundamentalists who long before had described their politics as 'liberal' and their religious attitude as 'American Islam', but also the conservative establishment.

Such was the show of support for the reform movement early after Khatami's election in May 1997. Yet they tended to underrate their opponents and the social, economic, political and military forces they could muster. Despite their serious electoral setback, the conservative establishment was far from beaten. They had the Majlis majority (until the year 2000 – see below), the Council of Guardians, the Expediency Council, the Assembly of Experts and the Judiciary; they largely controlled the bazaar as well as the *bonyad*s, the Revolutionary Guards and the regular army. Radio and television were under the command of the supreme leader, who was then following a centrist line but was more inclined towards the conservative establishment.

The reformists also faced the hostility of the fundamentalists. Although the latter did not as yet have a significant social base, they nevertheless controlled some important newspapers such as *Keyhan*, and could easily organize street gangs, which attacked authorized demonstrations by students and Khatami supporters. Khatami was later criticized for not having completely fulfilled his election promises (even though experience had impelled him to make fewer promises in his 2001 re-election), but it is unlikely that, against the active opposition of his opponents, he could have achieved much more than he did, short of a violent clash with them, which he would not enter upon, nor would he win even if he did.

Along with concepts such as 'rule of law' and 'civil society', a central ideal that began to be hotly debated was democracy. Was Islam compatible with democracy, and, if so, should the Islamic Republic be reformed to become one? The religious intellectuals had made a beginning with this debate under Rafsanjani, but it was during the Khatami years that it became a central issue. The less radical writers argued that democracy was possible even within the terms of the existing constitution; others believed that it would be possible with some significant changes to the constitution. Both the secular fundamentalists and the Islamic fundamentalists argued that Islam and democracy were incompatible. Some authorities such as Ayatollah Montazeri argued that the concept of Guardianship had been misapplied, and that, if rightly interpreted, it would be consistent with democratic government.

However, democracy and whether or not it was compatible with Islam remained the central issue. Abdolkarim Soroush along with other reformist religious thinkers made use of modern hermeneutics – which in religious studies and social philosophy is the study of the theory and practice of interpretation – to argue that the traditional readings of the Qur'an and Traditions were not necessarily the only possible or acceptable versions of the texts. Having rejected any and all conceptions of an Islamic ideology, he went on to argue that proper readings of the principal sources show that there can be democracy in an Islamic society.

Hasan Yousefi Eshkevari, the liberal cleric who was to be defrocked and imprisoned for several years, was another tireless contributor to the debate on 'the paradox of Islam and democracy'. There were three tendencies in the Muslim world, he said: those who 'considered democracy as permissiveness'; others who preferred 'liberal democracy in its Western form'; and a third tendency, which saw no contradiction between religion and democracy.

It was this third theory that Khatami was publicly advocating. He did not claim that the existing regime quite answered to that description. But, often emphasizing that 'democracy is a process, not a programme', he maintained that it was possible to promote it through a continuous process. It was this attitude which worried his traditionalist opponents the most, and especially the extremists among them.

On 21 November 1998, the people of Iran were stunned by the official announcement that Daryush Foruhar, the veteran dissident and labour minister in Bazargan's cabinet, had been viciously murdered together with his wife Parvaneh Eskandari – also a veteran Mosaddeqite activist – at their home in Tehran. Within the next twenty days the bodies of two dissident writers were found and identified, having been beaten and strangled. The deaths shortly became known as serial killings or chain murders. Tehran was gripped with horror, and fear spread everywhere that many intellectuals and reformist activists were on the killers' hit list.

It was widely believed that the murders were not just intended to terrorize reformist activists and intellectuals, but that they were part of a plot to force Khatami to resign. There had been a number of highly suspicious deaths, mainly of writers and intellectuals, for a number of years, perhaps the most celebrated being Ahmad Tafazzoli, a world-famous professor of ancient Iranian languages at the University of Tehran. Early in January 1999, less than a month after the two latest killings, the ministry of intelligence announced that they had uncovered the gang of murderers, and that they belonged to their own ministry. Although the revelation was shocking, it also brought quick relief to the community since the supreme leader had approved of the exposure. Sa'id Emami, a senior official of the ministry of intelligence, and a number of ministry officials were arrested and charged with the killings. It was later announced that Emami had committed suicide in jail. The others were sentenced to up to ten years in prison at their final appeal hearing. The victims' families boycotted the judicial process, arguing that there must be a search for those who had been behind the killings.

Dominated by conservatives, the judiciary assumed an executive role in trying to stem the tide of reformism. It was the judiciary's closure of *Salam*, the oldest and most influential reformist daily, which sparked a student revolt subsequently known as the 9 July (18 *Tir*) disaster. On 8 July 1999 the students at Tehran University, who at the time generally supported Khatami's government, held a protest demonstration without official permission against the closure of *Salam*. That night, their halls of residence were attacked by a unit of riot police, reinforced by a band of vigilantes who assaulted any and all students resting in their rooms. It shook the government and the university authorities, who condemned it; the police denied having issued orders to the unit, and even the supreme leader publicly expressed deep regret at the incident. Not satisfied, the students reacted by holding angry demonstrations the next day, which quickly led to riots in which other dissidents also took part. It took four days of street clashes before calm returned.

The eyes of the reformists were fixed on the parliamentary elections for the sixth Majlis in February 2000, apparently believing that they could then legislate as they wished. They did win a landslide victory, but had reckoned without the veto power of the Guardians Council and, ultimately, the supreme leader himself. Indeed, the first test came very early in the day when they tried to reverse the restrictive press legislation of the previous parliament. Quickly, however, the reformist Majlis speaker Mehdi Karroubi presented the House with an edict by Ayatollah Khamenei, forbidding them from changing the law.

From then on, the conservative Guardians Council and Expediency Council vetoed virtually every government, or Majlis-initiated, bill that was unacceptable to the conservative establishment. The judiciary, on the other hand, went on using its power to contain reformist activists, including outspoken Majlis deputies, by various means such as arrest and imprisonment. Meanwhile the campaign of radical reformists against the election of Rafsanjani as a deputy for Tehran had largely resulted in his being alienated from the reform movement, thus narrowing its political base, although many of his Servants of Reconstruction party continued to support Khatami's government.

In time, the obstructive attitude of the Guardians Council, the Expediency Council and the judiciary became known as 'blockage' or 'blocking'. In effect, it revealed the inability of the executive and legislative branches – the two elected bodies – of government to implement policies to which the conservative establishment was vigorously opposed.

Notwithstanding all of that, Khatami's popularity did not wane, not least because this was clearly the work of his opposition. He was able to fulfil a number of his promises, but there were some that were frustrated by his powerful opponents. His main domestic achievements included a relatively more open society, a freer press than before, the emergence of a large number of NGOs, cultural advancement and more social (though not legal) rights and considerable social opportunities for women. In the meantime, many of the reformists had organized themselves in the Participation Front, a coalition of reformist organizations and activists.

Thus Khatami was elected for a second term in the presidential elections of 2001, even with an improved majority compared to the 1997 election. And he still had a large parliamentary majority. But this did not impair the ability and determination of the conservative establishment to block any executive decision or parliamentary legislation to which they had strong objections, or of the judiciary largely to assume the role that, before Khatami's election, the ministry of intelligence had played in trying to deter the activities of dissidents and reformists, the last major episode being the death in judicial custody of the Iranian-Canadian photojournalist Zahra Kazemi in July 2003. Khatami pressed for justice, but the judiciary dragged its feet until 2005 when Khatami's term came to an end and Mahmoud Ahmadinejad became president.

Meanwhile the Council of Guardians' 'blocking' continued. In order to face this and the judiciary, Khatami submitted his 'twin bills' to the Majlis, which would have enhanced the executive and legislative branches vis-à-vis the Guardians Council and the judiciary. If successful, this would have radically altered the power structure in favour of the reform movement. The bills passed through the parliament, but were predictably vetoed by the Council of Guardians.

Thus, less than two years before the end of his term, Khatami had reached a dead end. The more idealistic reformists had already coined the phrase 'passing Khatami by'. The dreaded consequence of the failure of the twin bills came in January 2004. Vetting the candidates for the forthcoming seventh Majlis elections, the Council of Guardians disqualified about 2,500 candidates, including eighty sitting reformist deputies. At first they threatened to resign en masse; then they staged a *bast* or sit-in in the Majlis building, hoping for a robust show of public support, which, however, did not materialize. The people's lack of enthusiasm – arising from unfulfilled expectations from Khatami – had already been demonstrated the year before by their quiet but highly effective boycott of the Tehran Council elections, resulting in a landslide conservative victory and the appointment of the little-known Mahmoud Ahmadinejad as mayor of Tehran. And in line with the decline in the reformists' popularity, in the February 2004 parliamentary elections the turnout was relatively low (about fifty-one per cent, but less than thirty per cent in Tehran) and the conservatives won a handsome victory, partly for this reason and partly because approved reformist candidates were a small minority.

Khatami had inherited many problems regarding regional and international relations, even though the arch-realist Rafsanjani had managed to resolve or reduce the scale of some of them. Khatami considerably improved Iran's relations with its neighbours, practically apologized for the hostage-taking affair,

Mahmoud Ahmadinejad. (Source: Agência Brasil via Wikimedia)

publicly praised American values and resolved the Salman Rushdie conflict, which coincided with the resumption of full diplomatic relations with Britain. Thus, while Khatami might have provided a golden opportunity for improved relations with the US, domestic forces in both countries worked against rapprochement: in Iran, the fundamentalists and hard-line conservatives; in America, the neocons and pro-Israeli lobbies.

The presidency of George W. Bush made a slow start in foreign affairs, and no significant changes occurred in the US Middle East policy. The drama began with the great shock of the 9/11 terrorist attacks, inaugurating the era of 'the war on terror'. President Bush said plainly in a speech that others could be either with or against America. Nevertheless, in the beginning it looked as if the American tragedy could act as a catalyst for improved relations between Iran and America. The almost spontaneous sympathy displayed by Iranians – there were even candlelit processions on the streets of Tehran – surprised American observers and commentators. Khatami sent a letter of condolence to Bush, and the mayor and fire chief of Tehran sent their condolences to their counterparts in New York. Apart from plain human emotion, Iranian good wishes arose from an intense dislike of the Taliban and their terrorist allies.

When the war in Afghanistan began in early October, relations improved further due to the logistical assistance the Iranians gave the American forces. For a couple of months it looked as if there would be opportunities for a rapprochement between the two countries. Whatever the motivation, however, Khatami received a blow from President Bush's axis-of-evil speech soon after the fall of the Taliban.

> Our . . . goal [said the president] is to prevent regimes that sponsor terror from threatening America or our friends and allies with weapons of mass destruction. Some of these regimes have been pretty quiet since September 11, but we know their true nature. North Korea is a regime arming with missiles and weapons of mass destruction, while starving its citizens. Iran aggressively pursues these weapons and exports terror, while an unelected few repress the Iranian people's hope for freedom. Iraq continues to flaunt its hostility toward America and to support terror.

In May 2003, through the Swiss ambassador in Iran, the Iranians seriously offered to negotiate with America, suggesting an agenda that included all of America's concerns, including Iran's nuclear programme. But while the State Department looked positively on the offer, the office of Vice-President Cheney dismissed it out of hand. Clearly, regime change was still at the top of the US agenda. The easily won, American-led invasion and occupation of Iraq in the previous month is likely to have encouraged the dismissal of Iran's offer of negotiations, but events were to prove that the fall of the Taliban and Saddam Hussein in fact benefited Iran rather than the West, since they rid Iran of two hostile neighbours while the West got entangled in long-term conflicts.

The beginnings of the nuclear programme went back at least to the 1970s, when the shah took some preliminary steps towards building a nuclear power plant. In 1995, Iran signed a contract with Russia to resume work on the partially complete Bushehr plant. In August 2002, a uranium-enrichment facility in Natanz and a heavy-water facility in Arak were discovered, which had not been reported to the International Atomic Energy Agency. At the time, Iran was not even required to inform the IAEA of the existence of the facilities, which were still under construction, but in the circumstances their discovery made the Iranians look suspicious.

Western powers said that uranium enrichment was aimed at nuclear armament, whereas the Iranian government kept insisting that it was a peaceful programme. Under the terms of the November 2004 Paris Agreement, Iran announced a temporary suspension of its uranium-enrichment programme, even though enrichment as such was not a violation of the Nuclear Proliferation Treaty. Iran described the suspension as a confidence-building measure for a short period while negotiations with the EU-3 (France, Germany and the UK) continued. It lasted just as long as Khatami was still in office.

Khatami's presidency had begun with high hopes, but ended with the apathy or frustration of many of his erstwhile supporters. Addressing Tehran University students on Student's Day in November 2004, he had to face a hostile crowd shouting, 'Khatami, you liar, shame on you.' When he went there again in 2007, the crowd were shouting, 'Here comes the people's saviour.' It was a small reminder that Iranian 'short-termist' habits were still very much in place.

The turn of fundamentalism

In June 2005, seven candidates stood for the presidency, five of them regarded as possible winners, the favourites being the pragmatist Rafsanjani followed by the reformist Karroubi. Mahmoud Ahmadinejad, who had become mayor of Tehran as a result of a twelve per cent turnout in the city council elections, was closest to the fundamentalists and was believed to be the least likely to win. Yet he managed to attract many votes due to his modest lifestyle and his promise 'to bring the oil money to the ordinary people's dinner table' – Ahmadinejad came second to Rafsanjani in the first round, with Karroubi in the third place.

The run-off therefore was between Rafsanjani and Ahmadinejad, although Karroubi protested that his real votes in the first round had been higher than Ahmadinejad's. However that may be, in the event Ahmadinejad won 61.7 per cent of the votes against Rafsanjani's humiliating 35.9 per cent. Sensing the serious possibility of an Ahmadinejad victory, in the contest the reformists and Melli-Mazhabi leaders and the secularists – most of whom had boycotted the first round – rallied behind Rafsanjani. Too late! In fact, it was in the run-off that large numbers of ordinary people voted for Ahmadinejad, viewing him as one of their own.

MAHMOUD AHMADINEJAD

Mahmoud Ahmadinejad was born on 28 October 1956 in a village near Garmsar, eighty-two miles south-east of Tehran. In 1957, the family moved to the Narmak district of Tehran in search of better economic conditions. Ahmadinejad held no interest in politics as a young boy. He went to primary and secondary school in Tehran, and entered Iran's University of Science and Technology in 1975, receiving his undergraduate degree in civil engineering in 1979. It was as a university student that he became politically active and partici-pated in the February revolution, and during the war with Iraq he occupied a role as a fighter in various capacities. In 1986, Ahmadinejad began his master's programme in engineering at the university, and in 1989 he joined its academic staff. In 1993, he was also appointed governor-general of the newly established north-west province of Ardebil and served there for four years. He was removed in 1997 by Khatami as part of the general policy of replac-ing conservative staff with reformists. Ahmadinejad received his doctorate in transportation engineering in 1997 and returned to his teaching position at the university. In 2003, he was appointed mayor of Tehran by the city council. As mayor, Ahmadinejad began repeal-ing reforms put in place by the reformists, and imposed new cultural restrictions favoured by conservatives and fundamentalists. He was still mayor in 2005 when he was elected president.

After his inauguration in August 2005, one of Ahmadinejad's first acts as president was his speech at the UN General Assembly in September, in which he impressed his audience more with his messianic and apocalyptic sentiments than with his diplomatic skills. As a Holocaust-denier, he convened an international Holocaust-denial conference not long afterwards. Added to Ahmadinejad's simple and direct approach to politics was his apparent belief in the imminent advent of the Hidden Imam. In mid-2008, he even made a habit of saying that Iran was being run by the Imam, despite the fact that He was still hidden from view.

Back in August 2005, Ahmadinejad ordered the seals on the uranium-enrichment unit in Isfahan to be removed. The new Iranian negotiator was Ali Larijani, former head of the radio and TV network (*Seda o Sima*), who was not a radical fundamentalist but a member of the conservative establishment. Early in February 2006, the Board of the IAEA voted to report Iran to the UN Security Council over its nuclear activities. All this time, the United States had said that Iran was secretly engaged in making nuclear weapons, while the EU predicted that Iran's acquisition of nuclear technology could result in weaponization. Iran, on the contrary, kept insisting that its programme was purely for peaceful – mainly medical and electricity-generating – purposes. In late February 2006, the then IAEA director Mohammad El-Baradei suggested a compromise, whereby Iran would not resort to industrial-scale enrichment and instead limit its programme to a small-scale pilot facility, and would import its nuclear fuel from Russia. Iran expressed interest in this compromise solution but the US rejected it, thus making it clear that their real objection was not just due to fear of weaponization but to Iran's acquisition of nuclear capability, which would make it potentially possible to weaponize over a relatively short period. Two months later, Ahmadinejad surprised most people when he made a spectacular TV announcement to the effect that Iran had successfully enriched uranium, which indeed she had.

Negotiations not having succeeded, a series of UN sanctions were applied, the first one in December 2006, a second in March 2007, a third in March 2008 and a fourth in June 2010.

The sanctions would have been a good deal tougher had it not been for the moderating influence of Russia and China, with whom Iran had good diplomatic and business relations. In the meantime, Larijani had given up his post as Iran's chief negotiator as a result of disagreements with Ahmadinejad. However, a most unexpected event over the nuclear dispute was the publication in November 2007 of the consensus of US intelligence agencies that Iran had since 2003 ceased efforts to make nuclear weapons. One American journalist described it as a 'pre-emptive surgical strike by the intelligence community against the [US] war party'.

In mid-October 2011, the US accused Iran of a plot to assassinate the Saudi ambassador to Washington, a charge which Iran vehemently denied and which some Western observers regarded as being somewhat far-fetched. Shortly afterwards, the new IAEA report implied that Iran might be aiming for weaponization.

These events led to a new wave of Western measures against Iran, including British sanctions against the Central Bank of Iran. This was followed by the Iranian parliament's decision to lower the level of diplomatic relations with Britain, which, on 29 November 2011, triggered an attack by three hundred mainly Basij students on the British embassy compound in Tehran. In response, Britain shut down the embassy and told Iranian diplomats in London to leave within forty-eight hours. Other Western sanctions included the American and EU boycott of the Central Bank of Iran and the EU boycott of Iranian oil, which could cut demand for Iranian oil by up to twenty per cent of total exports. Thus the sanctions had now been raised to a severe level, although the Iranian government continued to respond with defiance.

Ahmadinejad was still popular in the first few months of his presidency, but he did not have a faction of his own in the Majlis, instead receiving support from the new conservative-fundamentalist faction called the Principlists, a coalition of the two factions which soon began to show differences among its members. Much of the bazaar and modern business community still made up the main social base of the regime, but Ahmadinejad's appeal was directly to 'the people', and there came a time when he would hold the Majlis as well as his own ministerial colleagues responsible for the failure of his own policies. In 2011 he caused serious controversy – to the point of receiving public rebuke from the Revolutionary Guards as well – by disputing the extent of the parliament's constitutional powers.

Nowhere did his domestic policies more quickly and clearly yield negative results than with his top-priority objective of raising the ordinary people's standard of living, providing affordable housing for the masses and creating new jobs to reduce unemployment. With oil prices continuously soaring (at one stage, in 2008, peaking at $149 per barrel) he would have been well placed for achieving these goals if he had chosen more appropriate economic policies. His vision of increasing social welfare resembled traditional charitable alms-giving in an otherwise complex political economy.

Still, in the new Majlis the sum of conservatives, reformists and independents made up the majority, and this was reflected in the election of Ali Larijani in March 2008 to the speakership of parliament. Countrywide, the four principal tendencies that materialized after 1988 – conservative, pragmatist, reformist and fundamentalist – were still in place, there being a greater chance of either a conservative-fundamentalist or a reformist-pragmatist alliance when the lines were drawn. But it was clear that the conservative establishment was still the strongest single political force in the country. By 2011, the fundamentalist faction became increasingly alienated from the Ahmadinejad group over its differences with the supreme leader and its nationalist postures towards ancient Iran.

More newspapers were banned. Human rights and human-rights activists suffered more than they had before. Despite systematic harassment and imprisonment, women's rights activists continued their efforts, centred on the 'one million signatures' campaign led by a group of feminist activists for the abolition of discriminatory laws. Secular and modern women had long been complaining about the compulsory Islamic dress code imposed shortly after the revolution. However, legal discrimination against women – much of which had existed in the former regime too – upheld male superiority in matters concerning criminal justice, divorce, inheritance laws and custody of children, among other matters. On the other hand, both modern and traditional women managed to increase their participation in the educational process to the extent that they outnumbered male students at the universities. A large and increasing body of female doctors, dentists, lawyers, administrators and business owners and managers thus entered the labour market, enhancing the status of women in society and adding to their voice for social and cultural development. Yet the paradox remained, for example, that while a man who murdered another man was executed, one who murdered a woman would not be put to death because in the criminal justice system a woman counted as one half of a man.

By January 2009, Iran's gaze was firmly focused on the forthcoming presidential elections in June. The incumbent Ahmadinejad was the fundamentalist-conservative candidate, but the leader of the highly influential Islamic Coalition party said at the time that they supported him, despite disagreements with many of his policies, solely in order to stop the reformists. The reformist Mehdi Karroubi had already declared his candidacy.

Khatami had now become the secularists' as well as the reformists' favourite candidate, and was under great pressure to come forward. But he was reluctant, and told a person very close to him that even assuming he were allowed to be elected, the day after he would have to face a 15,000-strong, shroud-wearing, hard-line crowd of activists pouring into the streets against him. And when the person told him that he would have millions supporting him, he replied: 'Ah, but they wear miniskirts', and would be no match for the fundamentalists' street gangs. In the end he did step forward, but shortly afterwards, when the one-time radical prime minister Mir Hossein Mousavi became a candidate, Khatami stepped down in his favour. Finally Mohsen Rezaee, a centre-right ex-Revolutionary Guards leader and now general secretary of the Expediency Council, was the fourth and last candidate to be allowed by the Guardians Council to stand.

It quickly became clear that Mousavi and Ahmadinejad were the real contestants for the post. Throughout his first presidency, Ahmadinejad had repeatedly toured the country, addressed the provincial people saying that he was their servant, spent money on public goods they asked for and, latterly, handed out cash in underprivileged areas. Many professional observers believed that the result was too close to call. Almost all were certain that neither of the two would make it in the first round, and that one of them (more likely Mousavi) would win with a margin of a million or two in the run-off. Their supporters were out in the streets, but the excitement and optimism of the young men and women who supported Mousavi were most evident. In his TV debate with Mousavi, Ahamdinejad made vitriolic personal attacks, not least on such non-candidate personalities as Khatami and Rafsanjani.

The great schism

When by midnight on 12 June 2009 the polls closed, Mousavi declared that he believed he was the winner. The count however put Ahmadinejad far ahead with nearly twenty-five million votes, Mousavi second with fewer than fourteen million and the other two candidates with a few hundred thousand votes each. The opposition was shocked, and there was a public eruption in Tehran and in other major cities the like of which had not been seen since the closing days of the 1979 revolution. The supreme leader had congratulated Ahmadinejad immediately after the election results were declared. On 19 June, in his address after Friday Prayer, he defended the election results and rejected Mousavi's and Karroubi's call, backed by street demonstrators, for a rerun of the election. Finally, he said that further demonstrations would not be tolerated.

However, both Mousavi and his supporters persisted and the next day there were bigger demonstrations across the country, which led to reports of up to twenty deaths and an unknown number of injuries in Tehran alone. In particular, the death of a young woman, Neda Agha Soltan, became the worldwide symbol of the Iranian protest movement. Meanwhile, protesters had begun to shout *Allaho Akbar* (God is the Greatest) from the rooftops, as they had done in the last weeks of the February 1979 revolution, a stark déjà vu.

Strict measures were taken to restrict the use of the internet and SMS (text) messages, the activities of foreign reporters and access to foreign Persian broadcasts, especially the BBC and Voice of America. The regime accused the opposition of – perhaps unknowingly – being agents of America and Britain for leading a 'velvet revolution'. They in their turn accused the regime of having instigated a coup against the constitution. The mass demonstrations stopped for a while, but there were still pockets of protesters in the streets and the chant of *Allaho Akbar* continued at night.

It was a major turning point in the history of the Islamic Republic. This time the opposition was led not just by disenchanted secular students, but also by some of the leading figures of the Islamic Revolution who believed that the elections had been a sham. It was not only a crisis of authority but also of legitimacy. The Islamic Republic was split down the middle, not just in a contest but in a confrontation. Millions of people led by sizeable Islamist reformist forces appeared to be alienated from the system itself. The difference with 1979 was that not the whole of the society but a large part of it was confronting the state. Nevertheless, a serious split had occurred which would leave its marks on future developments.

The protest marches were to continue erratically until December 2009 when there was a further big clampdown against the dissidents. Green having been Mousavi's chosen campaign colour, the movement that sprang out of these events became known as the Green Movement or Green Wave. Meanwhile, a significant number of dissidents – estimates vary a great deal – had been killed in the streets as well as in custody by the Basij militia and police. A large number of former high officials had been interned and reportedly mistreated, a few publicly recanting, while others, notably the former deputy home minister Mostafa Tajzadeh, received long sentences. It was the first time that several leading Islamist reformist officials, many of whom had served under Khatami, were being punished for what they believed rather than what they had practised.

By 2011, the opposition complained that their political dispossession was complete: they could have neither non-elective jobs and positions nor elective ones. They pointed out that not even Mousavi's fourteen million declared votes in the 2009 presidential election counted for anything, and that the regime neither understood the country's problems nor was it able to run it.

The great change brought about by the schism was reflected in virtually every aspect of society, including the censorship of press and publications, arrest and trial of dissidents as well as students returning home from abroad and a ban on public meetings and demonstrations called by dissidents. For example, following the movements leading to the 2011 fall of the Tunisian and Egyptian presidents known as the Arab Spring, Mousavi and Karroubi, citing the relevant provisions of the constitution, applied to the authorities for permission to hold an open-air meeting for a show of solidarity with the Tunisian and Egyptian peoples.

The government responded by describing them as 'leaders of the sedition', putting them under strict house arrest and saying that 'the plot' had been hatched in the UK. Nevertheless, on 14 February many thousands of protesters (again, estimates vary greatly) came out onto the streets and were attacked by police and Basij, resulting in two deaths, several injuries and many arrests. Mousavi and Karroubi's close advisers had already been rounded up before the event. On 15 February, 222 of the 290 parliamentary deputies passed a resolution to put Mousavi and Karroubi on trial for sedition. This was followed by a noisy demonstration of about sixty of them in the parliament's main hall calling for the execution of the two leaders. Next day, Khatami and Rafsanjani's names were added to the list. Shortly afterwards, Mousavi and Karroubi were completely shut off from the outside world, being put under an even stricter house arrest, which stopped them from communicating with their supporters. Following that, in early March 2011, Rafsanjani withdrew his candidacy for re-election as chairman of the influential Assembly of Experts. It looked as if another round of the age-old Iranian 'politics of elimination' had been completed.

Yet there were serious arguments and conflicts among the Principlists as well. It has already been indicated that the government's parliamentary majority was a coalition of conservatives (the bigger party) and fundamentalists. But there were many, some severe, disagreements and dislikes between the two groups as well as within each. For example, it was fairly clear that Ali Larijani, speaker of the parliament, and Ahmad Tavakoli, a senior deputy and head of a parliamentary committee, both disliked Ahmadinejad and disagreed with some of his views and policies, and this was reflected in occasional arguments and quarrels between the president and parliament. Another senior conserva-tive deputy, Ali Motahhari, persistently held Ahmadinejad partly responsible for the events that followed the presidential election.

Three issues in particular were battled over in such verbal conflicts. First was the argument over the relative powers of the executive and the legislature, given that the Iranian constitution is based on the separation of powers. On a couple of occasions Ahmadinejad strongly implied that the legislature should assume a lower seat than the executive. This led to fierce reactions from some deputies and others, and not least from the head of the Revolutionary Guards, whose response was almost scornful. It showed that despite the Guards' well-known support for the Principlists, they were not committed to the person of the presi-dent, only to the supreme leader.

Another source of controversy surrounded Esfandiar Rahim Mashaei, head of the presidential office and closest to Ahmadinejad among his colleagues. Indeed, the Majlis declined to ratify his appointment as vice-president, which led to Ahmadinejad's giving him his present position. Mashaei, whom it was rumoured Ahmadinejad was grooming to become the next president, was a controversial figure among the Principlists, not least due to the emphasis he put on ancient pre-Islamic Persia and Iranian nationalism. In this, he was shadowed by the president himself. Hence actions such as the official borrowing of the Cyrus Cylinder from the British Museum to put on public display in Iran, and convening large international conferences on Iranian studies with some emphasis on the pre-Islamic ancient past. Further than that, some ulama and Principlist leaders were highly critical when Ahmadinejad declared his intention to visit Persepolis at the Nowruz (Persian New Year) in 2011, such that he felt impelled to change his mind. It reminded many of the shah's various celebrations at the ancient site, and his famous speech at the tomb of Cyrus the Great during the celebrations for the 2,500th anniversary of the Persian empire; another déjà vu?

However that may be, both Ahmadinejad and Mashaei gave the impression that they did not set much store by the approval of the Shi'a ulama, except perhaps for one such as their mentor Ayatollah Mesbah Yazdi who consistently preached that, under Islamic government, the people must have no say in running the country's affairs, although he too joined the chorus of condemnation of these nationalist gestures. He also sharply criticized the rumour spread by pro-Ahmadinejad groups that the country was currently being run by the Hidden Imam, saying that that would imply there was no more need for His deputy, the supreme leader. The Principlist opposition to Ahmadinejad went on to describe the president's men as 'deviationists', and the judiciary gave his media advisor a jail sentence for insulting the supreme leader.

Now that the reformists were out of the way, rifts among the Principlist factions began to get wider as well as deeper, such that the Majlis election campaigns of early 2012 saw the emergence of various groupings, though none of them with a democratic tendency. The most important faction was the conservative coalition, mentored by Ayatollah Mahdavi Kani and described as the United Front, followed by the ultra-conservative faction mentored by Ayatollah Mesbah Yazdi and described as the Steadfastness Front, leaving Ahmadinejad's 'deviationists' as the third party. In fact what had happened was that the old conservative faction had united in one organization, while the old fundamentalist faction had split into two groups, led respectively by Mesbah Yazdi and Ahmadinejad. By this time there was little love lost between the supreme leader and the Ahmadinejad party.

This brings us to a consideration of Khamenei's rather complex role in all this. Before the June 2009 election, Khamenei had been acting more or less as if he were above political factions, although his increasing closeness to the radical conservative wing of the Islamic regime was manifest. However when he categorically committed himself to the election results and described the protesters' reaction as 'sedition', he unambiguously identified himself with the Principlist – the fundamentalist-conservative – coalition.

On the other hand, he generally backed Ahmadinejad – and quite firmly so in his New Year message in March 2011 – rather like the bulk of the conservatives, who seemed to be more wary of the tide of reformism than they were happy with Ahmadinejad's rising power within the regime. The conflict between Khamenei and the president reached its sharpest point in May 2011 when he did not let the president sack the minister of intelligence (apparently because he had sacked a relative of Mashaei), whereupon Ahmadinejad stayed away from his office for eleven days, apparently in protest at this public snub, and in his unfulfilled wish for loud popular support. Later developments led to the further isolation of the Ahmadinejad group, the 'deviationists'. The supreme leader's October 2011 statement that it was possible for the country's political structure to change from the existing presidential system to a parliamentary one with a prime minister elected by the parliament, left the impression that he was weary of a directly elected head of the executive.

At the same time, various political factions and groupings were preparing the ground for the forthcoming parliamentary elections. Some of the conservatives within the larger Principlist coalition were accusing Ahmadinejad's party of planning to cheat by spending large amounts of government money on their campaign. The elections were held in March 2012. Not surprisingly, the conservative United Front did well, the fundamentalist Steadfastness Front came second and the 'deviationist' Ahmadinejad group performed relatively poorly. The bulk of the reformists boycotted the elections, mainly because the candidates would be vetted first by the Guardian Council, the body that oversees parliamentary legislation and vets the eligibility of parliamentary and presidential candidates.

Analysts made much of the rising and spreading power of the Revolutionary Guards and the Basij militia under their command. The Basij was a volunteer force largely made up of young men aged between sixteen and twenty-five, and the figures quoted for their number ran into many millions. Deeply religious, devoted to the supreme leader, receiving their religious education at some especially designated mosques, they were used as auxiliaries to the police in combating street protests as well as at official rallies. It was believed that one-quarter of them carried firearms. Apart from religious devotion, they were encouraged by various official favours such as exemption from national service, priority in gaining public employment, easy admission to universities and the like.

The Revolutionary Guards had been the regime's most important military force since the 1980s. Not only did their numbers grow fast in the 1990s and beyond, but from the mid-1990s they began rapidly to widen their sphere of influence and activity, such that by 2011 their various business and industrial concerns – ranging from armament industries, car production and oil dealership to eye operations – were estimated to account for around one-third of non-oil GDP (Gross Domestic Product).

Added to the fact that they were also indirectly connected to the giant foundations or *bonyad*s, they naturally carried enormous weight in the economy and economic policy.

There was much speculation about the exact role of the Guards in behind-the-scenes politics and, in particular, their relationship to the supreme leader. As noted, on a few occasions Guards commanders publicly criticized, if not rebuked, Ahmadinejad himself, especially when they sensed that he had responded curtly to the leader's advice. A Guards' leader even went so far as to rebut a Khatami speech laying down conditions for the participation of the reformists in the next Majlis elections, an act that conflicted both with Ayatollah Khomeini's express views and with the constitution that the military should keep off politics. Some observers speculated that in reality the supreme leader was under the influence of the Guards. There was even talk of the militarization of the regime, and, further, of probable future Guards attempts to establish a military regime. However, in the opinion of other, more acute analysts the matter was more complex. In their view, the Guards were integrated into the regime itself in a way similar to the Spanish military under General Franco, and their relationship to the supreme leader was symbiotic.

On Nowruz (21 March) 2009, the Persian New Year celebrated in a number of non-Arab Middle Eastern counties, President Obama held out an olive branch to the Islamic Republic – so named for the first time by an American official – offering dialogue in a friendly tone. The Islamic Republic's reaction was that deeds rather than words were needed, citing some of their main grievances against the United States. Obama's offer did not bear any tangible fruit, yet despite the moral support expressed for the Iranian protest demonstrations after the 2009 presidential election, America said that they were still open to negotiations with the Islamic Republic. No progress was made in that direction, although disagreements with Western powers over uranium enrichment looked about to be resolved when, following negotiations, America, France and Russia proposed a deal which would result in some of the operations being carried out in France and Russia. For a moment the Iranians seemed inclined to agree, but it fell through due to differences on some important details.

China, as Iran's biggest trading partner, and Russia, as a major power with both economic and regional interests in relation to Iran, had consistently stalled and, in the end, watered down the previous three rounds of UN sanctions against Iran. However, in May 2010 the impression was abroad that they would soon reach an agreement with the West regarding sanctions. At the same time, the Turkish and Brazilian governments stepped into the breach and arrived at a proposed deal, not much different from the last one that had fallen through, except that this time some of the operations would be carried out in France and Turkey. The Iranians agreed, but, having by that time obtained the cooperation of Russia and China, the West tabled a new sanctions resolution at the UN Security Council which was carried against the opposition of Brazil and Turkey, and with the abstention of Lebanon. The new resolution extended the existing sanctions but was far short of the 'crippling' sanctions that had been threatened since the previous resolution. However, as noted above, both the US and the EU extended their own unilateral sanctions further than before, making them much more effective. The UN sanctions cost Iran in various ways – especially in restrictions on foreign investment and the transfer of technology, banning the purchase of certain weapons, banking and financial constraints, and the provision for other countries to inspect cargo ships bound for Iran – but it was difficult to know their practical effects against sanction-busting deals. In any case, by early 2012, the Iranians still looked able to live with the sanctions, but this was before the latest unilateral sanctions imposed by the US and EU which took matters much further, such that by early 2013 the situation was approaching a critical point. Also in early 2012 it came as a surprise that the American government did not think that Iran was engaged in weaponization, further supporting the notion that America and her allies were opposed to Iran's acquisition of nuclear capability whether or not it intended to make nuclear weapons.

Developments in Iran's regional relations were mixed. Relations with Saudi Arabia and other Persian Gulf states deteriorated, while in January 2011 Iran-backed Hezbollah helped to establish a cabinet acceptable to them in Lebanon. The Iranians had cordial, if not good relations with the Afghan government, while maintaining contact with other political forces in that country.

Most important of all, however, was that Iran maintained its ability to play a major role in Iraqi politics, including the formation of Nuri al-Maliki's government in December 2010. The fall of President Mubarak of Egypt on 11 February 2011 was welcomed both by the Iranian government, who compared the events with the Islamic revolution, and by the Greens who compared them with their own movement and aspirations. There was no noticeable Iranian intervention against persecution of the Shi'a majority in Bahrain which was openly supported by Saudi Arabia, though the Bahraini government put some of the blame for the unrest on Iran. But in late November 2011, the Bahrain commission of enquiry into the disturbances concluded that they had been a response to genuine grievances and that Iran had not been behind them. Iran did, however, support President Assad of Syria diplomatically as well as materially during the long political conflict in that country.

There was regional unrest, notably in the Kurdistan and Baluchistan provinces. The arrest and execution of the leader of the Baluch guerrillas in 2010 led to a decline in Baluch activity, but the campaigns of the Kurdish Pejak guerrillas intensified in 2011. At the same time, several key Iranian scientists and generals were killed by assassination and in explosions. The Islamic regime believes that all such campaigns, as well as highly damaging cyber-attacks, are part of a destabilization policy led by either America or Israel or both.

According to Iranian as well as international sources, in 2012 Iran was considered to be the world's seventeenth-largest economy, and held the third-largest oil and second-largest gas reserves. Its income per capita was in the region of $11,300, and around eighty per cent of its total exports and sixty per cent of government revenue were due to oil and gas exports. The rate of growth of between 2.5 and 3.5 per cent was considered high by post-world economic crisis standards; close to eighteen per cent of the population were below the poverty line; the unemployment rate estimates were between thirteen and fifteen per cent; the official rate of inflation was around twenty-five per cent but rising much faster in some sectors; and foreign exchange reserves were in the region of $100 million due to rising oil prices between 2009 and 2011. The youth and graduate unemployment rates were higher, the latter of which were partly responsible for the continuing brain drain.

It was as telling as it had been before the revolution that oil and services made up the lion's share of the GDP, while the main productive sectors, industry and agriculture, lagged behind. Oil contributed 27.2 per cent, services 45.5 per cent, industries and mines 18.1 per cent and agriculture, 9.2 per cent. While oil and services claimed more than seventy per cent of the GDP (as they did thirty-three years ago), with a share in the total labour force of only twenty-five per cent, agriculture's share in GDP was little more than nine per cent. It should be noted that Iran is not a tourist destination, which might otherwise have accounted for the enormous share of services. This share is largely explained by the consumer orientation of Iranian society motivated by the oil bonanza.

In the early months of 2012, the rate of exchange of the dollar to the Iranian rial began to rise sharply by around seventy per cent. The long-term reason behind this was the fact that the government-imposed rate of interest of fifteen per cent was five per cent below the official rate of inflation on the president's insistence, who believed it would make for economic justice as well as efficiency. As a result, the real value or purchasing power of bank deposits was actually declining by an annual rate of ten per cent, and so lenders began to withdraw their money and buy gold and foreign exchange to maintain its real value. The war scare of early 2012 added force to the loss of public confidence and intensified the flight out of the rial. Eventually, and after the governor of the central bank threatened to resign, Ahmadinejad caved in, the interest rates rose beyond twenty per cent and the foreign exchange market eased up temporarily. But the application of further sanctions against Iran – and most notably the EU boycott of Iranian oil – put further pressure on the rial's rate of exchange such that the government felt impelled to implement a multiple exchange-rate policy to ease off the pressure on consumer goods prices. Nevertheless, the price of the dollar went on rising sharply in the free exchange market, and the rate of inflation soared above thirty per cent.

With its great assets in oil, gas and other minerals, Iran has good potential for developing into a large industrial state within the next ten to fifteen years. But that would be contingent on political stability as well as many economic, social and cultural factors. The economy was still too highly state-dominated. Many privatized industries and services had ended up as subsidiaries of *bonyad*s and the Revolutionary Guards' economic sector. The market was weak, and this had led to many price and other distortions, which reduce efficiency. Due to the large number of public holidays, weekly working days averaged to four, and effective work done per hour was generally little. Private business activity was usually small-scale, and investment horizons generally limited for fear of unpredictable short-term political and economic changes.

In 2012 there were thirty-eight firms in the relatively large-scale car industry, compared to just a few in the advanced car-producing countries of the world. There was a considerable flight of financial and human capital for political, economic and cultural reasons. Investment in oil and gas development was far from adequate due to the sanctions against international investment and transfer of recent technology. Consumerism was very great among the high-income groups and the wealthy, while there was a huge welfare gap between the haves and have-nots.

The government's controversial policy of substantially reducing its $90-billion-a-year consumer price subsidies by targeting them to lower-income groups alone, was both economically and socially sound. But there was serious opposition to it from among the Principlists themselves, since it was bound to push up the prices of food, utilities and some other services, and would test the patience of the already malcontented middle classes. However, the Iranian economy's continuing long-term weakness was its heavy dependency on energy exports for foreign exchange and government revenue – in other words, the oil and gas rent – most of all because of the culture of dependency, inefficiency and unearned income and consumption that for decades it had led to as well as encouraged.

In September 2012 it became clear that the international sanctions were beginning to bite severely and had led to a number of significant economic problems.

Whither Iran?

An extremely difficult question to answer in the case of many countries but more so for Iran, precisely because of the short-term nature of her attitudes and behaviour, not just at state and society level but often regarding the most basic and widespread issues, such as the high frequency of divorce. Nevertheless, the level of Iranian political development is – in certain, though not all, ways – relatively significant compared to other countries in the region.

One hundred and fifty years ago, Iranian intellectuals discovered that establishing a government constrained by law was key to both political and economic development, and fifty years later the Iranian people rose up to make it a reality, though this move characteristically ended in chaos leading to the return of arbitrary rule in modern guise. The openness of the 1940s did result in some political development, though the Tudeh fast became a Stalinist party and the Popular Movement, led by Mosaddeq, became so bogged down with the details of compensation to the Anglo-Iranian Oil Company that, in practice, it wrecked its most cherished aspirations for independence and democracy.

The shah's dream of creating a perfect society – indeed 'the Great Civilization' – all on his own, was so deep-rooted that, paradoxically, he ignored the complex realities of a 2,500-year-old civilization together with its people whom he angered, most of all by humiliating them. It served to turn people of all classes, not least the intellectuals, to an emotional hatred of the West as well as ancient Persia, and to the naive hope that the Islamic, Marxist-Leninist or whatever 'ideal society' – the shah's perfect society by another name – was within their grasp once the shah had been removed.

There has been some political development among both rulers and ruled, or the present conflicts which even extend to the leadership of the Islamist movement would not have arisen. On the other hand, the traditional beliefs in the politics of elimination, lawless behaviour and its associated political perfectionism still flourish within state and society, except that, as under the shah, the Iranian people are fully capable of exposing the consequences of such attitudes if and when they manage to take power.

Many Iranians now desire democracy, but if one was to name the unique feature of democracy that has led to its success in terms of continuity and progress, it is the fact that it has no claim to being a perfect system. It is this very recognition of imperfection that enables mistakes to be corrected and further progress to be made. Democracy has always been achieved through a long as well as a rough process of political development, and wherever it genuinely exists it is blended with the cultural and historical characteristics of the society. If Iranians seriously desired democracy, they would need to try and begin this exacting process of political development and that would involve three basic requirements: tolerance, dialogue and compromise. These in their turn would become possible, over time, if two closely related historical traits of Iranian society were gradually abandoned: the age-old conflict between state and society, and the short-term outlook towards all that concerns individual as well as social existence.

And that is easier said than done.

Timeline

ANCIENT PERSIA

550 BCE	Cyrus the Great (**600–530 BCE**) founds the Persian empire, the very first world empire
550–330 BCE	Achaemenid Persia
330 BCE	Downfall of Achaemenid dynasty brought about by Alexander the Great (**356–323 BCE**)
312–150 BCE	Hellenistic interlude
247 BCE–CE 224	Arsacid Parthians
CE 224–651	Sasanian Persia

MEDIEVAL PERSIA

CE 651	Persian empire falls to Muslim Arabs
CE 651–1258	Age of the Arab caliphates during which the Arabs, the Samanids, the Byuids, the Ghaznavids and the Seljuk ruled Iranian lands until the Mongol invasion of Iran
1260–1340	Rule of Holagu Khan and his descendants (the Ilkhanids)
1370–1506	Rule of Timurid princes
1501	Ismail (**1488–1524**) revives the Persian empire and founds the Safavid dynasty (**1501–1722**)
1736–1785	Afshar and Zand dynasties

MODERN IRAN

1785–1797	Agha Mohammad Khan founds the Qajar dynasty

1797–1834	Rule of Fath'ali Shah
1813	Russo-Persian treaty of Golestan initiates the original 'Great Game'
1834–1848	Rule of Mohammad Shah
1848–1896	Rule of Naser al-Din Shah
1890–1892	The Tobacco Revolt
1896	Assassination of Naser al-Din Shah
1906–1911	The Constitutional Revolution
1907	Signing of the Anglo-Russian Convention
1908	Mohammad Ali Shah, stages a coup against the Majlis after an unsuccessful attempt on his life
1909–1921	Constitutionalism and chaos

IRAN UNDER THE PAHLAVIS

1921–1930	Reza Khan/Shah rules as dictator of Iran
1930–1941	Reza Shah's arbitrary rule by fiat
1933	Anglo-Iranian Oil Company agreement
1941	British and Russian forces invade forcing the shah to abdicate; founding of the Tudeh Party
1949	Formation of the National Front
1951	Nationalization of Iranian Oil
1951	Mosaddeq is elected prime minister
1953	Mosaddeq's government is overthrown
1955	The Baghdad Pact (Central Treaty Organization)
1962	The Land Reform Law is passed
1963	The shah's 'White Revolution' is launched
1963 June	Revolt against the shah's assumption of arbitrary power, led by Khomeini

THE 1979 REVOLUTION AND
THE ISLAMIC REPUBLIC

1978 January	Article commissioned by the shah and attacking Khomeini is published

1978 September	Black Friday
1979 February	Fall of the shah followed by the creation of the Islamic Republic of Iran
1979 November	Students occupy the American embassy and take its diplomats hostage for 444 days
1979 November	Constitution of the Islamic Republic is approved and put to popular vote
1980–1988	Iran–Iraq war

POST-KHOMEINI IRAN

1989 June	Seyyed Ali Khamenei is elected supreme leader
1989 August	Hashemi Rafsanjani elected to presidency
1997 May	Mohammad Khatami elected to presidency
2001 September	The 9/11 terrorist attacks inaugurate the era of the 'war on terror'
2005 August	Mahmoud Ahmadinejad elected to presidency

Further reading

Abrahamian, Ervand *A History of Modern Iran*. Cambridge, Cambridge University Press, 2008.

Adelkhah, Fariba *Being Modern in Iran*. London, C. Hurst, 1999.

Afary, Janet *The Iranian Constitutional Revolution, 1905–1911*. New York, Columbia University Press, 1996.

Amir Arjomand, Said *The Turban for the Crown: the Islamic Revolution in Iran*. Oxford and New York, Oxford University Press, 1988.

Amuzegar, Jahangir *Iran's Economy under the Islamic Republic*. London and New York, I. B. Tauris, 1993.

Ansari, Ali. M. *Modern Iran: The Pahlavis and After*. London, Longman, 2007.

Arberry A. J. (ed.) *The Legacy of Persia*. Oxford, Clarendon Press, 1953.

Axworthy, Michael *Empire of the Mind: A History of Iran*. London, Hurst & Co., 2008.

Azimi, Fakhreddin *The Quest for Democracy in Iran: A Century of Struggle against Authoritarian Rule*. Cambridge, Massachusetts and London, Harvard University Press, 2008.

Bakhash, Shaul *The Reign of the Ayatollahs: Iran and the Islamic Revolution*. London, Unwin Paperbacks, 1985.

Banani, Amin *The Modernization of Iran*. Stanford, California, Stanford University Press, 1961.

Bausani, Alessandro *The Persians from the Earliest Days to the Twentieth Century*, trans. J. B. Donne. London, Elek Books, 1971.

Boroujerdi, Mehrzad *Iranian Intellectuals and the West: The Tormented Triumph of Nativism*. New York, Syracuse, Syracuse University Press, 1996.

Browne, E. G. *A Literary History of Persia*, vols. I–IV. Cambridge, Cambridge University Press, 1920–1924.

—— *The Persian Revolution*. London, Frank Cass, 1966.

Cronin, Stephanie *The Making of Modern Iran: State and Society under Riza Shah, 1921–1941*. London and New York, Routledge, 2003.

De Bellaigue, Christopher *The Struggle for Iran*. New York, New York Review Books, 2007.

Frye, Richard N. *Persia*. London, Allen & Unwin, 1968.

Gheissari, Ali *Iranian Intellectuals in the Twentieth Century*. Austin, University of Texas Press, 1998.

Karshenas, Massoud *Oil, State and Industrialization in Iran*. Cambridge, Cambridge University Press, 1990.

Katouzian, Homa *The Persians: Ancient, Mediaeval and Modern Iran*. New Haven and London, Yale University Press (paperback edn), 2010.

—— *Iranian History and Politics: the Dialectic of State and Society*. London and New York, Routledge (paperback edn), 2007.

—— *State and Society in Iran: the Eclipse of the Qajars and the Emergence of the Pahlavis*. London and New York, I. B. Tauris (paperback edn), 2006.

Keddie, Nikki, R. *Roots and Results of Revolution*. New Haven and London, Yale University Press, 2003.

Marin, Vanessa *Creating an Islamic State: Khomeini and the Making of a New Iran*. London and New York, I. B. Tauris, 2003.

Menasheri, David *Post-Revolutionary Politics in Iran*. London and Portland, Oregon, Frank Cass, 2001.

Milani, Farzaneh *Veils and Words: The Emerging Voices of Iranian Women Writers*. London, I. B. Tauris, 1992.

Mir-Hosseini, Ziba, and Richard Tapper *Islam and Democracy in Iran: Eshkevari and the Quest for Reform*. London and New York, I. B. Tauris, 2006.

Mottahedeh, Roy *The Mantle of the Prophet: Learning and Power in Iran*. London, Chatto & Windus, 1986.

Pahlavi, Mohammad Reza Shah *Answer to History*. New York, Stein & Day, 1980.

Rypka, Jan *History of Iranian Literature*. Dordrecht, Holland, D. Reidel Publishing Company, 1968.

Soudavar, Abolala *The Aura of Kings: Legitimacy and Divine Sanction in Iranian Kingship*. Costa Mesa, California, Mazda, 2003.

Tavakloi-Targhi, Mohamad *Refashioning Iran: Orientalism, Occidentalism and Historiography*. Basingstoke and New York, Palgrave, 2001.

The Cambridge History of Iran (various eds), vols. I–VII, Cambridge, Cambridge University Press, 1968–1991.

Index

References to images are shown in *italic*.